T0386300

THANK YOU MR CROMBIE

MIHIR BOSE

Thank You Mr Crombie

Lessons in Guilt
and Gratitude to the British

HURST & COMPANY, LONDON

First published in the United Kingdom in 2024 by
C. Hurst & Co. (Publishers) Ltd.,
New Wing, Somerset House, Strand,
London, WC2R 1LA
© Mihir Bose, 2024
All rights reserved.
Printed and bound in Great Britain by Bell and Bain Ltd, Glasgow

Distributed in the United States, Canada and Latin America
by Oxford University Press, 198 Madison Avenue, New York, NY 10016,
United States of America.

The right of Mihir Bose to be identified as the author of
this publication is asserted by him in accordance with the
Copyright, Designs and Patents Act, 1988.

A Cataloguing-in-Publication data record for this book
is available from the British Library.

ISBN: 9781911723004

This book is printed using paper from registered sustainable
and managed sources.

www.hurstpublishers.com

To Father Fritz for making me believe I could be a writer

CONTENTS

CONTENTS

A LETTER OF THANKS AFTER 49 YEARS

Dear Mr John Crombie,

This is the most extraordinary letter I have ever written. For a start, I do not know where to send it. When you were in contact with me, there was no internet. I do not have your email or home address. I do have your office address, that of the Home Office in Croydon, but it would be astonishing if you are still there. To be very frank, I do not know you at all. I have never met you. Nor do I know whether you are still around.

I am writing to thank you for a letter you wrote to me on 27 February 1975. That letter means so much to me that ever since I received it, I have taken great care to preserve it. As I write, it is spread before my computer, frayed at the edges but the paper still a lovely, light beige colour and the typing in very clear black letters. I have kept it in a plastic cover, and I have carried it with me wherever I have gone.

At that stage, having lived in this country for six years, I was planning to return to the land of my birth. A year earlier I had qualified as a chartered accountant. My brother-in-law Amal Chakrabortti, a partner in S.R. Batliboi and Co., one of the most prestigious accountancy firms in India, had come to London the previous summer with my eldest sister and offered me a partnership. It was the only job I ever got in the land of my birth and was a classic case of Indian nepotism. In order to prepare me, "Amal-da", da as a suffix denoting respect, secured me a year's training at Messrs Arthur Young McClelland Moors & Co., whose Indian associate Batliboi was. My parents had also visited me and made it clear that as the only son of Hindu parents I had an obligation to leave Britain and finally return home and settle down. It was time to fulfil the duties my Aryan ancestors had imposed on a Hindu son. They talk of Jewish mothers. When it comes to moral blackmail, a Hindu mother wins hands down.

I was expecting a letter from the Home Office in response to my request to renew my visa, as I had done every year since my arrival in Britain in January 1969 on a student visa.

On 27 February 1975 you wrote two letters. One was to Arthur Young McClelland Moores and one to me. I was touched that in both of them you wrote my name and the address by hand. My father, who wanted me to have good handwriting and made me practise on scrolls, would have been proud to see that people still valued handwriting. Your letter to me read:

> Dear Sir,
>
> I am writing to say that the time limit and conditions attached to your leave to enter the United Kingdom have been removed. An appropriate endorsement has been placed in your passport which is enclosed.
>
> You are now free to remain permanently in the United Kingdom. You do not require permission from a Government Department to take or change employment in England, Wales or Scotland and you may engage in business or a profession provided you comply with any general regulations governing the business or professional activity.
>
> In Northern Ireland however you would have to consult the Department of Manpower Services; if you are thinking of going to live or work in the Isle of Man or one of the Channel Islands, you should first consult the Island's Immigration authorities.
>
> If you leave the United Kingdom at any time you will normally be readmitted at any time within two years of your departure provided you hold a valid passport endorsed where necessary with a United Kingdom re-entry visa. It will be helpful if you can produce the enclosed passport to the immigration officer on your return.
>
> Yours sincerely
>
> John Crombie

Your letter transformed my life. This is because I had secretly hankered to become a writer ever since, as a ten- or twelve-year old, I had copied an article from the *Times of India* Sunday magazine onto my scrap book and put my name on it. Tuludada, my eldest cousin, reprimanded me, saying that was plagiarism. That determined me to one day write an article on which I could by right put my name. And amazingly, after qualifying as a chartered accountant, I had during the summer of 1974 found work as a journalist, becoming the first cricket correspondent of the recently formed London Broadcasting Corporation, LBC. When your letter came, I was doing hockey reports for LBC and had been commissioned by a British publisher to write a biography of Keith Miller, a legendary Australian cricketer.

Until your letter of 27 February, I had no reason to think I would be allowed to live in this country as I was no longer a student and thought that once I returned to India my dream would be over. Now, on reading your letter for the first time I saw a chink of light in what had been a dismal landscape. If things did not work out in India, and I still hankered to become a writer, I could return and try to fulfil my dream. You had made me part of that most privileged caste, even higher than the Brahmins, the "RR", Returning Resident, an immigrant who could live in the United Kingdom without any restrictions and enter and leave as they wished.

I preserved my RR caste by a later visit in 1976. Then in 1978 I returned to this country and became a writer. Without your letter, I would today still have been in India, a millionaire with servants and chauffeurs, who turned left when boarding an airplane, as I would always have travelled first-class. But all the time I would have reflected on why Father Fritz's grand prediction in my Standard XI class in St. Xavier's, my Jesuit school in Mumbai, that I would become a writer, had not come true.

It has always intrigued me that all the talk of immigration to the United Kingdom, which has been going on since I arrived here in 1969, is of people coming here to make money. In my case, I sacrificed money and lived in a Maida Vale bedsit because of the intellectual riches this country provides. But why is this country, the land of Shakespeare, not proud of those riches? Why does the west, whose historians wax lyrically about how Europe made the modern world, not make more of them?

Mine is a convoluted story, but it also reflects Britain's relationship with its empire and the products of that empire, like me.

Every time I read your letter, I think how that phrase "time limit has been removed" is such a very cosy British way of describing momentous developments. So, during the Second World War the Defence of the Realm Act was called Dora. Or the BBC is referred to as "Auntie". The phrase is like a parent writing to say the time limit on little Johnnie's sleepover has been removed. I am so grateful, Mr Crombie, I was allowed to sleep over in Britain. It has not always been full of sweet dreams, but I have fulfilled the dream I had as a child that Sunday morning in Mumbai. It could only have happened in the United Kingdom in quite this fashion. It is what makes this country unique.

Regards

Mihir Bose

2

WANT SONS, HATE DARK SKINS

The day I was born, *Baba*, my father, sat cross-legged on a Mumbai stone floor praying to a collection of Hindu gods at the Ramakrishna Mission, set up by Vivekananda, one of Hinduism's most revered figures. On the walls was also Jesus on the cross, reflecting Vivekananda's amazingly inclusive religious views. Just before my birth Baba had had *diksha*, blessing, from a guru Maharaj of the Ramakrishna Mission. Just after his bath, his hair still wet and astray, his dhoti flung carelessly around him, he would count on the fingers of his right hand while reciting the names of one of the various Hindu gods. Only the right hand could be used—the left is not allowed for such sacred purposes as it is considered unclean. Then he would apply lavish quantities of Brylcreem on his hair. He rarely spoke to me about religion except to say in Bengali, "*Raka Hari Mara Key, Mara Hari Raka Key*", "If God preserves you, who can destroy you? If God destroys you, who can preserve you?"

My birth was a relief. Ma had already besmirched her fragile reputation. After nine years of marriage she had produced two daughters and no son. Baba was the eldest son of the family and, if his wife were not to produce a male child, it would be a disgrace.

When my eldest sister Didi was born, Baba's stepmother had sat on the courtyard of the house, spread her legs wide on the cement floor, and wept loudly and bitterly at the news.

My grandmother wanted a fair grandson and had gone to the temple before I was born to promise that, if Ma finally produced a son, she would perform a special *Kartik Puja*.

She did not, however, perform a *Ganesh Puja*, which shows how much Hindus value fair skin and the good looks they assume come

5

from a fair complexion. When it comes to love and devotion for Hindu gods, Ganesh stands on a pinnacle. His little idol is to be seen almost everywhere, from the dashboards of taxi cabs to homes, restaurants and offices, while images of his brother Kartik are rare. What is more, Ganesh is the really clever and resourceful one. When Parvati, who is also revered as the great goddess Durga, set her two sons the challenge of circumnavigating the globe with the promise that the winner would rule the world, Kartik set off on his peacock, while Ganesh—fat, dumpy, with a huge elephant head—slowly walked round his mother. But Kartik returned to find his brother already proclaimed the winner. "Simple," explained Ganesh. "While you wasted your time actually going round the world, I merely walked around mother—after all, she is the world."

But still my grandmother would not have thought of offering puja to Ganesh. What she wanted was a grandson with good looks, and in that respect Kartik soars over almost every Hindu god: fair, sharp-featured, his bow slung over his left shoulder in a way a Bollywood actor would envy. And while Ganesh rides a rat, Kartik rides a wonderful peacock, the national bird of India. His intelligence may leave much to be desired, and in his duels with Ganesh he has always come out worst, but of his looks there is no doubt. After two granddaughters and one miscarriage from the wife of her eldest son, my grandmother wanted a grandson to look like Kartik, not the elephant-headed Ganesh, however much he was held to be a harbinger of good fortune. Some ten years after my birth, my grandmother celebrated the Kartik Puja in honour of my birth in some style, and her happiness at propitiating Kartik for finally giving her a grandson was very evident.

She was always particularly fond of me though I never reciprocated her feelings. She was small, weedy and shrivelled up, the blackness of her complexion a contrast to the regulation white sari she wore to convey her widowhood, and not a person I found it easy to relate to. Also, she was a stepmother. I was told my father's mother, who had died young, was fair and considered a great beauty, whereas my step-grandmother was dark.

* * *

I was born in a small lane in Kolkata, so small that a large car could cause an obstruction, in the smallest room of a house. Called *Majar Ghar*, Middle Room, it was in the middle of a row of rooms. By the time I was born, Majar Ghar had established itself as the maternity ward of my grandfather's house. It had seen the birth of both my sisters and my various cousins. *Dadu*, my maternal grandfather, didn't believe in hospital births. His eldest daughter had died in childbirth in a hospital; after that he had decreed that all his daughters, wherever they lived, on becoming pregnant would return to his home and would be delivered by his own doctor in his presence.

However, one of his sons-in-law defied this injunction, and while my aunt was safely delivered of a son this, far from reassuring Dadu, merely reinforced his fears about hospitals. The story went that soon after my aunt had given birth to her son, Uncle Upan, Upan *Mama*, went to visit her in hospital. But instead of rejoicing over the birth of a son, he returned looking very sombre. He told Dadu that he feared his grandson might have been switched. Asked why, he said the grandchild had an exceedingly dark complexion and no grandson of Dadu could possibly be so dark. Dadu required no further proof that the hospital had lost him a beautiful, fair grandchild and never held the child. When I was growing up this story was often told to us, and my poor cousin bore this cross of the Hindu fetish about skin colour. He could never reveal he was gay and as I was writing this book he died in a car accident outside his house.

I too was born with a dark complexion, but this was balanced by very sharp features, which may explain why Dadu did not shun me. Some months after Ma and I returned to Mumbai, one of Ma's sisters came from Kolkata to visit us. Ma was bathing me in the approved manner in a basin. My aunt asked Ma "Where is he?" Surprised, Ma replied "Well, here he is."

"My god!" she said, "What happened to his nose, he had such a lovely nose. But never mind, his skin colour is just like a sahib's", the word used in India to denote white men. The gain in complexion had more than compensated for the loss of sharp features. In a society which so values fair skin this was considered an excellent bargain.

In our family the colour lines were drawn easily. Baba could have passed for a light-skinned European; Ma was dark, and Baba would often joke about it: "Who else would have taken care of her perma-nent colour?" he would say, bursting into loud laughter. Ma, far from being upset, would join in the laughter, conveying her delight that she had fulfilled her ambition and married a fair man. This was, of course, in the reverse order as men are supposed to marry fair women.

Skin care to preserve beauty was an obsession with Ma and her sisters. They would apply all sorts of lotions, cream of milk and, often in the middle of hot Indian afternoons, shut themselves up in a darkened room and lie in bed, their faces covered with a hideous mixture of cream and other milk products to improve their com-plexion. One of my aunts, who was the darkest of the sisters, would sometimes have cucumber liberally coated with cream on her face. I found wandering into the darkened room a voyage of discovery, and once, I could not resist eating one of the cucumbers I found, causing my aunt to yelp with anger that I was a thoughtless child ruining her chances of getting a fair skin.

In the Indian tradition of showing respect, I, like all Indians, call my older sisters not by their names but by a special title, my eldest sister Didi, and my youngest sister Chordi. Didi's fair complexion, complementing her natural airs, made her a beauty, in contrast to Chordi, who was considerably darker. Ma would stroke Chordi's skin, saying, "What a pity you are dark!" As if to make up, Ma would also say, "Her complexion is dark, but otherwise this daugh-ter of mine is 'square'," using the English word, as she often did in the middle of talking in Bengali, and in describing Chordi as "square" she was complimenting her. Ma was also keen I should maintain my fair skin, and when I was growing up her frequent admonition to me whenever I played cricket or other games in the sun was, "Don't do that, you'll spoil your complexion." Then I railed against it. It took an Englishman to make me realise what a hypocrite I was.

It came at a party in our flat in London, which I was then sharing with Chordi. Neil, a very urbane civil servant whom I had met when we were both part of an am-dram group, after being introduced to Chordi came up to me: "Your sister is really beautiful." I thought he was mocking her beauty and very nearly hit him. I restrained myself and realised that, despite having experienced colour prejudice in Britain, I could not shake off my own Hindu obsession with fair skin, thereby showing how deeply ingrained this bigotry was.

Yet Hindus consider people who are very white ghostly. Their preferred colour is the Mediterranean, what in matrimonial advertisements is called a "wheatish complexion".

HOW SCOTLAND GOT MY PARENTS TOGETHER

Some years ago, the Society of Authors held a talk by a BBC producer who was very proud that the BBC had recently broadcast a series on Sir Walter Scott, a novelist whose works had been forgotten. He then asked his audience if anyone knew who Scott was. I was the only one to put up my hand, which astonished him. But for Sir Walter Scott, my parents might never have got married.

Unlike modern Indian arranged marriages, neither an agent nor advertisements in newspapers brought my parents together. It was done in the more traditional way. One of *Ma's* uncles knew someone in *Baba's* family, and, in the course of the conversation, Ma's name came up. It was quickly agreed that Baba and Ma would meet to see if they liked each other. This, in India of the 30s, was very progressive.

Baba was due back in Kolkata for a holiday and a date was set. So, sometime on a hot summer's evening in September 1938, Baba came to Ma's house.

Such visits had a well-established ritual. The visitors would be met by a servant, who would then inform *Dadu*. He would welcome the guests, order the servant to bring sweets and tea—hard liquor being absolutely taboo—and then usher in Ma. Ma was Dadu's favourite daughter, on whom he absolutely doted. He had once told her, "If you want the moon, I will get it for you." He wanted her to marry a husband of her choice. But Ma was proving difficult to please and Baba was not the first suitor.

Ma had set her heart on marrying a fair handsome man. Ma immediately fancied Baba. He was tall and fair and very good looking. He was wearing a shirt with dirty marks on it, but that was something any good woman could fix. There was one problem.

Baba was accompanied by Dhiren, his younger brother. Baba didn't say anything. Dhiren, acting as if he were the head of the family, grilled Ma.

Ma, having done very well in her matriculation, had just entered a prestigious Kolkata college to study for a degree. Among her specialist subjects was English, and she had, as she proudly told everyone, got a "letter" in English—a certificate of excellence awarded by the Bengal Matriculation Examination Board. Dadu was very proud of this, but no sooner had he mentioned it then Dhiren, speaking in Bengali, as all of them did that evening, turned to Ma and said, "So you have got a letter in English. Well, you know my brother lives in Mumbai, which is a very cosmopolitan city. He runs a business making raincoats, gumboots, and mixes with people whose mother tongue is English. Indeed, he meets people who are pure English people, *sahibs* and *memsahibs*. It is very important for him that his wife should be able to speak English and speak it well. You may have got a letter in your English exam, but all that means is you can write English. But how well can you speak English? I would like you to read something in English."

Ma read from Scott's novel *Ivanhoe*. It is possible Dhiren had brought a copy with him, but I suspect that in the literary Bengali house of Dadu this would have been the just sort of book on his bookshelf. Contrary to the claims of Scottish nationalists, the Scots were great imperialists. They dominated the commerce of Bengal, then India's richest province, owning many jute mills and racially discriminated against Indian rivals. However, literary Bengal made a distinction between the racist, arrogant, Scottish businessmen and Scottish men of letters, whom they liked. The result was that Sir Walter Scott was very popular with Bengalis of that generation. Ma knew *Ivanhoe* and liked reading Scott. She never told me which passage she read. Although Ma didn't like being put through this test, whatever passage she chose, she must have read it well.

Like Scott, Ma liked to travel and she was the first person in our family to fly overseas. Scott made three trips to Europe and Ma visited England on three occasions, which filled her with pride as none of her siblings ever went abroad.

MUMBAI'S VERY OWN DOWNTON ABBEY

In December 1958 Arthur Koestler, then a great British intellectual figure, visited India. His book, *The Lotus and the Robot* described what he saw on his first night in the city, looking out of the balcony of his air-conditioned hotel, The streets were full of Mumbai's homeless who looked so resigned that Koestler thought they were "etchings of mediaeval towns in the grip of the Plague". In a friend's house he stepped on one of them in a hallway and the sleepless figure "did not stir." There were actually five of them and Koestler thought their "ribs (were) sticking out like Christ's on the Cross."[1]

I was eleven when Koestler recorded these scenes. He never visited Sailor Building, where we lived. Had he done so, he would have found many such bodies. They were mainly workers employed by Parkes, which was both the local store and a restaurant. These workers shared the pavement with the destitute souls who called it their home.

Koestler would also have found another damning piece of evidence to prove his thesis that western values are superior to Indian ones. Well-off Indians considered cars more valuable than human lives. So, while humans slept unattended on the pavements of the city at night, Baba would not leave our car unattended outside Sailor Building then, despite the fact that there was plenty of parking space. Nobody in Mumbai would do that. As evening fell and the people left Flora Fountain, so did the cars, including ours.

Stories were common of the theft of tyres, other car parts, even engines, from cars parked on roads at night. There being no garage in the area where we lived, Baba hired one nearly a mile away in a block of flats. Every evening Shankar, our driver, would drive the car there. On the odd occasion when it had to be parked outside Sailor Building, a servant slept in the car. He would stretch out on the back seat and act as our human shield. We were confident that with a man in the car no thief would dare steal it. We were ready to sacrifice the servant to protect our car.

* * *

Our house was very much the Indo-Victorian house Koestler's friend lived in but made more distinctive because we were one of the few residential flats in what was largely an office building. The floor below us was occupied by a firm of solicitors which, like all offices in India, had *peons*. The peons, an essential part of an Indian office, are office servants who do the fetching and carrying of files, make tea, get snacks and generally run errands for the babus, the office workers. The lawyers and their legal clerks would have been highly offended had they been asked to perform what they felt were menial tasks. In many offices there is a bell on the desk of the officers. It rings in the kitchen and the peon comes running to serve his master. Although we did not know it then, the word *peon* was Spanish and had originally meant involuntary servitude of labourers with little control over their employment conditions.

The peons have no homes to live in. So, at night the office is their home. They sleep on the floor; to prepare their meals they use the kitchen where, during the day, they make tea, coffee and snacks for their bosses; and when they get married, their wives and children also live there. It is as if there were two worlds. A day-time office, which bears many similarities to an office in the west, is at night converted into a home for people who know they will never have a home in the city.

On most days, by the time we got up the peons of the law firm had folded up their mattresses and got the offices ready for the arrival of the bosses and the start of the day's work. Although we knew the names of the peons, we never mixed with them socially. Years later, when Didi had her first child, a girl, we found one of the peons also had a little girl, and Ma encouraged her to come up to our flat to provide my niece some company. But even that was limited. Baba and Ma were proud they treated their servants with great kindness and generosity, but no real friendship could develop. Years later in London, a university friend of my wife's, a gentle, kind English woman, would tell me how her mother had lived in India and her servants adored her. For her this was evidence that Indians liked British rule.

* * *

What made these peons different from the servants who adored my English friend's mother during the Raj was they were free people. This meant they were *ek din ka sultan*, king for a day. That was the day Indians went to the polls. The most dramatic evidence of this came during the 1967 general election. The south Mumbai seat was held by S.K. Patil, a cabinet minister and Congress heavyweight. The constituency, which included our house, was one of the richest seats in the country. Patil could not have had a safer berth.

Baba knew and liked Patil who professed socialism but really believed in free enterprise and was a friend of America. Baba had always felt Nehru should have cosied up to America after India's independence. Patil's opponent, George Fernandes, was a militant trade union leader. Baba and Ma went off to vote confident Patil would win.

But at the polling booth Baba found the peons, normally so deferential, behaving as if they were Baba's equal and openly saying they would vote for Fernandes. Fernandes had got them to register and also those Koestler thought were lifeless corpses. On election day these peons and the supposedly dead voters rose and ambushed Patil.

Koestler was sure democracy would not work in India and warned about the dire consequences of trying to ram democracy down the country's throat ignoring the fact that it had taken western countries centuries to learn to work the democratic model. The best hope for India was to be ruled by dictators as Pakistan and Indonesia were. If not it faced the prospect of becoming another totalitarian state like China.[2]

Just as peons ambushed Patil, Indian voters ambushed Koestler and the *Times* correspondent in India who had predicted that 1967 would be the last general election in the country. These Indians may sleep on the streets looking lifeless and know nothing about the renaissance and the enlightenment but value democracy as much as, if not more, than the Europeans.

* * *

Baba's firm employed a number of *Ghatis*, people from the Ghats, the mountain range that stretched for nearly 1,000 miles and effectively sandwiched Mumbai between the sea and the rest of the mainland. It is older than the Himalayas, is a UNESCO World Heritage site and rated as one of the eight hottest biodiversity hotspots in the world. But for us it was the place where the Ghatis, who did all the manual work in Baba's firm came from. Some also came to our flat and performed various household tasks.

It would start early in the morning with the arrival of Dharma. Ever since he had fractured his hand, Baba had decided he needed a daily massage. And Dharma, a stocky Ghati, wearing his dhoti pulled up to his stomach, would massage him. He would first massage Baba's chest, stomach, thighs and knees while Baba, holding the *Times of India* above Dharma's head, would read the paper. Not being literate, Dharma could not, of course, read the paper. Then he would massage Baba's back and Baba would put the paper to one side. I looked forward to this as it meant I could now read the *Times of India*, turning first to the sports pages.

As Dharma finished his massage, several other Ghatis would trudge up the stairs to our flat to be given their duties. Baba, still not completely dressed, would gather them round him and, in a language that was his own, a mixture of English, Marathi, Bengali and Hindi say: "You are all cows, what did you understand? I am God. Now, do you understand that? Now go and do your work." It was to be years before I realised how feudal it all was.

Ma had devised an elaborate regime for the Ghatis. One Ghati would go round with a duster and diligently dust all the furniture every morning. Living in the land of the dust, this was very important, and Ma would run her finger through the furniture to make sure there was not even a speck of dust. Another Ghati would first sweep the floor with a broom then take a bucket of water and a cloth and wash the floor. Ma would make sure we did not walk on the floors until they were dry. We would dump our dirty clothes on the floor in the bedroom and a Ghati would pick them up and wash them.

Soma, the favourite, would come early in the morning, wearing a pair of dirty brown shorts and faded brown shirt, and sweep and clean the flat. He was also a wonderful packer and would pack for all our trips. One of my abiding memories is of Soma packing my case when I came to England in 1969. Ma was particularly fond of Soma and affectionately called him "Somaraj", King. After he had finished his work, Ma served him tea and sweets and watched over him as he squatted on the kitchen floor consuming them. Ma provided food for all the Ghatis, and for her this was evidence of how much she cared for all those who served her.

It was Soma my heart went out to. He was very small and rather sweet and always had a smile on his face, his head bobbing from side to side as he spoke, and nothing seemed to faze him. Once, while he was washing the floor in the Indian way, dipping a piece of cloth in a bucket of water then applying it to the floor, I threw up in his bucket, but without batting an eyelid, he changed the water and just carried on as if nothing had happened.

The Ghatis had a hierarchy. Tukaram was the head Ghati, who would not have been called on to do any cleaning or dusting.

Tukaram played a very important role in Baba's business. Whenever a customer came in complaining their raincoat was leaking, Baba would say, "We shall test it immediately in our testing department." "Tukaram!" he would shout, and Tukaram would emerge from the curtained-off back of the shop and Baba would thrust the raincoat in his hands. Tukaram would go back to the rear of the shop, making sure to close the curtain so the customer could not see what he was doing. Then he would upturn an old leaky bucket and balance a tumbler on it. He would place the raincoat over the tumbler and slowly pour water on the raincoat. Then, after what seemed an inordinately long time, he would gently lift the raincoat. If there were drops in the tumbler, the complaint was justified; if it was dry, it wasn't. Mostly, Tukaram could report there was nothing wrong with the raincoat, and Baba would hand it back to the customer: "This raincoat does not leak. Our experts have tested it. Did you perhaps leave your coat unbuttoned—it often happens—then water may have sneaked in or maybe it was through the collar." The customer, now no longer sure when faced with such expert testimony, would relent. Baba's triumph was complete: "If a raincoat of ours ever leaks—and it never does—we shall immediately replace it." Thanks to Tukaram, he rarely had to.

Tukaram was lovable, if dull, and the man I loved was his brother, Shankar. Shankar had started as an office boy, learnt driving, and became my favourite person. It was appropriate Shankar should have become a driver. His surname was Cadillac, the same name as the luxury American car much featured in Hollywood movies which we all coveted. And while we did not have that American car, Shankar lived up to his name and was always fetching and carrying us in my father's Ford Anglia.

He took me to school every day, even bringing me back for lunch in the afternoon—I must have been the only one in my school to enjoy such a luxury—and he took me wherever else I wanted to go. I was an avid follower of cars. I would sit for hours beside my window, looking down on Dadabhai Naoroji Road and watch them go by, quickly seeking to identify them. My great joy would be to sit on Shankar's lap while he drove our car or stand next to the driver's seat and peer intently through the windscreen. Once, on a trip to Pune, which involved negotiating the steep ghats where Shankar and the Ghatis came from, I did the entire journey of nearly four hours standing in front next to Shankar and holding on to the dashboard.

All Shankar's complaints I took to Baba in the hope they would be redressed. I desperately sought his friendship and found the way to his heart lay through his stomach. Shankar, who had an enormous appetite, and found food absolutely irresistible, would often say, "*Pate ma chua goom rehe hai*," "In my stomach the rats are moving round." It provided me an easy way of winning his friendship. I would pocket the odd mango or orange and give it to him. Mostly I did this surreptitiously. Once he remonstrated: "Am I a thief? Why are you presenting it to me so surreptitiously?" From then on, though I stole it without telling Ma, whose wrath I feared, I presented it in grand style hoping this would impress him. Our relationship, of course, was defined by our respective positions. I was the boss's son and it paid him to please me, yet on my part there was a genuine desire for friendship. I sought no favours, and when one day he told me "You are like a telephone, you relay from one person to another," I was greatly shocked and hurt.

* * *

Aside from the Ghatis there were other servants, but unlike the Ghatis, who had committed their life to work for Baba's firm, our turnover of these servants was high. Their relationship with Ma would begin brilliantly but then quickly deteriorate, and we were always adjusting to new cooks. The servants usually came via Ma's friends, although on one occasion Ma took on a young Bengali boy without any recommendation. Ma quickly found he was not up to the jobs she had given him and was mystified. The mystery was solved when, a couple of days later, we were visiting friends in a Mumbai suburb. There was a gentleman from Kolkata who said he had come to Mumbai looking for his son who had disappeared. He felt he might have been attracted by the glamour of the city, that it was the movie capital of India. As he began to describe the boy, Ma recognised this was the very same young man she had hired: "I knew he could not be a servant. He just did not know how to do anything I asked him to do." Father and son were soon reunited.

It was many years later that Ma finally found a servant she could cope with and he with her. He was Gobardhan, from Orissa. The Bengalis have always been contemptuous of people from Orissa, calling them "*Oriya*" and considering them stupid. But Gobardhan would get his revenge on my fellow Bengalis. We became aware of his shrewdness when he went back to his *desh*, meaning his home in Orissa, for a holiday. Normally the Ghatis, being office employees, would feel superior to these servants, but on this occasion they were carrying Gobardhan's considerable luggage to Victoria station from where Gobardhan was to catch a train home. It turned out the Ghatis had been borrowing money from Gobardhan and did not want to upset their banker.

Some years later, when Didi had her second child, a son, Ma let Gobardhan work for Didi, who after her marriage had gone to live in Kolkata. Gobardhan became such an important part of her household, helping Didi bring up my nephew and niece, that they called him "GoMama", treating him as if he was almost equivalent to me, their Mama, their mother's only brother. By then Gobardhan was more than a servant; he was a member of the family, a status he had till his death a few years ago.

* * *

In 1947, when the British left India, it was an impoverished nation (its per capita income was £20 and it had a literacy rate of 12 per-cent as opposed to £6,636 and literacy of 81 per cent now), and growing up we were aware we were beholden to the generosity of the west. In the 1960s the country waited anxiously for word from the Aid India Club which would meet annually in Paris to decide how much money to disburse to India.

Everybody had a ration card, which was required to buy "essen-tial" food stuffs such as rice and wheat from government-licensed shops. Unlike most Indians, we could always buy food on the black market; Ma used the ration card for food for the servants, but the public message that Indians should eat less was constantly stressed. In cinemas, before the main film started, there would be govern-ment advertisements warning us it was criminal to eat too much or waste food. The partition of India had lost the country some of its rice growing areas in the east.

There were also guest control orders: no more than fifty people could be invited without the special permission of the Home Minister. At weddings and other such occasions only ice cream could be served. The only occasion I remember this being set aside was in 1964 for Didi's wedding in Kolkata, when Dhiren *Kaku*, a prominent member of the West Bengal Congress, made sure it did not apply by inviting the West Bengal chief minister and most of his cabinet. The police could hardly arrest the chief minister for break-ing the law.

* * *

As if to compensate, weddings were converted into very efficient business meetings. As the waiters served ice creams, the guests were ushered to meet the bride and bridegroom, who, wearing heavy garlands, were sitting on a dais on chairs with gold-coloured coverings. The guests congratulated the newly married couple, slipping an envelope into their hands. The donors did not know the bride or bridegroom. They were business contacts of the bride's father. An attractive young girl would sit on a table next to the podium taking down the names of those who had given the presents. Ostensibly, this was to send printed cards of thanks, though the bride's father was more interested in knowing how much money his business cronies had given in those white envelopes. Those who gave the most were the ones with whom it was worth preserving the business relationship.

When the children of business contacts of Baba got married, Chordi would always be the person sitting at this table. She was considered completely trustworthy and would not try and steal any of the money. Every now and again the father of the bride, or the groom, would come and ask what so-and-so had given. He would either smile or scowl: a smile if the money had come up to expectations, a scowl if it had fallen short. As a child going to these weddings, I looked forward to the ice cream and felt very proud my beloved sister was the one trusted with this delicate task. Now I can see how skilfully Indians had woven their pursuit of money into the wedding ceremony.

* * *

My own birthdays had a touch of these weddings. As I was the only son, Baba and Ma both made it special, but it meant my birthdays were not like other children's, for there were no other children present.

On that day I would become a vegetarian. I dined on silver plates, drank from silver glasses, ate with a silver knife and fork, and silver cups and saucers were brought out from Ma's cupboard. Then, in the evening a large cake with candles would arrive and two feasts would be arranged. I would be dressed up very prettily, generally in a new suit. Didi and Chordi would decorate my face with sandal paste, and for most of the evening I would wear a heavy garland.

The two feasts were entirely separate. First Baba's office staff would be fed. This was the day when Baba's white-collar assistants would sit in the living room and be served high tea, emphasising once again Baba's Englishness. Tasty, delicious, abundant Indian snacks served at 7 in the evening—high tea that made dinner redundant—while in the other room, abode during the day of his clerk Mr Rao, the ghatis and Shankar were catered for. I would be paraded through both groups to receive the presents and good wishes. After the staff there followed Baba's friends and acquaintances. All of them would bring costly presents for Junior Bose or "Master Bose".

Ma kept a careful watch on the presents. The ones she coveted were the ones that contained money in little white- or buff-coloured envelopes: Rs.25, Rs.35, occasionally even Rs.100. I would give these envelopes to Ma, who would quickly put them away in her cupboard to be stored for my future use. Years later when I asked her for the money, Ma affected total surprise. Occasionally, when I received not cash but presents Ma didn't like or didn't consider useful, Ma would seek to trade them in for cash.

* * *

There was only one kind of wedding ceremony where such naked materialism was not evident and where food was served. That was at a Parsee wedding. They were held in the *agiari*, where, being a religious place, food restrictions did not apply. The Parsees made the most of it and served a wonderful meal of starters followed by several courses, with fish, chicken, meat all being served. There were so many guests that people were fed in batches. The only problem was that just as the sweet was being served, the next batch of guests would arrive and stand behind the chair of those finishing their meal, as if to remind them not to linger too long over the sweet. But the one thing the Parsees could not serve was alcohol.

When the British ruled India such Parsee weddings would be awash with liquor, and the Parsees served the best Scotch. But freedom from the British had meant the freedom to drink had been outlawed. The India I grew up in had long since discarded all Gandhi's ideals, including his plan to return the country to a pre-industrial rural age of supposed bliss, and opted instead for Nehru's socialist path of industrial development. The one Gandhian idea Nehru held on to was *Sharab haram hai*, Drinking is evil. Mumbai had some of the tightest prohibition laws in the country. No bars. No public drinking.

To drink in Mumbai, you had to get a permit which was in the gift of the Collector of Customs. Baba had such a permit provided on the strength of his doctor's certificate, which said Baba needed two pegs of whisky every evening for his health. He also had a number of naval friends, and the Indian Navy still maintained the old British naval tradition of drinking. Every now and again Shankar would drive us to the Gateway of India. We would take a small boat to one of the ships commanded by my father's friend, and there, while I played round the ship, Baba and his friends would drink. Even then Baba missed Parsee weddings, where drink flowed so freely, this was another imperial legacy he had to discard.

Freedom came with a price.

5

DO IT FOR ENGLAND

The scene is the Oval Maidan in Mumbai in 1961. A maidan is, probably, the most evocative place in Indian urban life, a vast, open area, very often at the centre of cities, reproducing Indian city life with all its noise and clamour. The grass is matted, raggy, struggling to stay alive amidst the dirt and rubble. Flowing through the maidan are little canals, the surface is pock-marked with ditches, even what looks like small ravines, and the whole area is filled with people from every walk of life. In one corner a vendor could be selling cakes from a tin box, in another a couple might be furtively holding hands, which is about as much open affection as they dare display. In the land of the *Kama Sutra* public display of sex is taboo. It is amidst such confusion and noise that Indians learn to play cricket, the English game they now control and which is like a religion in the country.

This is highly appropriate, for the maidans are a classic illustration of the legacy the British bequeathed. They had borrowed the term maidan, meaning "square", from the Persian, but the development of the physical maidan was very British. Long before the English ruled India and even when they were traders, they developed armies and constructed forts. They kept an open field in front of their fort onto which they could train their guns on any Indian hordes likely to emerge from the interior. It is these fields of fire that have become maidans.

That day in 1961 a cricket match is taking place at the Oval between a group of boys. The batting side is struggling. At the end of the over, the batsman's partner walks down the wicket and, leaning on his bat, says, "Do it for England." The batsman who keeps failing to put bat on ball is me, and my partner invoking England is Eddie, a Catholic boy who is part of the cricket team I have put together. Eddie, like me and my other friends, had seen *The Guns of Navarone*, which had just been released, and fallen in love with it. For us it was magical that a handful of British, and a sole American, despite losing their leader, outwitted German defences and took over a heavily fortified German citadel. We would retell scenes from the movie to each other. Of particular interest was the character of the British explosive expert played by David Niven. One of the most fascinating scenes was when Niven told Gregory Peck, the American, that he must kill the traitor in their midst, a Greek woman who Peck had fallen in love with. Peck was reluctant. Niven, staring hard at Peck, fairly barked out: "Do it for England." Eddie, who had seen the movie several times, was captivated by the words, and whenever we batted together at the Oval Maidan he would walk down the wicket and try to imitate Niven, treating me as Peck. We had not seen England but felt part of it, and at that particular moment, like Niven and Peck, were trying to defeat a superior cricketing foe.

We were part of the first generation of free Indians for two hundred years. It was 1961, only fourteen years since the British had left India, yet we craved things and ideas from Britain and desperately wanted British acceptance.

* * *

All about us, in the streets below and around our house, from morning to evening could be heard the cries of hawkers. They could not be more *desi*, Indian, wearing a long white shirt that hung over their loose white trousers, their goods spread out on a large sheet, and bargaining in Hindi with their customers. Yet they knew three words of English: "Foreign, imported, novelty". This is what they shouted all the time. These words would entice customers eager to get goods made abroad, particularly in England, as they must by definition be better than anything India had to offer. Today our attitude would be called self-hatred; then we saw it as a mark of sophistication.

Baba thought nothing could match Gabardine and Burberry coats. And the only car worth possessing was an English one. "Whatever happens," he would say, "an English car will always start first thing in the morning." His best friend had a Sunbeam sports car and, while Baba did not approve of the flashiness, he was reassured that it was English.

For Baba, England also had superior moral values. Recalling that Edward VIII had not been allowed to ascend the throne because he wanted to marry Wallis Simpson, a divorced American, he confidently predicted that a divorced woman would never be Queen of England. Had he been alive today, Camilla as Queen would have made him wonder what had happened to English moral values.

* * *

The man I called "*Dadu*", grandfather—he was really Baba's uncle and had served in the British Indian Army—introduced me to Richmal Compton's William Brown by giving me two books. If I remember right, they were *Just William* and *William in Trouble*. I immediately fell in love with William, Douglas, Ginger and Henry and was reassured that life in England was not all that different from India. After all, didn't William have a cook and housemaid, and didn't he tussle with his parents about school as much as I did?

I had already started borrowing *Biggles* books from my school library. To read about Biggles killing Huns was exciting. Soon there was P. G. Wodehouse and Jeeves.

We longed to be sixteen so we could become members of the British Council Library. Such was the demand that the British Council had rationed membership and you had to be sixteen to join.

And it was while I was waiting to be sixteen that, suddenly one Thursday, I discovered a British library which was a cultural nirvana.

* * *

It came about quite by chance. I was still chaperoned wherever I went. But on Thursdays, when our school had a midweek holiday, after lunch I was allowed to wander out into Dadabhai Naoroji Road on my own. There I stumbled across the offices of the British Deputy High Commissioner, just opposite our flat and the other side of Flora Fountain, located on the second floor of a marvellous white stone building—the rest of it was occupied by the Hong Kong and Shanghai Bank. It had a small library, which housed all the latest English papers, printed on paper so thin I felt I could eat them. The newspapers were all broadsheets rolled round a large wooden stick which had neatly spaced holes and hung from a wooden rack. The exception was the *Daily Mirror*, where the whole week's issue was bound together with a yellow cover.

The journey to the library was like going to the source of the river. The *Times of India* had a weekly "Letter from London" from its correspondent. Now I realised they were no more than a summary of the British press. Newspapers in India regularly reprinted articles from the British press. Now I could, thrillingly, read the originals.

What gave me the most pleasure and made me feel very privileged about visits to this library was knowing it was a secret treasure trove to which I alone had the key.

My reading was voracious and undiscriminating, and the high point was the *New Statesman* and the political commentaries of Anthony Howard. I had read that Nehru had the *New Statesman* airmailed to him every week and of the enormous influence its then editor, Kingsley Martin, had on him. Harold Macmillan was then mired in political problems—soon the Profumo scandal would break—and Howard wrote in a style at once intelligible and accessible. Political commentaries were not unknown to me. The *Times of India* carried one almost every day, and the editor wrote his long weekly piece taking up almost the entire leader page and setting right the nation and the world. But they were written in a heavy neo-Victorian style that was quite difficult to fathom. Howard was like a ray of sunshine cutting through a dense fog.

As I read, I imagined him to look like David Niven, our idea of the typical Englishman.

My interest in that library was not merely intellectual; there was also a quite unexpected and deliciously sensual side to these visits. The Swinging Sixties were upon us, and the English girls of the High Commission had taken to wearing short skirts—if not quite mini, certainly much shorter than anything to be seen in Bombay. Lunchtime was a good time to go, for at 1 pm they went out for a group lunch and returned at 2 pm. I only had to glance up from Howard's political commentary to see a generous flash of thighs as they paraded past. The combination of Howard's brilliant prose and the promise of those thighs made me long for Thursdays.

But just as the promise of the thighs never turned into reality—and I never imagined they would—so, for very different reasons, I was shocked when, years later, I got to London and made my pilgrimage to the *New Statesman* offices at Great Turnstile Street. I was ushered into Howard's office. He received me with great kindness, but I could hardly take in anything he said. Far from looking like Niven, he looked like one of our Nepali servant boys, and to my utter shame—although I did not say this to him—as I left his office, I told myself, "How can a man who looks like Ramu write so well?" I now understood why *Private Eye* had always called him "Sherpa".

* * *

Such was the legacy of the empire that English words would impress even powerful politicians, many of whom had fought against British rule.

In 1964 the All India Congress Committee (AICC), the party's decision-making body, held a meeting in Mumbai's Shanmukhananda Hall. Dhiren *Kaku*, who had recently been elected as a member of the AICC, came for the meeting. It was held just weeks before Nehru died, and in the months leading up to the meeting there had been an explosion of Hindu-Muslim violence. For a time, there were fears the dark days of partition might be revisited.

Like Baba and all his family, Kaku had warm memories of his upbringing in pre-partition East Bengal, enjoying the great wealth the family then had, and felt deeply about the Hindus being driven from their homes in East Pakistan and seeking shelter in West Bengal. But he was also a secular politician. He asked me to write a speech taking all this into account. I was thrilled that at the age of sixteen I was asked to do so for such a prestigious political event. I wrote that "Pakistan is guilty of genocide." Kaku read the speech while Nehru, Indira Gandhi and the other Congress bigwigs reclined on mattresses covered with pristine white sheets on the dais behind him.

After the speech, Kaku was very chuffed that a prominent Congress politician had first asked him what the word meant, and then gone round repeating it with great relish. One of his Congress colleagues, an old man, patted me on the back and said, "'Genocide, appeasement', very appropriate words. You write like an Englishman." I felt so proud.

* * *

In the late fifties and early sixties, Mumbai had little to offer in terms of entertainment. Cinema provided our great window on the world, and snobbery pushed us in the direction of Hollywood. In posh south Mumbai, the cinemas did not screen Hindi films. They were regarded as strictly for the servants and the hoi-polloi: those who could not boast our faultless English or pedigree.

Hollywood movies opened up a world at once alluring and irre-sistible, where there was no dirt, beggars, pollution, crime, poverty, disease or death; where roads were broad and cars big enough to fit them; where men were always handsome, and women beautiful and tender; where the villains were nasty; and where it all ended happily. Such was our love for cowboy movies that I forced Ma to take me to a restaurant that served "cowboy breakfast", only to find it was raw eggs. Ma was furious I had made her pay for me to eat them.

So heavily did Hollywood influence our tastes that when *The Spy Who Came in From the Cold* was screened, its portrayal of life in 1960s London—people living in dirty bedsits, wearing old clothes, agonis-ing over petty domestic issues and riding on overcrowded buses and tubes—was so alien that within fifteen minutes of the start the audi-torium resounded with boos and catcalls.

* * *

The question I am asked more often than any other is "Why do you support Tottenham? You were not born in North London." Nor am I Jewish which could explain my loyalty given the club's large Jewish following. I started supporting Tottenham on 8 May 1961, when the *Times of India* led its sports pages with a report of Tottenham becoming the first team in the twentieth century to do the double of wining the English First Division and the FA Cup. The report was accompanied by a picture of the team parading the League trophy and the FA Cup through the streets of North London.

I had never heard of Tottenham, but I immediately fell in love with the club. I had my favourite Indian football club, East Bengal, which Baba supported as it reminded him of his homeland. I soon cared for Tottenham more than I had ever cared for East Bengal. We felt we would only be complete if we acquired knowledge of England, and the more we knew about it, the more superior we felt. English sporting stars were like gods who occupied a special plane, epitomising the promise the English sporting world held out to me, namely to open the door to the unique, wondrous world where skill reigned supreme and sportsmanship was never in doubt.

This was reinforced by the whole host of signs we received at home and at school which made England seem like the veritable factory of sporting dreams. After I played in my first football match at St. Xavier's, Father Fritz, who took us for sports and English, fixed a photograph on the school noticeboard purporting to be from the match. It turned out to be one of an English First Division game reproduced in an Indian sports magazine and, if my memory serves me right, showed Dave Mackay, Tottenham's great midfielder, tackling some other burly player. Fritz had just scratched out their names and replaced them with those of two of my school team-mates. He explained it was not meant to deceive. He wanted us to look at the photograph of those huge British players, study their technique and seek to emulate them.

Reports and descriptions of England at play were, in our minds, all about us. We read articles from the *Daily Express* and the *Daily Mail* in *Sport and Pastime*, India's premier sports magazine. It made us feel we were not 6,000 miles away but in the grandstand.

In the summer, even the *Times of India* easily, effortlessly, allowed English sports like cricket and tennis to take over its sports pages. In general, foreign news always took precedence over domestic news—500 deaths from cholera a small news item, 16 miners killed in Belgium meriting big headlines. V. S. Naipaul has seen this as a sign of the displacement of Indians in their own land, people trying to mimic mature societies. But this was an expression of our searching for what we considered the best. And the best was in England.

K. N. Prabhu, The *Times of India's* legendary cricket correspondent, borrowed English imagery to validate Shivaji Park, the vast, teeming maidan in congested central Mumbai which can claim to be the greatest cricket nursery in the world. He called it "the Pudsey of Mumbai". Pudsey was the birthplace of Len Hutton, one of England's greatest cricketers and the first professional to captain England. Should a journalist on the *Yorkshire Post* dare to call Pudsey "the Shivaji Park of Yorkshire", he would be denounced as "woke".

We felt things that were wholly English really belonged to us. I hankered after a copy of *Wisden*, the great cricket almanac. There was a perfectly good Indian equivalent—*Indian Cricket*—, but growing up I never considered buying it.

* * *

Curiously, the disdain of Indian politicians for popular culture forced us even more towards England. Gandhi had no time for the cinema and, while I was growing up, for many years All India Radio eschewed Hindi film music, considering it unworthy. This gave Radio Ceylon, which was beamed to India, free rein. It broadcast Hindi film music. And programmes from the World Service. We could not wait for the BBC *News* to come on. The joke about the All India Radio news was that if World War Three broke out, it might just make the closing headlines after the latest production figures for rice and wheat. To listen to the BBC *News* was to feel I was a citizen of the world, and I can remember my excitement when I heard the Russians had erected a wall in Berlin. I rushed in to tell Baba and his friend, who gazed at me in wonder, curious to know how I had discovered this amazing information. When they heard it was the BBC, they had no doubt it was true.

The shining jewel of the World Service was "Saturday Special", the sports programme presented by Paddy Feeny. It would start at round about 4.30 pm Indian time on a Saturday afternoon and end at around 10.30 pm with the "Sports Roundup". Then, with the streets of Mumbai hushed for the first time and a single overhead lamp burning over my desk, I would listen to a stentorian voice reading the English football results. As the announcer said "League Division One", I stopped everything I was doing and tried to picture the matches that had been played that Saturday. The English results would be followed by the Scottish ones, and I was fascinated by a team called the Queen of the South. Was there, I wondered, a

Queen sitting in the stands watching the match? If so, what sort of a Queen was she and why was she only Queen of the South and not the entire country? Years later, when Queen of the South made it to the Scottish Cup Final, as BBC Sports Editor I persuaded the *Today* programme to broadcast an item on the club. When I went there, they proudly mentioned they were the only team in the Bible.

Colonialism had made us doubt ourselves. This explains why, after coming to England, when asked what languages I spoke, I said only English. It required my wife, who is English, to make me realise I also spoke a host of Indian languages and to overcome my deeply ingrained belief that these Indian languages could not be equated with European languages.

We were, as my friend Vidya, a physicist, puts it brilliantly, looking for the *thappa*, the stamp, of foreign approval.

We fell in love with foreigners who acclaimed India and Indian culture. When I did my degree in Physics and Maths at St. Xavier's College, I was drawn to the story of Robert Oppenheimer, the American physicist who headed the Manhattan project, which produced the atom bomb. As the Americans exploded the atom bomb over the New Mexico desert, Oppenheimer quoted from the *Bhagavad Gita*, the nearest the Hindus have to a Bible, where Lord Krishna tells Arjuna why he must wage war. As the unearthly mushroom cloud soared into the heavens, Oppenheimer thought of the words of Lord Krishna: "Now I am become death, the destroyer of worlds." It made us proud that a western scientist recalled words from a Hindu text, and I later learnt Oppenheimer had learnt Sanskrit, part of his wide learning and eclectic thinking.

We were proud of the great Indian mathematician Ramanujan and the story of how Cambridge mathematician G.H. Hardy took him to England making him known to the wider world. We endlessly repeated the story of when Hardy came to see Ramanujan when he was in a nursing home in Putney. Hardy told Ramanujan that his taxi number was 1729 and that it was a dull number and hoped it was not a bad omen. Ramanujan immediately said, "No, Hardy. It is a a very interesting number. It is the smallest number expressible as the sum of two cubes in two different ways." This in mathematics is not easy until you reach 1729. To us it showed how Ramanujan was superior to Hardy, which Hardy acknowledged.

Hardy, who was also very interested in cricket, became a particular hero of mine. But while India hails Ramanujan and has a stamp in his name there is not even a biography of Hardy. I have never been able to persuade a publisher to commission me to write one.

Proud as we were of our culture, and did not agree with Naipaul's view that India had a wounded civilisation, we instinctively accepted it needed to be validated by its former conquerors.

6

CHAINED TO THE COLONIAL LEGACY

I was seven months and three days old when the British left India and like Saleem Sinai, Salman Rushdie's great fictional hero, consider myself a "Midnight's Child", India having attained freedom on midnight of 15 August. Sinai claimed to be chained to the destiny of India. I was chained to what the departing conquerors had left behind. And not just the British but also the Portuguese.

My early upbringing was entrusted to ayahs, Mary and Marie, both Goan Catholics. Goa was still a Portuguese colony and would remain so until the Indian Army marched into Goa in 1962. There is an old sepia print showing Mary and Marie on either side of me when I must have been no more than one. They were dressed in the frocks so characteristic of that era, a cross round their necks, their faces and hands carrying evidence of their years of labour. I remember almost nothing of how they brought me up. Ma had no worries that Mary or Marie would convert me—and in any case, if she felt it would be helpful, she was always ready to go to a church to pray. Told by either Mary or Marie that, if she offered candles to Mother Mary, I would do brilliantly at school, she hurried off to St Mary's church in Bandra, nearly an hour away by car. In this case, however, and for whatever reason, the offerings did not quite do the trick.

Mary and Marie's influence meant that as a Bengali child I did not speak Bengali but a curious Hindi nobody understood. When I was about four Baba employed another Goan Catholic, older, heavier, who would sit on my bed eating poached eggs, which the servant had brought her, and teach me the English alphabet, the workings of a clock and, above all, the power of God. It could not be more incongruous. In a corner of the room were the Hindu gods Ma worshipped, in particular Lakshmi, the goddess of wealth. That morning Ma would have prayed to Lakshmi asking her to make us rich. Now this Goan Catholic taught me about the Christian god.

All the deeds of an individual, whether good or bad, were entered into huge ledgers and, on the day of reckoning, the scales would be brought out, the good deeds placed in one pan, the bad in the other, and the good would go to Heaven, the bad to Hell. Her description of the horrors of Hell was so real I felt it had been designed exclusively for me. "Everything that is done is put down in the ledger?" I would ask, trembling.

"Yes, everything". There was no escape. Hell was unending torture, everlasting pain, eternal roasting on the spit. Heaven, on the other hand, was an unspecific, unending bliss. It was years before I was to lose my fear of the God with a flowing beard, looking like Charlton Heston, totting up the sins on a scale—curiously, this was when I realised what death actually meant. Years later my girlfriend, Margaret, like my Goan teacher also a Catholic but from Ireland, would tell me she had been brought up to believe Heaven meant eating oranges all the time. By then I could laugh and wonder where they came from and, as apartheid still existed, whether the Christian Heaven allowed South African oranges.

In contrast to the revealed religions of Judaism, Islam and Christianity, Hindus had no concept of Hell and Heaven. But my parents had no fear that my Hindu faith would be subverted.

Today, though I can speak Bengali with reasonable fluency, complex conversations see me lapse into English. I can neither read nor write Bengali, which still produces the familiar lament: How can a Bengali who cannot read Tagore in the original be considered a Bengali?

* * *

I went to primary school two years after India had become a republic with a Constitution saying Hindi was the national language. I should have been sent to a school where the medium of instruction was either Hindi or Marathi or Gujarati, the two vernacular languages of the state.

Baba decided that I, like Didi and Chordi, would also be educated at an English school. It was important to be educated in the language of the departed conquerors. I cannot thank Baba enough for making that decision. It meant I could become an English writer.

My parents had thought of sending me away to a Indian boarding school, modelled on British public schools. But they were put off because they felt I might like Bhanu, Baba's cousin, rebel against his father. He had married a non-Bengali girl—a Punjabi—, resigned his army commission and settled in England. The moral he drew was simple: children sent to boarding schools become alienated from their parents. He could not have imagined that, despite not going to a boarding school, I would follow Bhanu's example.

Baba decided I would go to St. Xavier's, Mumbai's leading Jesuit school. The Jesuits said, "Give me the child of seven and I shall give you the man of seventeen." The ditty Baba often recited was "*Porasuno kora jey, gadi ghora chorey shey*", "Those who study hard get to ride in a carriage." Jesuits, he was sure, would help me ride in carriages. As far as Ma was concerned, divinity in any shape was welcome as long as it brought prosperity to the family.

* * *

So, I went to a Jesuit school, where the medium of instruction was English, and Indian languages, like Marathi and Gujarati, were optional languages. The school was administered by white-robed priests, many white, whom we called "fathers", assisted by the odd "brother", a priest who had yet to make the grade. Not all our teachers were Jesuits, or even Catholics, and a good many were female. Our non-Catholic teachers were mostly Parsees, who had been the most prominent collaborators of the Raj and were keen we should learn British ways. A stern Parsee female teacher—attractive in a curious sort of way—made us learn the whole formal letter of invitation for dinner parties: "Mr & Mrs So-and-so request the company of Mr and Mrs So-and-so" by heart, complete with commas and all other punctuations. One class was spent repeating the letter loudly, and those who could not were punished. I had never ever seen anyone in India send such a letter and now, even in Britain, very few do.

* * *

We were, naturally enough, susceptible to Catholic influences. In all our classrooms, just above the blackboard, there was a crucifix. Four times a day we bowed our heads before it, crossed ourselves, and said the prayers of the Lord. Twice a day we sought blessing, before class, and again after lunch; twice we sought forgiveness for our sins, just before the lunch break and, finally, before going home at 4.30 pm. In unison we all learned to mumble our prayers in low monotones, quickly cross ourselves and get on with more desirable pursuits. But this ritualistic Christian prayer was not meant to convert us: our parents never feared it; our school certainly did not want it.

The school also cultivated a feeling of reverence for the Christian faith, presenting it as very different to the Hindu one. The chapel radiated a sense of calm, very removed from the raucous noise and bustle of a Hindu temple, and I often went there when I wanted some peace and quiet. I did not believe in Christ, but I did seek solace gazing at the figure of Christ on the cross.

There were subtle suggestions which questioned traditional Indian beliefs such as arranged marriages. Father Fritz would often try to convince us it was natural for a man to choose his own wife: "Your parents may tell you that the female is a cow, and for years you will believe it, but the day will come when you will tell your parents that, even if all females are cows, I would like to have a cow."

Father Fritz's greatest legacy to me were his remarks after he had read what I had written about Shelley's poem "Ozymandias". He looked down from his seat on the podium and said "You will be a writer." Words that would sustain me over many years when it seemed I could never fulfil that dream.

The Catholic boys went for catechism classes, we non-Catholics had Moral Science. I loved Moral Science as I discovered that, by answering that God was omnipotent, and omnipresent, I could score as much as 95 per cent. It helped convince me that talking of such a God was particularly useful for scholastic success.

* * *

I learnt more about Catholics not through school but because my best friend at school was Hubert Miranda. They were poor and lived in two small rooms above a rickety house in a narrow, stench-filled lane. By the side of their house was the communal sewer.

It was when talking to Mrs Miranda's daughter Juliet that, for the first and only time in my childhood, my Hindu faith was questioned. In our friend's circle we never discussed religion although we were from diverse religious communities. But Juliet felt her religion required not merely justification but advertisement.

She was always keen to prove that Hinduism was inferior to Christianity. "How is it," she asked, "that in your religion a man can be named after a god?"—referring to the fact that many Hindus are called Krishna, Ram, Shiva or Vishnu. This was impossible in Christianity. Nobody could be called Jesus. He was the one and only son of God. I was aware of how Christians saw Jesus. The school had taken us to see Ben-Hur, which has a scene in which Jesus appears, but only his back is shown. A priest had explained, "No man can play Jesus, so he can only be seen from behind."

Juliet eventually left home and married a middle-class Hindu. I would have loved to know if her husband was called Krishna.

Mrs Miranda, too, when talking about her faith, could make argument difficult and reasoning redundant, but my most abiding memory of her is not of her Christian faith but her belief in superstitions. One day she saw me put my hands on my head. "Never put your hand on your head," she told me, "For if you do, it is very likely that your parents will die very soon." This put such a fear in me that I quickly abandoned the habit—one that can be very comforting indeed—and for years afterwards shuddered whenever I saw people do it. How curious now to think that, despite the vast religious gulf separating Ma from Mrs Miranda, when it came to superstition Mrs Miranda and Ma were not all that different.

* * *

Our school attracted the best of upper-middle and middle-class society of Mumbai. There was a fair sprinkling of upper-middle-class Muslims. Throughout my school career a Muslim was often the head monitor of my class, equivalent to a prefect in England, one of whom would migrate to America and become a very keen supporter of Donald Trump. There was a sharp divide between them and the poor Muslims.

Just down the road from our school was Muhammad Ali Street, which was the main Muslim area of Mumbai and had the city's most colourful market, called "*Chor Bazaar*", Thieves' Market, Mumbai's equivalent of London's Portobello Road market, where all sorts of things could be found. Had Boris Johnson ever ventured there, he could have pointed to any number of women wearing letter boxes. We did not find them remotely strange. One of Baba's best clients had his shop there and on Muslim feast days would bring us the best biryani I have ever had. Yet these Muslims would not dream of sending their children to our school. They went to a Muslim school whose prowess in sport, particularly cricket, we feared—but we also thought they cheated and did not have our high moral standards.

* * *

Every teacher at St. Xavier's instilled in us the fear that if we didn't study hard, we would be sucked into the quagmire of poverty that surrounded us. Nobody did this more than Father DeMello, an Indian priest, short, fat, dark, whose hands locked together were always held just over his nicely rounded paunch. Though after primary school he rarely taught us, throughout our school career he was the one priest we dreaded. His demeanour was stern, his admonition never varied: "Why don't you all study? Do you want to become boot polish wallahs? (shoeshine boys). If you do not study that is what you'll become, and then one day, when I am walking down the street, you'll be waiting to polish my shoes—only I mean slippers." We shivered. Boot polish wallahs! A life spent polishing shoes! In many ways DeMello was saying what Baba had been saying, except more dramatically. We turned to our books, aware of the jungle that awaited us if we did not study and pass the Secondary School Certificate (SSC), our school leaving examinations, with flying colours.

The jungle where the shoeshine boys came from was literally next door. For that was where the municipal school was located.

Indian municipal schools are for the urban poor and provide a few years of unsatisfactory education to people who will never make much use of it and do not, in fact, have the means to do so. The municipal school was just beyond our playground and along one side of it. During our recess, it was part of our pastime to watch the students there. They were poor—they looked poor. They were hungry—they looked hungry. They were ill-educated and ill-mannered, and they looked it. From our side of the fence there was pity, and I suspect they envied us. They were part of the unnamed and never-mentioned enemy of our wider struggle against those who did not speak English and were incapable of assimilating our westernised thoughts.

* * *

We despised those who did not speak English. Not all of the non-English speakers were poor, indeed some were very rich, and in despising them, we were proclaiming what we saw as civilised society. We called them "*Guju Bhais*" and "*Mani Bhen*", literally "Gujarati brothers and sisters". Not that they were all necessarily Gujaratis— they covered a wide spectrum from different communities in the city, but in our imagination they all belonged to this class of Mumbai citizens who may have great wealth but no learning or sophistication.

This fight between those who spoke English and those who did not was symbolised in our dealings with our Hindi teacher, Parekh.

* * *

Hindi was the one compulsory Indian language, and we had to get at least 35 per cent to pass our SSC examinations. Parekh came into our lives in the 7th standard, by which time we were thirteen, that difficult age when, as teenagers, we wanted to be adults but were not treated as adults. He would shrug his shoulders while he walked, as if exercising them. We mocked this, calling it "U-U", symbolising the way he twisted his shoulders. He also had a nickname, "*Ayo*", He has come.

My relationship with Parekh was established immediately. I knew he could be provoked; he knew I was a troublemaker. He felt that in order to control me he had to launch a pre-emptive strike. My neighbours, who were generally docile, would be called up to his table and questioned about what I was up to. Once, as soon as he entered the class, he asked me to leave and kneel outside the classroom.

"But I have done nothing."

"You have not done anything, but you are likely to cause trouble." So, I did. Of the 35-minute class we spent no more than fifteen on actual work. I constantly interrupted the class to fetch various things I had left behind.

Our teachers were allowed to beat us, and they did. I was caned only once, when I was about seven, an event I can barely remember: a long, thin cane, a white priest beating it against my open palms. The main physical chastisement was with the ruler. Our teachers would hit us hard on our knuckles with the edge of a wooden ruler. This was the most painful of the physical punishments. Occasionally there were slaps and a few blows with the wooden ruler, but the most potent weapon used by our teachers was humiliation. Boys who were considered naughty would be sent out of the class and made to kneel. Parekh loved inflicting this punishment, and I spent many a Hindi class kneeling outside the classroom.

We in turn tormented Parekh. We carried small compass boxes, which we would place at the edge of our desks. As he passed down each row to check on our work, we would gently tap them, and they would fall with a crash on the floor. His reaction would be immediate. He would turn around, seize the smallest boy and thrash him.

With Parekh we could not have the normal teacher–student relationship we had with our other teachers. Nor could we indulge in banter; no question was harmless, no answer free of loaded meaning. When Parekh taught us Hindi, we were not learning India's national language, which the constitution had decreed would replace English, but defining ourselves in relation to a great mass of Indian humanity who spoke Hindi not English.

Language was an explosive issue. Many in the south did not want to accept Hindi as the national language. In Mumbai, many Maharashtrians did not want to be part of the British-created Bombay province, which also included Gujarat. The agitation led one Sunday to a march going past our flat in Flora Fountain. Trying to contain the crowd, which was throwing shoes, always a great mark of disrespect in the east, the police reacted just as the Raj police often did. They first fired tear gas, which flooded into our flat and made Baba cough incessantly. Then they started shooting, killing a young boy who could not have been more than twelve. I saw his body, naked from the waist up, a red streak across his chest, lying at Flora Fountain. It was my first sight of death. The agitation would lead to Bombay province being divided into Maharashtra and Gujarat, and Flora Fountain being later renamed "Hutatma Chowk", Martyrs' Square, with an eternal flame burning.

But in the end Parekh had the last laugh on us. It concerned the most sensational murder during my childhood with an Englishwoman at the centre of it.

* * *

In 1959, Commander Kawas Nanavati, a high-flying naval officer, killed his wife's lover, a Mumbai businessman called Prem Ahuja. Nanavati's wife was an Englishwoman called Sylvia whom he had met when undergoing naval training in England. On hearing of the adultery, he took a Smith and Wesson .38 revolver from his ship, drove to Ahuja's flat and shot him. Despite this he pleaded self-defence.

But in the media Nanavati was presented as a rising naval star with Sylvia, grieving for him. It was Ahuja who was portrayed as the scheming businessman. The fact that Sylvia could be presented as this beacon of goodness despite her infidelity showed how Britain was still regarded in India, twelve years after the Raj had ended. That Ahuja was painted in lurid colours reflected the general distrust felt towards Sindhis, a classic story of hating successful immigrants.

The Sindhis had migrated to Mumbai following partition and within a few years become the most prominent business group in the city, displacing the Gujaratis, the previously dominant business group. We could not believe they could have obtained such success fairly. As Baba put it, "They came with only a shirt on their backs, now they own all the shirts in Mumbai." And he didn't mean it as a compliment.

Parekh was part of the nine-man jury in the Sessions Court, and to the astonishment of nearly everyone, the jury returned a "Not Guilty" verdict.

Parekh always refused to tell us why and how the decision was made. As a Gujarati he may have felt it was good Nanavati had killed a Sindhi. On the day of the judgement, his fellow Gujaratis gathered around Flora Fountain, onto which I gazed every day from my bedroom, and distributed ladoos and other Indian sweets celebrating the fact that Nanavati had killed a Sindhi.

The judge refused to accept the verdict, and it was referred to the higher courts, where Nanavati was convicted. Four months later the jury system, yet another legacy of the empire, was abolished. I wonder if the Nanavati case provided Parekh an opportunity to get his revenge on people like us who had mocked him by helping produce a judgement which shook up the legal system the British had bequeathed.

7

BENGALIS IMITATING BRITISH COLONIALS

My life has been one of being an immigrant in two different countries, one in the land of my birth and one in Britain. In Britain, almost from the moment I arrived, I was told that the problem with the immigrants was that they did not integrate but lived in ghettoes of the mind.

Yet this is just what the British did when they lived in India, except their ghettoes were lavish homes in white-only areas of town where the only Indians were servants. British writers like Malcolm Muggeridge and Alan Ross have written of how little contact they had with Indians.

While we could not maintain such a distance from our fellow Indians, Baba's non-Bengali acquaintances were business contacts. I cannot recall Ma having a non-Bengali close friend. Just as the British residents in India were very hospitable to visiting Brits, our home was open to anyone from Kolkata. Many came, like the Kolkata sweet-makers visiting Mumbai, meeting Baba on Marine Drive and then staying with us and forming a remarkable bond. There were others whose arrival in Mumbai reflected Mumbai taking over from Kolkata as the centre of the film industry. Bengali directors, music directors, artistes, film stars, made the journey my parents had. Hemant Kumar, one of Bollywood's greatest music directors and playback singers, stayed with us when he first arrived in the city. By providing hospitality Baba and Ma were keeping in touch with a world they really craved and deeply missed.

They also copied another trait of the colonial British.

Neither Baba nor Ma learnt to speak Marathi, the language of the majority in Mumbai and those Baba employed, including the ghatis who worked for Ma. Nor did they speak the other major local language, Gujarati. The spoke a *Bazaar ka Hindi*, Hindi for shopping in bazaars. They could not have sustained a long conversation in India's national language. The Maharashtrians addressed Ma as *"Maiji"*, respected mother, but Ma hated that term and preferred the Bengali term Ma or Didi, which she considered sweet. As if to compensate, I opted to learn Marathi as one of my additional languages in school and was very proud I came first, beating even boys whose mother tongue it was. It made me feel I really belonged to Mumbai. At home I spoke Bengali, but with my friends and at school it was always English as all my friends were non-Bengalis. Didi's two closest friends were Zubeda, a Muslim girl, and Shirley, a Jewish girl in love with a Hindu.

* * *

And while the Raj did take to Indian food, no Maharashtrian or Gujarati food was ever served by Ma. Bombay duck never entered our home as it was considered unworthy, smelly and something only poor Catholics ate. Ma would occasionally buy pomfret, a popular Mumbai fish, but made it clear it did not compare to the fish all Bengalis loved to eat, the hilsa. Shopping for fish was a very special Bengal tradition which must always be done by the man of the house. While Ma did all the shopping, it was Baba who went to Crawford Market, Mumbai's great market, a 5-minute drive away, to buy fish. Baba could not even make a cup of tea or boil an egg, but he knew how to buy fish. As he told me, you judge how good the fish is by looking into its gills. You only buy it if it is bright pink inside. The fish market floor can be very slippery. Once, in the course of shopping he slipped and broke his arm, but when he recovered he resumed a practice he believed defined a Bengali male. Buying fish was important because no Bengali meal is complete without *macher jhol ar bhat*, fish curry and rice, and we had it every mealtime, at lunch and dinner. Even when Ma served chicken or "mutton", which was goat's meat, there was always a fish dish. Ma on her shopping trips would buy a live chicken which would then be slaughtered by the cook.

The problem was that despite being by the sea, Mumbai did not have the great rivers of Bengal which produced hilsa. It had to be imported from Bengal. When, finally, the local government started a fish farm to develop hilsa, Baba felt Mumbai was at last becoming a place where a Bengali could get a proper meal.

We dismissed the many sweets of Mumbai as far too sweet and unworthy of our delicate palates. They could not compare with *rasgullas*, *rajbhogs*, *sandesh*, *cham cham*, *ledikeni*, *payesh*, Bengali rice pudding, *or misti dahi*, sweet yogurt. Ma did make delicious *payesh* at home, far superior to any rice pudding I have had, but rasgullas, the king of Bengali sweets, was beyond her culinary skills. Every now and again a middle-aged man wearing a dhoti and carrying a big pan on his head would come and squat in our kitchen and Ma would buy rasgullas. They were not quite as wonderful as the ones she had tasted in her youth in Kolkata, but still much superior to the sweets of Mumbai. We children did not need convincing.

* * *

We lived far away from the Bengali exiles' heartland in Mumbai, which, in the era I am writing about, was concentrated in Shivaji Park, Dadar, Parsee Colony, Parel and the other congested central districts of the city. Shivaji Park is the great maidan which has produced some of India's greatest cricketers. But for Baba and Ma what mattered was the nondescript two-storey building with grilled windows and a grilled veranda which was the Bengal Club. Bengalis when they go abroad always like to build a *Kali Bara*, Kali temple. But the Bengalis of Mumbai had not managed that, and for them Bengal Club was home. It was also near where my parents' Bengali friends lived. Every Sunday we would travel to these parts of Mumbai, nourishing our Bengali roots.

The only non-Bengali we met during these visits was the Parsi wife of a Bengali friend of Baba who, not surprisingly, was given the nickname *Dustu* Guha, naughty Guha. His Parsi wife, a demure woman who always wore the sari the Parsee way, was aware that her children could never become Parsees but would also struggle to be accepted as Bengalis. Just as the British were horrified by interracial marriages, the Bengalis always felt a Bengali marrying a non-Bengali was the ultimate sin.

* * *

Our colonial Bengali way of life was reinforced by the nature of Hinduism, which is vastly different from other religions and little understood in the west. Hindus call their religion Sanathan Dharma. Both Hindu and India are foreign names, one Persian, the other Greek. The word Hindu comes from the Persians, who unable to pronounce the name of the river Sindhu aspirated it and it came out as Hindu. The Greek softly breathed the word Sindhu, it became Indus. The west took the Greek word India to describe the country, the Persian word Hindu to describe the religion. In reality, both words mean the same thing. Hinduism, unlike the revealed religions of Judaism, Christianity and Islam, is probably the world's only federal religious system where, while there is a centre composed of gods accepted by all Hindus, the different regions have great autonomy worshipping their own special deities and celebrating their own religious festivals. There is no single religious date, like Christmas or Easter for Christians, that unites all Hindus.

While we Bengalis celebrated *Durga Puja*, which is held round about October, the other Hindus in Mumbai did not join in: they had their own religious festivals held at very different times of the year. Growing up, this did not strike me as odd. So, the Bengali Durga Puja is sandwiched between the *Ganpati Puja* of the Maharashtrians, which is held just as the monsoon ends round August, and the Gujarati festival of Diwali, round about November. For us Bengalis in Mumbai, neither of these festivals had any religious significance, except that Diwali coincided with *Kali Puja*, the worship of the goddess Kali. I realise this statement will surprise many in this country where Diwali is seen as the Hindu Christmas but that reflects the Gujaratis, the most successful Hindu community, making much of their great festival. Had my fellow Bengalis been as successful, Durga Puja could have been seen as the Hindu Christmas. Yet another illustration of how religion is always influenced by money.

While Diwali is the Gujarati New Year, it is not the New Year for all Hindus. The Bengali New Year is in April marking the start of spring while Diwali is in autumn. Diwali was in essence no different to the Muslim Eid. In Diwali Baba's Gujarati clients gave us sweets. In Eid, Baba's Muslim clients brought us delicious biryani. The one thing that made Diwali stand out was that Gujaratis always opened new books of account living up to their reputation for combining pleasure with business.

We Bengalis, proud of our status as the intellectuals of India, looked down on this, and there would be many snide comments that this is what you would expect from *Baniyas*, the less than complementary nickname for Gujaratis. Every year Baba's bookkeeper, a Gujarati who came to work wearing a dhoti, would take us for a meal in a famous Gujarati restaurant. We knew Gujaratis were vegetarians so there would be no fish, but what really distinguished the Gujarati meal was reversing the normal order of eating, starting with sweets and ending with a savoury dish of rice and ghee. Baba would say that is how Gujaratis do business. Before you do the deal, they lure you with promises, and then, just as you sign the contract, you find it has a clause which has taken away all the sweetness of the early promises and that you have signed a deal which is not quite as favourable as you thought it was when you started the negotiations.

The only time religion really impinged on us was during Durga Puja. It has been described as the Bengali Hindu equivalent of Christmas, Eid or Passover; my experience of it was that the religious element was completely overshadowed by the social and cultural aspects. Yes, it is about the worship of goddess Durga for killing Mahishasura, a demon, half-man, half-buffalo, while her four children, Lakshmi, Saraswati, Kartik and Ganesh, all of whom are goddesses and gods, look on. The story is meant to represent a triumph of good over evil, and I duly paid homage to that, which meant taking part in the *anjali* ceremony—standing with some flowers in front of the goddess Durga, repeating verses recited by the priest I barely heard, let alone understood, and then, with a bow to the mother goddess, throwing the flowers at her feet and repeating them three times.

Bengalis call the puja the *Sarbojanin Durga Puja*, a community festival. But while Durga Puja is celebrated in some of the great temples of India, like the Kali temple of Kolkata, in the main it sees Bengalis construct hundreds of temporary temples for *Ma Durga*, Mother Durga—a makeshift *pandal*, marquee, on a maidan, or in Britain in a community hall. At one end are the images of Durga and her children; at the other is a stage for musical shows and plays. When I was growing up, it was this aspect of the festival, in addition to the new clothes—my sisters got wonderful saris—and unlimited, delicious food that always meant more to me.

Christmas is a time for gifts and food but there is also carol- and hymn-singing and nativity plays dramatizing the Christian story. Though the story of Durga flouncing off from her matrimonial home with Shiva to go to her parents, then returning after killing a demon, would make a grand play, I never saw one performed. Neither Baba nor Ma told me any religious stories. It was Bhai, Ma's mother, who first recounted stories from the *Ramayana* or *Mahabharata* which I found fascinating.

What is more, Puja does not end when the religious part of it closes with what is called *Bishorjon*, in which clay images of Durga and her four children are immersed in the river to mark the return of the mother goddess and her children to the abode of her husband, Shiva. As the images float away, the devotees shout out "*Durga Ma ki Jai*", "Hail, Mother Durga", knowing that next year new images of the goddess will be made. Kolkata has a potters' area, Koumurtuli, which specialises in making the images. The goddess and her children will return and the entire process will be repeated. In Kolkata the immersion is done in the Adi Ganga, as the Bengalis still call the Hooghly. Mumbai with no river, the idols are taken to the Arabian Sea. Bengalis cannot take the images of Durga and her children in a procession through London and immerse them in the Thames. They lock the idols in a cupboard, and bring the same images out the following year, pretending they are new.

The worshippers do not disperse after the immersion. They return to the makeshift temple where the Puja had been celebrated. The end of the hall where the images stood is now bare. The devotees do *kulo koli*, embrace each other, there is more food although no longer blessed by the gods and the organisers of the puja present a show which they hope will be the best of the four-day festival with a top singer, dancer, or magician performing. Imagine if just after Christmas Day all images of Christ, Mary and the Christian saints were removed and the church used to stage an entertainment. It would be blasphemous.

You only have to visit the Durga Puja held every year in Hampstead Town Hall to realise how very distinct it is. At one end it is mostly women who congregate round the images of the mother goddess, the only man amidst them the priest who is performing the puja; the priest has to be a man despite the worship of a goddess; the men are all at the other end of the makeshift temple, collecting donations, making sure everyone has *prasad* and that the entertainment has been properly organised. And it is these men who are also very keen to become president of the organising committee.

Baba was also keen to become president of the main puja in south Mumbai. But the president was the manager of his company's bank, which provided overdrafts and Baba had to keep on his right side. Almost as a sop, the bank manager allowed Baba to organise the Lakshmi Puja of South Mumbai, which followed days after the faithful had bid goodbye to *Ma Durga* and was always held in our house. Baba did eventually become president of the entire puja committee, but of a puja in another part of the city. Who had what position in the puja committee always concerned the men and the religious part of the festival did not much concern Baba, or most Bengali men.

But even as the Bengalis of Mumbai celebrated pujas they longed for the pujas of Kolkata. Ma, lapsing into English would say wistfully, "Home sweet home".

This explains why when it came to owning a house they choose Kolkata not Mumbai, notwithstanding the fact that Ma lived most of her life in Mumbai watching the city overtake Kolkata as India's economic capital. As Mumbai tore down its old colonial homes and built New York-style skyscrapers, one of Baba's friends offered him a flat which would now be worth millions. He turned it down and, giving into relentless pressure from Ma for years, bought a plot of land in Kolkata and built a home, designing it himself and calling it The Rising Sun. He had fulfilled Ma's great dream. Just as the British returned home on long leave, Ma, every summer, took us to Kolkata to remind us where our real home was. The homage paid by exiles forced to live far away from their beloved motherland.

8

BENGAL ONLY KNOWS HOW TO CRY

Bengalis have a word for people like me: *Probashi* Bengali. It is not a compliment. It denotes a person who lives in a faraway land and is to be pitied for missing out on life in "*Sonar Bangla*", Golden Bengal. And nothing was more *sonar* than Kolkata.

During my childhood Bhai summed up this attitude when we left Kolkata to return to Mumbai. As the train left Howrah station, she would fight back the tears and mutter, "Oh, poor dears, going away to a foreign land." The way she said it, Mumbai seemed a place she knew nothing about. Yet she had visited the city twice, even lived there for long stretches of time, but Mumbai remained an undesirable foreign land where her beloved daughter and her children were condemned to live. It comforted Bhai that Ma joined in the lamentations, but what she or Ma did not know was that I could not be happier as the train picked up speed and Howrah receded. I was returning to the city I considered home, the place I loved. I saw myself as a Bombaywallah, or a "Mumbaikar", as natives of the city are now called. It was Kolkata that was a foreign land for me, and it has remained so. I was born there, I lived there for three years between 1975 and 1978 and, while I have never shared Kipling's view of Kolkata being "The City of Dreadful Night", I have never warmed to it.

Kolkata should have been a place of joy. For we were travelling to *Mamabari*, maternal uncle's Home. The word *Mama* releases the sweetest emotion in India, for it stands for one's mother's brother. In Bengal the wife's brother is especially important and immune from the normal family quarrels. The sister dotes on him, and even the brother-in-law treats him with indulgence. When a child has its first morsel of proper food, a ceremony called *Annaprashan* is held in which the child sits on the Mama's lap and is fed by him. There is the most moving of ceremonies every year when the brother sits on a small wooden seat on the floor and the sister puts a dot on her brother's forehead and says, "*Jomduara poralo kata.*" It means "I have struck a knife through the door of the god of death," and it is a wish for her brother's long life. This is accompanied by the most lavish of parties for the brother. Yet, in Kolkata there was no Mama. He lived in Kanpur some six hundred miles away, and to the chauvinistic Bengalis this was as remote, as inhospitable, as foreign as Mumbai. And he, far from being a success, had caused much trouble.

Baba had got him a job in a firm owned by one of his friends, but his first task there was to organise a strike. The factory closed down. Baba's friend was outraged, and Baba felt humiliated, more so as this friend was a haughty Bengali who gloried in being a rich Brahmin and was also one of the few Bengali industrialists. And the house that we called "Mamabari" was rented, a living indictment of the spendthrift ways of *Dadu*. So, arriving in Kolkata we were assailed by the most persistent of all Indian emotions—self-pity. My *Mashis*, maternal aunts, would say as they cuddled me, "Oh, poor lad, he doesn't know what Mamabari's affection should be. How could he? If only your Dadu had been alive, this would never have happened. But he died only a year after he was born and of course his Mama is not here."

The heavy presence of the long-departed Dadu was symbolised by the obeisance we were made to pay to his photograph, which hung on a wall next to the dressing table in the *boroghor*, the big room which Bhai used as her bedroom but which became our bedroom during our stay.

* * *

The photograph must have been taken just after Dadu died. It showed a man lying on a four-poster bed, naked to the waist, his lower part covered in a dhoti held together by a large knot just above his belly button. In the west such photographs of the dead, unless it is through accident or war, would be considered distasteful. In India it is the norm, as if to record a sort of finality. The photograph appeared to have been taken without flashlights, for his features could hardly be made out and his whole body seemed to emerge from a pit of darkness symbolising death and destruction. However, on important occasions like feast days and birthdays, it would be brightened up, candles would be lit, a garland of marigolds would be put round it and all of us grandchildren would be made to go through a ritual of obeisance.

We stood in front of it, bent down low, then touched the inert feet in the photograph with our fingers, which we then applied to our forehead, a gesture meant to say we were wiping the dust off his feet although, as it happened, just before we did this the photograph would have been wiped dust-free with a soft velvet cloth. What we were doing, as my Mashis said, was giving Dadu a call. And in case he did not hear this as we touched the photograph, somebody—either Bhai or more likely one of my Mashis—would say in a loud, ringing voice, "Say after me, Dadu give us your blessing and make us good and rich."

We were never taken to the theatre or films, but this was drama that would have fascinated the greatest of directors.

It is always twilight as we make our ritual obeisance to the photograph. The air is filled with the incense of joss sticks from the evening prayers offered by Bhai and, as she places the sticks next to the photograph, thin wispy smoke rises in the air, weaving patterns of light and shade round the gloomy frame. And accompanying this, like an impromptu orchestra producing supporting sound, are long sighs from my Mashis, regretting the lost world of Dadu.

Bhai and my Mashis would look at the photograph longingly, then gently squeeze my cheeks saying, "Oh, *sonarmoni*, treasure of gold, how much your Dadu would have loved you, how unfortunate we are that he is not here to host you. If he had been alive, the whole world would have been your oyster."

These remarks were also made by Bhai every morning of our stay in Kolkata, just after Bhai had returned from the corner shop down the road bringing *danadar* and *jeelapies*, balls of extremely sugary sweets. In the complex Bengali hierarchy of sweets these were considered low-class, sweets usually given to servants, in comparison with more desirable sweets such as *rajbhogs*, its very name meaning "food for rajahs", kings.

* * *

My grandmother and my aunts were not the only ones bemoaning a lost world. The past hung over the city like a dark cloud. All round us in Kolkata we seemed surrounded by tales of families once rich who had been suddenly ruined, matching the mood of a city in decay whose glories as the capital of the Raj were fading fast. In the great contradiction that marked how Bengalis saw the Raj, they were simultaneously proud of being the first province to challenge British rule, yet also gloried in Kolkata being the second city of the Empire and the Paris of the East. But in 1911, it all changed.

That year, Lord Curzon, the Viceroy, was forced to undo the partition of Bengal, which had led to the Swadeshi movement, the first ferocious nationalist agitation against British rule. But, as if in retaliation, Curzon shifted the capital to Delhi. As a Bengali wittily put it, "We asked for the moon. The British gave us the moon but took away the sun." Half a century later Kolkata was still coming to terms with the setting of the sun except that now, a decade after India's freedom, their anger had shifted from the British to their fellow Indians for daring to usurp their place as the leaders of India.

They moaned about how businesses were being taken over by the ruthless *Marwari* trading community from Rajasthan, of whom it was said that if in a jungle you see a Marwari and a tiger, shoot the Marwari first. They hated the Marwaris despite the fact they were Indians replacing the departed Scots, who had been the great business owners of the city. Their anger was also directed against Gandhi, who was held responsible for the partition of Bengal. Such was the Bengali anger towards Gandhi that when Baba heard Gandhi had been assassinated, he was convulsed with fear the assassin was a Bengali. He returned anxiously to his office to be told by his deputy, Pradhan, that it was not a Bengali. "*Seth*," Pradhan said, "it is a Maharashtrian, Nathuram Godse." Pradhan, a Maharashtrian, seemed to take great pride in Gandhi's murder.

What was shocking was to hear in Kolkata vile, unprintable, remarks about the man I was brought up to consider the "Father of the Nation". One phrase I often heard about Gandhi was "*Gujartika bacha, kabi nahi chhaha,*" "A son of a Gujarati is never honest," Gujarat being Gandhi's state. Once when a relative arrived in a very small brown car, my Mashi Nanu immediately dubbed it "Gandhi's *goo* [shit]".

Baba would vividly illustrate how Bengal's status had changed. Baba, born in 1911, grew up being told "What Bengal thinks today, India thinks tomorrow", but by the 1940s things had changed so much that Gandhi's right-hand man, Sardar Vallabhbhai Patel, a fellow Gujarati, dismissively said "Bengal only knows how to cry."

* * *

Mamabari was a house to be pitied. It had no male adult in charge. In Hindu society a household without a male adult is immediately suspect: it is considered either a house of prostitution (otherwise why should unattended women congregate together?) or uniquely unlucky. So, Bhai instead of being the queen mother, felt that as a widow her status was unenviable and her life a failure. A Hindu widow wears the marks of Cain. For Bhai to have outlived Dadu meant her past misdeeds had been so dreadful that they disturbed the natural order of things in the Hindu world, where a wife dies before her husband. Hindu society can never forgive a woman for being a widow. But while Bhai would not have dreamt of committing *sati*, which contrary to what the British said, was always a rare thing, from the moment Dadu died she conveyed the grief she felt for allowing her husband to die.

I can understand how Bhai felt. She had married aged nine, had not seen her husband until her wedding night, and had had her first child aged ten. She had known no other man. When I once asked her how she could marry at the age of nine she smiled and said she and Dadu were children, just playing, and the innocence with which she said it was touching. I did not have the courage to ask her what it was like to have a child at the age of ten. So, after Dadu's death Bhai wore only white clothes, cooked her own food, ate separately and lived on vegetables. For her as a widow there was to be no enjoyment, she would attend no functions, she could not remarry. She lived for nearly twenty years after Dadu's death wearing her widowhood as a badge advertising her sins. She proclaimed her simplicity, her poverty, bemoaned her fate and demanded pity, which she received in copious measure from friends, from casual acquaintances, above all from her daughters. Hindu society with its folk memory of deprivation and sorrow instantly understood and sympathised and elevated Bhai, treating her as a person who could do no wrong.

To make up for a husband who had left her destitute and a son who had failed she showed remarkable determination. Shortly after partition, despite news of the violence inflicted on Hindus by Muslims during that traumatic period and the rape of many Hindu women, she had bravely ventured to East Pakistan, as East Bengal had become, to see if she could reclaim anything from the land the family had once owned there which had now been taken over by Muslims. Despite being a lone Hindu widow, she had returned with stories of how she had been treated with kindness by Muslims, but she returned without any money.

Bhai, small, fragile—I often, to her alarm, lifted her clean off the ground—the fairness of her skin setting off the stark white of her sari, went about her routine. I can picture her climbing the stairs to her small prayer room on the terrace, in the kitchen bending low over the earthen stove as she cooked, searching for her "chemise", that nondescript white undergarment she wore next to her skin, or lying curled up, her knees very near her chin, next to her favourite grandchild, Ashok. This despite the fact that every now and again, in the midst of having a dream of playing in a football match, he would shoot out his left foot smack into her stomach and, still asleep, scream "goal".

* * *

The only male in the house was Upan. His name had also been given by Didi. He was said to be Ma's uncle, though there was no blood relationship. He had served with the King's forces in Mesopotamia. But then things had gone wrong and he had been discharged, although nobody talked about it. He had arrived when Dadu was alive, probably meaning to stay a few weeks and hoping to find a job in the big city. But he had found none. The weeks had become months and then years. Dadu had passed away. Upan had stayed.

He did no work, contributed nothing towards the household expenses and even borrowed money from Bhai.

He had two remarkable characteristics. For much of the time he was naked from the waist up in the style of Gandhi. In the evenings he would venture outside, a ritual he enjoyed. He would comb his long, curly locks, which reached down to his shoulders—he was genuinely the first long-haired person I saw—and sprinkle powder over his hairy chest, making certain it was visible. Then he would don his kurta, exchange his heavy slippers for shoes, untuck one end of the dhoti from the small of his back where it had been securely placed, take it in one of his arms and slowly, methodically, venture out of the house.

Despite never wearing a watch, he always knew the time, particularly mealtimes. Bhai called him "*Garribabu*", Watch man. At 7 he would have breakfast, at 10.30, lunch, at 3.30, tea, at 8, dinner. He never lent a hand in their preparation, but at the appointed hour he would be at the rickety table in the dining room expecting to be served. By 10 he was in bed.

At precisely 7 in the morning, his cups arranged on a stainless-steel tray, he would climb the stairs from the kitchen to the main bedroom. He would repeat this at 3 in the afternoon, and Upan bearing the tray of teacups would mark the end of the post-lunch siesta time.

He attended to my cousins' education, admonished them to study, cleaned their shoes, looked after their uniforms and acted as sentinel. His domain was the drawing room, a rectangular room on the ground floor which had a divan at one end and several cane-backed easy chairs dotted round. At night the divan would be Upan's bed, and anyone trying to get into the house would have to get past him.

On our visits to Kolkata, we proclaimed that all the families on my Ma's side were one family, and we did this by never calling them by their names but gave them special titles. The eldest son of *Boromashi* we called "Dada", which meant we were saying he was our oldest brother not just a cousin. My cousins reciprocated by calling my two sisters "Didi" and "Chordi", which indicated they had been drawn into their family.

* * *

And then there were "*Nanu*" and "*Bimashi*", names given to them by Didi when she was a child. Bimashi, the youngest of Ma's sisters, was at birth called "Baby", the whole family using that English term. She did have a proper Indian name, but all her life she was called Baby. Didi, as a child, unable to pronounce "Baby" called her "Bimashi", Bi Aunt, the name by which we always called her.

Nanu and Bimashi formed a very interesting pair of aunts. Nanu's marriage was in tatters. But Nanu knew she could never divorce her husband. That would cast such a shadow it would make it impossible for her daughter, Momo, to find a husband. So, unable to defy established convention, she defied society in the stories she told and the language she used, which in polite Indian society was outrageously profane. If anyone went to the loo after a meal, she would loudly say "Keha haga", having a shit after food, which was not considered a good habit. And talking of Muslims, she would say how they loved to lift the saris of Hindu women and fuck them. If somebody farted, Nanu would say, "Tumi ke padaso?" "Have you farted?" Nanu was careful not to make such remarks in front of Baba, as he was the husband of an older sister, and therefore to be treated with respect.

She could also be very assertive and once, while travelling in a crowded bus, she squeezed herself onto a seat and landed on the thigh of a passenger seated in the next seat who cried out in agony. A few days later Nanu accompanied Baba to one of his office functions only to find that man there. When Baba introduced the man to Nanu, the man said, "We have met, have we not?" Nanu, with a very straight face replied, "No, we have not. You must be mistaken. But very nice to meet you." And although Nanu would mock me as "haggo muttu", piss and shit, I enjoyed her company and loved to sit next to her as she spread out her legs and rolled a pan, betel nut leaf, which she then, with great relish, chewed, while entertaining us with her tales. Unlike Ma, she exuded fun, and what I liked best was she did not make you feel that spending money was sinful.

* * *

Ma was always trying to marry Bimashi off, but she rejected all suitors. One because she did not like the colour of the socks he wore. While she liked his looks, how could she spend her life with a man showing such a poor taste in socks?

She would have really liked to become a singer. But Bhai thought singers and actresses were no better than prostitutes. It would have brought in much needed money, but for Bhai some means of earning money were unacceptable.

* * *

Kolkata did give us the opportunity to show off our connections and our prosperity. Amongst cousins, whose poverty was advertised, we were rich, sophisticated, worldly. Mamabari did not have a telephone, the bathroom and the loos were primitive, the room where we had our bath being under the staircase, where there was a large water tank. Nakuleshwar Bhattacharjee Lane was remote from the city centre, our aunts didn't have cars and only one maid servant. We brought glamour.

Baba's friends included the city's leading sweet-makers, so we could entertain Mamabari people with sweets they could not afford. Baba's friends were also part of the elite of Kolkata. They provided us cars, some of them so large they caused terrific traffic problems in Nakuleshwar Bhattacharjee Lane. The children from the houses nearby, in particular the *bustee*, slum kids, would gather round to look at the car, the like of which they had never seen before.

But despite my cousins envying us, they insisted Kolkata was better than Mumbai. On every visit there was an argument about which city had the best mangoes. Baba would take Alphonso mangoes as gifts for his friends and relations. He would buy unripe mangoes and carefully pack them in cases filled with straw so they would ripen by the time we arrived. An Alphonso is ripe when it is bright orange. But in Kolkata there was a rival, Langera, eaten when green. Baba's friends, unaware a green Alphonso was not ripe, would eat it and complain it was not good. When I pontificated about their ignorance, my cousins would insist Langera was the better mango.

Kolkata, they claimed, is the biggest city in India. Mumbai, I insisted, was bigger in area; Mumbai they dismissed as all length and no breadth. When I retorted that Mumbai was disciplined, their answer was in Kolkata people may hang on to the footboards of buses, but at least they get on; in Mumbai the conductors push you off buses if they are full. Surely they could not argue with the fact that Mumbai had the sea. But who wants the sea, they said, Kolkata has a lake, an artificial lake but it is much better than the sea. And then came the clinching argument, Kolkata has life, it has soul, in Kolkata we may burn buses, but it shows we are not apathetic. Mumbai is soulless; they only care about making money.

I thought I had played the ace when, in 1956, Khrushchev and Bulganin, the leaders who had taken over the Soviet Union after the death of Stalin, came to India. They received a tumultuous welcome. In Kolkata, long regarded as India's centre of left-wing thinking, crowds pressed onto their car and threatened to overwhelm them physically with their welcome. The Chief Minister quickly transferred them into an accompanying police van and saved them from being crushed. So, caged like animals they rode into this city of culture, intellectuals and fervent left-wing ideology. I would repeat the story with some pride, believing there could be no retort. "But tell me," said my cousin Ashok, "where else but in Kolkata would this happen: a foreign dignitary entering a city in a police van?" In vain I searched for irony in his voice.

Kolkata would also lead to one of my most humiliating moments at St. Xavier's. The geography teacher was talking of Kolkata. Who has visited Kolkata? I put up my hand.

"Have you been to the Victoria Memorial?"

"Yes."

"Tell us what is inside it."

What is inside the Victoria Memorial? I had seen the Memorial often but only as we had driven past it, never inside it. We never did the tourist things in Kolkata. The question did not make sense.

"Go on, tell us. We haven't got all day."

My moment of triumph was over. Slowly, hesitatingly, I replied.

"I have never been inside."

"Never been inside the Victoria Memorial?" the teacher snarled.

The class erupted. For days I carried the memory of that shame. Years later as a grown man I would venture inside the Victoria Memorial and find it dreadfully disappointing, the hideousness of its inside matching the incongruity of its outside. A monument, dwarfing its surroundings and built by Lord Curzon to advertise British power, which appears absurd in that very Indian setting. It was the

British talking to the British, not to the Indians. In the words of V.S. Naipaul in *An Area of Darkness*, "Not worthy of the power they celebrated." It displayed "the peculiar quality of the Raj: the affectation of being very English, this sense of a nation at play, acting out a fantasy."

It could have described Mamabari. Pining for the lost glory of Bengal which was long gone and which had never appealed to me.

In Mamabari I could not also conceal a dreadful secret that I was a bedwetter and continued to be one until I was twelve. It was with great joy that I arrived in the summer of 1959 and, before we went to bed, paraded round in my pyjamas making my cousins exclaim in astonishment. The night-time drama they had enjoyed on previous visits was over. That year also marked the last time we went on annual summer trips to Kolkata.

9

THE BABA–MA PLAY ON THE TRAIN TO KOLKATA

What did appeal to me was the train journey to *Mamabari*. In the India of my youth, we loved visiting family and friends but never wanted to be tourists. For us this was a western custom which our puritanical code found repulsive. Four hundred miles from Bombay there are the famous Ajanta and Ellora caves—a unique representation of the much-advertised classical Hindu and Buddhist culture; we never visited them. I can remember only two journeys in early childhood to a hill station. But Kolkata was different.

Twelve hundred miles separate Mumbai from Calcutta and there were three daily trains. The railways the British had left behind had been nationalised and called "Indian Railways", but we still clung to the names of the old British companies. The two mail trains were the Bengal Nagpur Railway and the Eastern India Railway, and the third was the Bombay–Calcutta Express, which for reasons nobody could explain to me wasn't much of an express and slower than the mail trains. We travelled on the BNR train, which I loved all the more because there was also a BNR football team which had, in their wonderful winger Balaram, a player whose dribbling skills I wanted to emulate but never could.

Our journey to Kolkata was like a play with which we were very familiar but which never failed to entertain us. The two principal characters, Baba and Ma, did a neat role reversal: a frenetic, agitated Baba, a calm, unfussed Ma. I can see now that Baba didn't view going back to Kolkata as a return to his homeland. That was Barisal, then part of East Pakistan and lost for ever. For Ma, Kolkata was the homeland she so dreadfully missed.

Baba's great worry was missing the train. Three hours before it was due to leave Shankar would drive Baba to Victoria Terminus.

Baba arrived so early that rail officials would tell him, "Sahib, the train has not yet returned from its previous trip." Ma, who all this while was back in Sailor Building supervising Soma and other Ghatis packing our cases full of goodies for Mamabari, would arrive a few minutes before the train was to leave, which would drive Baba into a frenzy.

As Ma arrived, Baba would be pacing the platform, counting the number of bags we had. And we had many. Not once on our many journeys to Kolkata did the total number of our bags and other packages fall below fifteen. This greatly added to Baba's worries. To transport our luggage required all the resources of Baba's company. A handcart carried our heavier trunks, Shankar, in the car, our personal suitcases, and the Ghatis would carry the bedding and mattresses, balancing them on their heads as they walked the mile from Sailor Building to Victoria Terminus.

The train journey was long—two nights and a day—, our requirements plentiful. We carried a stove, buckets, cutlery, crockery, food, gifts, blankets, and Alphonso mangoes. Baba was fastidious: he liked everything to be neatly packaged, properly labelled, correctly counted. "How many packages are we taking?" Baba would ask as he walked round the platform counting "fourteen, fifteen". Where is the bedding? Where is the sugar? Where is the bucket? And then, his patience exhausted, he would shout at Ma. Ma, who had been an oasis of calm compared to Baba, would react strongly: "Is all the packing for me? Who wants to eat all the time? How am I supposed to feed you between stations? If I do not carry a stove, how will you get your cups of tea? Who wants hot water for his bath—none of this is for me. They're all for you and your children."

Watching the scene would be the coolies, with their white dhotis, red tops and red caps, who, as our bags arrived, had expected to make a fortune in tips carrying them to our compartment, only to find themselves being shooed away as we had the Ghatis to do that.

Amidst Baba's worry and Ma's feverish packing, and servants wandering here and there, we would be settled in our first-class "bogie", which in those days, long before the advent of corridor trains, meant that once the huge doors were shut, it was like a little house on wheels. Nobody could come in or out except when the train stopped at a platform. Didi and Chordi would quickly make the bathroom homely, Ma would light the stove to make Baba a cup of tea, and he would soon settle on a bunk, cross his legs and drink his cup of tea. I loved getting up on one of the top bunks and looking down on the activity below.

There was one curiosity. We travelled in a four-berth compartment, but we were a family of five. We were entitled to an attendant ticket which, illustrating the Indian class system, was a ticket for the third-class compartment where he was supposed to go and sleep once he had finished his work. We never travelled with an attendant, although Baba did once go to look in the third-class compartment to make sure we had a berth.

The range and diversity of the various classes was a microcosm of Indian life, distinguishing between the haves and the have-nots, and the Indians even catered for a new aspiring class. The haves travelled in first and second class, aspiring people in the intermediate class with its wooden benches and grimy toilets, and in third class journeyed the have-nots, for whom even the intermediate class would be a world they could only fantasise about. Gandhi, seeking to identify with India's teeming millions, travelled in the third but this was exclusively reserved for him and came with luxuries that made it much better than any first class. As Sarojini Naidu, a poetess willing to mock her fellow politicians, would tell a British administrator, "If only you knew, Sir Richard, how much it costs Congress to keep him in holy poverty."

We left Mumbai at around 6 pm, the steam engine slowly gathering speed, and I loved watching the local stations pass. The first night out from Mumbai we ate food cooked at home. This for me was always a sore point because I longed to sit in the restaurant car eating railway food. Yet this was denied me. The very homeliness of our compartment imposed its own limitations. To travel to the dining room we would have to get off when the train halted at a station then board it again at some other station. We never knew exactly how long the train would stop to be confident of making it to the restaurant car—or making it back. I was considered too young to make such a journey, although Baba once did, and so the restaurant car remained an elusive dream. By the time it was fulfilled, a lot of its charm had vanished. Two delights compensated for this: the excellence of the restaurant car food that was delivered to our compartment, and the tiffin-carrier full of food we knew waited for us at Nagpur.

This came around midday the second day. It was the main stopping point of the journey. The steam engine that had brought us from Mumbai was replaced by another one; sweepers would come and clean our compartment of coal dust, which even three layers of windows, one glass, one wood, one net, couldn't keep out. But above all, waiting on the platform was a well-dressed man with a servant next to him who wore khaki clothes and held a white tiffin-carrier. The man was Mr Das, "*Daskaku*" as we called him, who had once come and stayed with us and been lavishly entertained by Ma. He was determined to match the hospitality of "Mrs Bose", as he called Ma. Since then, whenever we travelled to Kolkata, he would be at Nagpur station. After Daskaku had greeted Baba and Ma, and we had touched Daskaku's feet, we would settle down to a sumptuous, delicious, home-made meal of rice, various vegetables dishes, meat, and fish, all cooked in pure ghee, and he would watch while we ate. This was a ritual we looked forward to. Once, on our journey back from Kolkata to Mumbai the train ran late and arrived past midnight, yet Daskaku and his servant with the tiffin-carrier were still there on the platform. Not far from Nagpur Gandhi had built his ashram, where he spent his last days. But we never thought of visiting it. For us, Nagpur meant Daskaku and his servant's tiffin-carrier. It was only in 2015, when I wrote on Gandhi in my book *From Midnight to Glorious Morning?* that I first broke journey in Nagpur to visit Wardha, Gandhi's ashram.

We knew that after Nagpur we had a whole afternoon and another night on the train, but, as if fortified by the meal Daskaku had provided, we felt we were on the home stretch. Over the years, as we made the journey to Kolkata we saw India changing, becoming like the industrialised west Nehru wanted and Gandhi detested. The Indian Institute of Technology was being built at Rourkela, the steel mills constructed in Bhilai. If it was summer, and it generally was, we would order ice blocks. These would come in packs and, in a compartment tightly sheltered against the sun and heat, provided some relief. But then, in the evening these packs would melt. Water would run, and just when the evening turned cool, we would have the problem of mopping up the compartment. By then we knew Kolkata was just a night away.

The next morning, as the train neared Kolkata, Ma, Didi and Chordi would get busy. They would put on their make-up, wear fresh sarees, make sure they had the right shoes. For me it was the sights and sounds of this strange world we were entering that were bewitching. I was used to seeing people use umbrellas in Mumbai during the monsoon. But here were men in the middle of a fiercely hot day using umbrellas to protect themselves from the midday sun. Then, as Didi and Chordi got ready, Howrah Bridge—that symbol of Kolkata and another "British gift to India", as the empire-lovers describe it—loomed into view. Ma, expecting the train to pull in at Howrah station very soon, would start shouting instructions as to what we should do when we arrived. But the BNR train would tantalise us. Having provided us with a glimpse of Kolkata, it would make us wait. Our train would come to a complete halt. All Indian trains bear the legend: "Trains running late are liable to make up time." But the wait with Howrah Bridge in sight was always the most galling. Eventually, we would slowly pull into the station and, as I was to realise years later when I came to England, this was the most English of Indian stations, where cars could pull up next to the platform. And there, waiting for us, would be Mamabari. The exiles had returned home. Ma couldn't contain her delight.

10

INSTANT FAMILIES AND MA'S TWO FACES

Some years ago Atlantic Books commissioned me to ghost the cricketer Moeen Ali's autobiography. When his agent Kamran took me to Birmingham to meet Moeen's father, Kamran called him "Uncle". I thought they must be related. Then I realised, after nearly fifty years of living in Britain I had forgotten how people in the subcontinent address parents of friends. I had grown up with it.

There was a well-defined structure to this sudden creation of new family members. Friends of Baba became "*Kakus*", Uncles. Female friends of Ma became "*Mashis*", sisters. Their male children, if older than us, were called "*Dada*", older brother, the females, "*Didi*", older sister. Once they were family they always had to be part of all family occasions. The only family photograph we have is one taken when I was about five. We were dressed in our finery; I wore my best suit, selected for the occasion by my sisters, with polished black shoes. My sisters wore their lovliest frocks and we went to a studio in Mumbai for a very formal portrait showing our entire family: Ma, Baba, Didi, Chordi and me. However, while we are seated there is also a man in a dark suit standing behind us. He was another Mr Das, no relation but a family friend, who, of course, we called "*Daskaku*". He had arrived just as we were about to set out for the studio, and, since Ma felt it was bad manners to exclude him, he was invited along. I now have it in the hall of my home in London; when I explain to my English friends that Mr Das is not a relation, they look stupefied.

But while we extended this privilege to all Baba's office staff, making them all Kakus, uncles, the line was drawn with the ghatis.

However old they were, we called them by their name. They could not be family, they were, after all, servants.

* * *

Having defined the relationship, we provided a physical demonstration of our love and devotion. The moment we were summoned in front of a guest, Ma would say *"Pranam karo,"* "Touch their feet," and we would stoop down in front of the guest and touch his or her feet.

We would touch their feet with the tips of our fingers and then touched the fingers to our foreheads.

The strangers knew they had to play their part in the performance of this stylised pantomime. The older ones, who had become our Kakus or Mashis, even though they expressed polite surprise, would speak of how heart-warming it was to see such respect for elders in this heartless western-influenced world, so keen to reject ancient customs.

But the younger ones, who had become our Dadas or Didis, would react with mock horror—or, at times, real indignation—and try and prevent us from touching their shoes. This often added an unexpected Laurel-and-Hardy touch to this ancient Hindu ritual.

The zenith was attained one evening when, as so often, I was suddenly presented with a new Dada. He was not just a manufactured member of the family but a first cousin of Ma's. He worked in the merchant navy and had just returned to India from many months abroad, during which he had developed a great distaste for many of the old Hindu rituals and customs.

I was totally unaware of all this. I had never seen him before and, until Baba summoned me, I did not even know he existed. The moment I emerged in the drawing room and saw him I marched up to him and bent low to touch his highly polished shoes. He had not expected it, but once he realised what was happening he did something I had not anticipated.

He was sitting on the three-seater sofa that was Baba's pride and joy with his legs crossed. Seeing me bend down to try and touch his feet, he uncrossed his legs, spread them wide, bent down himself, and with both hands tried to push off my hands. I had never experienced such resistance before. This was not part of the script and I was determined not to give in. I spread myself wide, like a goal-keeper facing an onrushing forward, and, extending my arms on either side, tried to touch his shoes. By this time he had raised his feet and they were waving gently in space. He spread his hands and our fingertips met. Also, in order to avoid my hands, he moved to the left, while I countered by moving to the right and tried to find a gap between his hands to reach the tips of his bootblack shoes. He countered by moving right and I moved left. The game could have gone on endlessly had not Baba intervened and said "That's enough." My newly acquired cousin laughed but I felt cheated, for it seemed to me these declarations of loyalty and respect enhanced my faith. I was greatly concerned about preserving our customs. I did not know much about them but was convinced they were threatened by the rational western order.

However, as I grew older my belief in these customs vanished and I rebelled. After much argument with my parents I convinced them this was an extreme form of devotion and should only be shown to people you really cared for, ones who were close rela-tions, such as parents. Therefore, I said, I will only touch your feet. From then on, I observed this ritual nightly before going to bed, but I stopped touching the feet of strangers. However, I con-tinued to maintain the fiction that total strangers could become members of my family by calling them Kakus, Mashis, Dadas and Didis as appropriate.

* * *

Baba enjoyed entertaining guests, and we had the means to enter-tain. The location of our flat meant we attracted visitors. It was smack in the middle of the city, what we called "the heart of Mumbai". "All roads lead to Flora Fountain," said Baba. "And all of them end up in my kitchen," moaned Ma. The result was that friends, exhausted from shopping or work or just a visit to the city centre, were always dropping in for a lunchtime or teatime tiffin, confident that the generous Boses would provide a cup of tea and a plateful of snacks and sweets, if not lunch or even dinner.

We were in awe of the English custom of making appointments over the telephone, but most of our friends rarely did. Ma called them "untimely guests", using the English phrase. The ones she held in even greater contempt were those who took "undue advantage". They would borrow our car, servants, and on one occasion, woke up Baba from his siesta to borrow money. This guest never reappeared and never repaid the money. But it was the eating habits of guests that truly infuriated Ma. "Always eating, always wanting to be fed. These are not friends, they are not humans, they are demons. Look how they eat. Eat, eat, eat, eat! How I hate eating! If they want to eat so much, I say let them eat shit".

To placate Ma, Baba would say she could hire more servants and he would, if necessary, pay them *Rs.*500 a month, a princely sum. This would enrage Ma even more. "My mother can't eat, my sisters are starving, and you want to feed people and hire servants at 500 rupees a month. My father fed people, fed Brahmins all his life, did it stop him becoming poor? Oh, God, what have I done to deserve this? I wanted a husband who was handsome and was like my father. Handsome he is, but he has taken to my father's worst sin, feeding people. Oh God, are you punishing me for wanting a handsome husband?"

Such was her remorse at the plight of her family that she could never enjoy the finer sides of life Baba was so keen for us all to have. Baba liked eating out, Ma hated it. And even when we ate out, she could never relax. Baba always took us out for a meal on New Year's Day, but Ma would throw the entire restaurant into confusion by suggesting she would share. Waiters would look dumbfounded and explain there was no real way a Chicken Kiev could be shared between three people. While we ate extremely well and had four meals a day, including a very substantial tea, Ma drastically limited her own food intake and would often finish off the food we couldn't. She gloried in saying, "I am like the rubbish bin, I eat leftovers."

However, Ma was shrewd enough to know it was important for Baba's business that he entertain. Upwards of a dozen people would dine with us at least two or three times a month, sometimes as often as once a week. This was in addition to the "untimely guests", which meant it was rare for us to have dinner or lunch on our own. Ma would moan and rage before they arrived, but once they arrived her entire demeanour changed, and this is where the other, public face of Ma emerged.

* * *

Five hundred rupees for a cook being out of the question, ghatis would be dragooned in for the party. To make them look present-able, they would change from their dingy brown shorts and a thin brown singlet into a uniform which Ma had designed: starched white trousers, a stiff starched white jacket, a jaunty white cap. An hour or so before the guests arrived, they would be made to wear these clothes and stand in a line, much like waiters in a restaurant, ready to serve drinks and then the food.

We, too, would be made to wear our best clothes. The mother who had told us how feeding people was a sin now converted these guests into instant members of our family, as if in so doing she had washed away the sin of entertainment.

* * *

Ma's final moment as the supreme hostess came just as the guests were about to depart. This was another wonderful Ma pantomime, but one which required the participation of the guests, who, as if this was the price for their supper, joined in enthusiastically.

Picture the scene: we are all standing on the landing outside our flat. The members of the family are arranged along the staircase all the way back to the entrance of our flat. The guests are at the top of the stairs with some on the steps leading to the floor below.

The physical set now erected, Ma's theatre begins. Ma has served a sumptuous meal of about a dozen courses which has included fish, chicken, lamb, several vegetables, parathas, pulao rice, biryani and her great speciality, stuffed pomfret. This has been followed by at least two or three different varieties of sweets. But now, as the guests are about to leave, she says: "I am so sorry, we could not really serve you anything. But we did not have much time to pre-pare. You cannot get good help these days and I can only apologise for this wretched meal."

The guest immediately says, "What are you saying? This is the most wonderful meal we have ever had. I have eaten so much I have food up to here," and with that the person gestures towards his throat, as if to suggest the food is banked all the way up from his stomach.

"No, no," says Ma. "Please do not shame us by being so polite. You have eaten nothing, you eat like a bird. You know, my father used to say when you feed people they must go away belching to indicate they have eaten the greatest meal of their life. I cannot entertain like my father. But you must come again, and maybe then I will be able to give you something to remember us by."

The guest once again protests that this is indeed the best meal he has ever had, and this Bengali version of "No, no it is not" and "Yes, yes it is" goes on for some minutes until mutual exhaustion sets in and the guests finally walk down the stairs and to their cars waiting at street level.

* * *

Such was the lavishness of the entertainment that Baba's parties were legendary in Mumbai, though it was not Baba who got the credit but Ma. The guests had seen a face of Ma that was totally unrecognisable from the hard-faced woman who constantly warned of the perils of spending too much money and was grudging with her favours to her own family. She had been transformed into this luminous lady of munificence, someone generous to a fault, and, not surprisingly, all the guests fell in love with Ma. By the end of the meal she was no longer just Mrs Bose but had become part of their family, and they would call her *Sovadi*, *Bordi* (older sister), *Chordi* (literally "third sister"), *Kakima* (paternal aunt), *Mashima* (maternal aunt).

In contrast, Baba would appear remote, almost standoffish, and the guests would leave still calling him "Mr Bose". Many came to the conclusion that Ma was generous while Baba was a Scrooge who had only reluctantly agreed to have the party at his wonderful wife's insistence.

After the guests left the ghatis would immediately discard their smart white uniforms for their dingy brown shorts. They would sit in a long line on the floor in the office room and eat some of the leftover food. For Ma this was being a benevolent woman who looked after her servants.

* * *

The inner Ma re-emerged when dealing with the presents the guests had given us. Guests were not supposed to come "empty-handed", and she judged them by how full their hands were. Generally, they brought sweets and often a tin of assorted biscuits from Parkes store, below our house. I, as the youngest in the family, would be given the tin, which I always took as a reward for bending down and touching their feet. I looked forward to opening it and gorging on the delicious biscuits inside.

However, even as the guests were walking down the stairs and the ghatis were shedding their posh uniforms, Ma would take the tin away: "We have enough biscuits, we don't need them." She knew the people who ran Parkes very well, and sometime the following day she would go there and exchange it for something she felt we needed. If I complained, she would say, "These biscuits are no good for you. You must not think of eating all the time. Remember, the stomach is an elastic muscle, the more you feed it, the more it expands."

The private Ma with all her rage was back with us until the arrival of the guests for the next dinner party. When people talk of the hypocrisy of the British, I always think of Ma.

11

WHY THE WEST GETS CASTE WRONG

In the winter of 1959 Martin Luther King went to India. It was a pilgrimage because Gandhi's non-violent campaign to free India from British rule had inspired him. But when he visited a school in the southern state of Kerala he was "a bit shocked and peeved" that the principal of a school introduced him as "a fellow untouchable from the United States of America", untouchables being the caste the Hindus had for centuries oppressed so cruelly. Then, thinking about life in America he accepted that, "Yes, I am an untouchable, and every Negro in the United States of America is an untouchable."

The American writer Isabel Wilkerson has used this story in her book *Caste, The Lies that Divide Us* to argue that the problem in America is not race but caste: "Caste is fixed and rigid. Race is fluid and superficial."

There can be no question Hinduism's treatment of the so-called lower castes, the Dalits, is its original sin and has caused untold misery to millions of Indians for centuries. However, Wilkerson's presentation of the Indian caste system is very simplified. It is part of a historical misrepresentation of caste which started with the British. Even the British who claimed to know India could get caste wrong. Francis Tuker, who spent thirty-three years in the Indian Army and was General Officer Commanding-in-Chief Eastern Command for the last two years of British rule, in his 1950 book predicted that Hinduism, "Its religion, which is to a great extent superstition and formalism is breaking down." Not only has he been proved wrong but he did not know the difference between Brahmins and non-Brahmins, converting Subhas Bose, not related to me but, like all Boses, a Kayastha, into a Brahmin.

* * *

I had grown up with the big-C of Indian life. Which Indian has not? The Aryans may have invented caste, but it is not confined to the Hindus; there is a caste system even among Indian Christians and Indian Muslims. All through my childhood I was acutely aware of how caste distinctions affected social life in very different ways.

The first awareness of this came every morning when a woman came to our house to clean the lavatories. Ma was proud she treated the sweeper woman well. After she had finished her work, she would give her a cup of tea and something to eat. She would squat in the kitchen sipping her tea and having the food. Ma would chat to her with great affection. However, the sweeper woman was of such low caste that nobody else in the house used the cup from which she drank. This is despite the fact that the leader of her community, Babasaheb Ambedkar, having overcome horrendous prejudice to become a lawyer had drafted the Indian constitution. Yet nobody could rescue the sweeper woman from the misery she had inherited because of her birth. However, the story of another servant shows how complex the Hindu caste system can be.

* * *

This servant, a Brahmin, was our cook. He was known as "Thakur", the generic name given to Bengali Brahmins who cook for a living. I cannot remember if he was a good cook. But he was a tremendous card player.

Didi and I loved playing cards with him on Sunday afternoons. Our game of seven hands was Bridge without bidding and Thakur was exceptional. He partnered Didi, while I partnered one of the other servants or Shankar.

He had a very distinctive style of playing, dealing the cards with the one hand, shuffling them on his thigh, while in his other hand he would hold a little bundle of tobacco mixed with *chuna*, lime paste, which he chewed incessantly. He had an uncanny knack of producing the ace of trumps which often won him and Didi the game. We thought he had hidden it in the folds of his dhoti, which was often very dirty, but could never prove he had cheated.

But while a Brahmin, complete with a sacred threat that Brahmins wear, and the only ones allowed to be priests, he was a Brahmin servant who worked for a Kayastha. Didi and I sat on chairs, as a servant he in the presence of his master sat on a stool. When Baba or Ma came into the room, particularly Baba, Thakur would quickly get up from his stool and stand at the edge of the table. It seemed he was apologising for playing cards even though he was doing it in his free time.

But even as he did this, he kept to his Brahminical status, and while he cooked for us, he cooked his own meal separately in pots and pans reserved for him.

Baba had other Brahmins working for him in his office and while they could sit on chairs they all called him Seth, boss. One of them regularly took me to see cricket matches.

Perhaps the best illustration of how the British do not understand the complexities of Indian society is the story of Saurav Ganguly, the former Indian cricket captain. Ganguly played for Lancashire but the English players felt, as Andrew Flintoff put it, that he behaved "as if he was royalty—it was like having Prince Charles on your side." The British media dubbed him Lord Snooty. My relationship with him could not be more different. Despite being a Brahmin he calls he me "Mihirda", the term of respect for an older brother, and has never behaved as if he is royalty and I am a courtier.

* * *

Even among us Kayasthas there were caste differences. We were proud of being Kulins, the highest caste among the Bengali Kayasthas. And even among Kulins the Boses were special. My aunts always used to sing an old Bengali ditty, which went:

Ghosh bongsho boro bongsho,
Bose bongsho datta,
Mitra kutil jat,
Dutta sala haram jadha.
The Ghoshes are high caste,

The Boses are generous,
The Mitras have low cunning,
And the Dutts are bastards.

Indeed, among Kulins a Bose marrying a Ghosh was considered the best match and other marriages a sign of a Bose demoting himself or herself and doing the lower-ranked family a favour.

* * *

Contrary to the general belief in the west, castes are not hermetically sealed. Castes can move around. The Kayasthas, for instance, did once rise from a lowly position centuries ago to their current more exalted status. True, Brahmins are the only caste that can officiate as priests. They are Hinduism's amazing closed shop that no one has managed to break into. But many centuries ago there were some non-Brahmin, non-Aryan priests of the local sects. Non-Brahmins can also breach the Brahmin fortress.

One of Bollywood's greatest actors, Ashok Kumar Ganguly, claimed that his own family became Brahmins when his great-grandfather, the *dacoit* Raghunath, seeking shelter from the Raj's police, took refuge in a temple. He posed as a Brahmin and the police, taking him to be the temple priest, left him alone. Rogho celebrated his escape by giving thanks to the gods, deciding to give up dacoity and become a Brahmin priest. This made Ashok Kumar, Amathe Brahmins not real Brahmins at all.

Within the Brahmins there are also differences with two distinct sects of Brahmins in Bengal who do not intermarry. The Bengali Brahmins are also different to other Brahmins in that, unlike most other Brahmins, they are not vegetarians but eat fish and meat.

* * *

Where British writing on caste is really deficient is that it has never explained why it never comes up during a Hindu religious ceremony. All the years I saw Ma praying, the Brahmin priest officiating at the ceremony never asked her what caste she was. His only question—and it was always a he—was "What is your gotra?"

The historian Abraham Early has written, "The Gotra—literally a cow pen—is a lineage group, a clan, like the gens of ancient Rome."[1] It is generally thought to signify which *munni*, guru, the person's ancestors belonged to. Brahmins can have the same gotra as a Kayastha and other Hindu castes, and Kayasthas, can belong to different gotras. So, while we Boses are Gautam gotra, Chordi's husband, who is also a Kayastha, is from the Kashyapa gotra, Gautam and Kashyap being two ancient munnis whose devotees our ancestors presumably were. But with Hindus relying more on oral rather than the written tradition of recording history westerners have been able to set the agenda even in matters of caste. This was, perfectly illustrated by how the term used to denote lower castes was invented in the House of Commons by white British MPs, many of whom had never visited India or knew anything about it.

This came about when the House of Commons passed the Government of India Act, 1935 which, defined the lower castes, listing them under a list (or Schedule) of castes throughout the British-administered provinces. The result was the deprived castes of India began to be referred to as "Scheduled Castes".

When I was growing up in India, that was what we called the sweeper woman. In recent years this British definition has been done away with and the word *Dalits* has come into use. It is a perfect illustration of Indians finally breaking free from the centuries of British intellectual stranglehold.

12

NOT UPSETTING THE TRAVEL GODS

As long as I can remember, we were always travelling on January 15. It was like no other journey I ever made. It lasted only a few hours. It invested mundane events in our everyday life with an extraordinary glow, and I remember the trips in the early hours of that day more vividly than many others lasting days and weeks that I have since made.

The fifteenth of January in the Bengali calendar marks the first day of the month of Posh. Dadu had drummed into Ma that if she did not travel on that date, then she could not travel for the entire month of Posh. Worse still, by staying at home that day she would be throwing a challenge to the travel gods and nobody could be sure how they might react. They might be so enraged that they could easily decide to visit all sorts of awful curses and miseries on us.

Ma, keen to keep the travel gods happy, devised a strategy that took advantage of the fact that, unlike the rest of the world, for the Hindus the start of a new day is marked by the rising of the sun every morning. It was this system that had made India declare independence from Britain at midnight on August 15. When Britain decided that India would be free on August 15, the Indian astrologers immediately declared that it was an inauspicious day. However, the solution was simple. Celebrate independence, they said, at midnight on August 15, for the Hindus this would still be August 14 and would have none of the astrological problems supposedly associated with the next date.

This belief that the new day dawns with the rise of the sun would be exploited by a Hindu fantasist, P. N. Oak. to claim that Britain had once been a colony of India. Oak articulated his theory many years after Independence. As he consumed cake in Gaylord, a Delhi restaurant, he told me, "Do you know why in Britain midnight marks the change of dates? Surely that is a very odd time to do that? The reason is because midnight GMT is 5.30 in the morning in India. For Hindus, sunrise marks the start of the day, and when the Hindus had their world empire, as the sun rose the call would go out from the Ganges all over the world, and the British, then under Hindu colonial rule, would change their date, even though for them it was midnight."

Ma decreed that while we could spend the night of January 14 in our beds we had to be out of the house before the sun rose on the morning of 15 January.

Ma arranged this unusual journey with great precision. The previous evening Shankar who lived some ten miles away, and normally did not come to work until about 8.30 in the morning, was made to sleep in our flat with the other live-in servants. Ma served dinner early and we were made to retire well before 10 with the alarm clocks set for 4 in the morning. Ma's great nightmare was that we would oversleep and still be in our beds when the sun rose and thereby arouse the wrath of the travel gods. So, just to make doubly sure that we did not commit such a sacrilege, Ma would get one of my sisters to ring Mumbai Telephones for a 4am wake-up call.

Ma always woke before the alarm, and the moment she was up she would rouse the rest of the household starting with the cook and Chokra, the little servant boy, who did the basic fetching and carrying. The cook would first make a cup of tea for Baba and Ma would then wake him up. Baba would be served the tea while he was in the toilet. He normally liked to read the *Times of India* and have tea, a combination he felt was crucial to help him clear his bowels, something he said was very important at the start of the day. I once accidentally opened the toilet door and saw him sitting on the toilet; next to him on a little stool was a cup of tea, while in his hand he had folded the *Times of India* and was reading what looked like a long column. When I later picked up the paper it turned out he was reading the "Letter from London" by Girilal Jain, then the *Times of India's* London correspondent.

However, 4 in the morning was too early for the paper boy to deliver the *Times of India* so Baba had to be content with a cup of

Darjeeling and hope it would do the trick. And as Baba moved his bowels, Ma would come and wake us up.

We had to be ready to leave by 4.30. Ma could not stop looking at the clock and would keep shouting out the time every few minutes, while warning us that we had to be down the stairs and in the car by 4.30.

Normally, when we left the house on everyday journeys, we would leave by the kitchen door at the side of the flat. But on this occasion Ma said we had to leave by what we called the "main door". This was a big, heavy, wooden door which covered nearly one side of a wall and had all sorts of locks on it, including an incredibly heavy iron bar across the door bolted to the frame on either side. Every night before going to bed Ma would make sure the main door was bolted. Had there been a fire at night we would have roasted, unable to open the door in time, but that did not enter our heads. Ma was only concerned about keeping thieves and burglars out.

The main door was rarely opened except when important guests arrived, or when we were going away on a long holiday. The fact that it was now being unlocked marked this trip as out of the ordinary.

It was as the servant began to unlock the door that I came in my childhood to having some sense of what a military operation must be like. Ma would assemble the entire household at the main door with one servant at the head carrying a battery torch and another servant at the rear carrying another. Yet another of the many customs Dadu had drilled into her was that when the family left the house on important occasions, as the journey on January 15 undoubtedly was, it should not only leave together but once it had crossed the threshold of the door and stepped outside the house, it should not look back. So even if we had forgotten something, no one was allowed to turn back, or even look back, and Ma would get furious if anybody was called back after he had stepped out of the house. Ma knew nothing about what had befallen Lot's wife, but the way she pictured our fate suggested turning into a pillar of salt would be one of the more attractive options. As far as Ma was concerned, calling a person back as he was setting out on a journey meant casting a bad omen which could mean the journey might be interrupted or go badly. We had to step out of the main door like an army that never looked back and was marching boldly to the sounds of glory to come.

The only problem was that at 4.30 in the morning of January 15 we had to be careful not to step on one of peons sleeping on the floor below as we made our way down the stairs.

That should have been easy. The stairways were well lit, but Ma would not allow us to put the lights on. Ma would shout, "Who is going to turn the light off when we get into the car? You want me to keep the light burning all the while we are away? How much electricity would that cost? I am not made of money to give it away to the Mumbai Electric Supply Company. Is it my father's company that I should give them money for nothing? Why should they have it when I could give it to my mother and my sisters? With that money my mother could have a gallon of pure milk."

And so in order to make sure that Mumbai Electricity Supply Company did not damage Bhai's chances of having a gallon of pure milk, Ma came up with the idea of torches. As we assembled just inside the main door, Ma would switch off all the lights, including the stair lights, and the torches would be switched on. The servant at the rear would lock the main door. Then after one final call, "Got everything," and having said, "*Durga, Durga,*" calling for the blessing of the Goddess Durga, she would shout to the servant at the head of the file, "*Chalo,*" Go, and in single file we would begin to walk down the stairs.

The torch would create little pools of light in front of us, into which we would step gingerly, but despite our best efforts we would occasionally miss it and step on a sleeping peon, raising a cry. Sometimes they would wake up, sit up bolt upright and become very angry. Then Ma, in a soothing voice, would say, "Oh, oh, my child, it is all right, nothing has happened, go back to sleep." Then, as the pools of light from the torch danced on, we would scamper after it hoping to reach the safety of the car before we disturbed anyone else.

We would emerge on the pavement, dodging yet more sleeping bodies, to find Chokra, and the cook placing the thermos and hamper in the boot of the car. Ma had made sure we were well wrapped up. January in Mumbai was supposed to be the cold season when the temperature could occasionally dip just below 70 degrees and invariably produce at least one front-page *Times of India* headline: "Cold Snap hits City."

Chokra, who would travel with us, would shut the car doors behind us as we got in then get in himself in the front seat, next to Shankar. The cook would stand on the pavement waving to us, encouraging the illusion that he would not be seeing us for weeks when in fact we would be back in about three hours. Then, Shankar would ask Ma, "Marine Drive, Maiji?" Ma would nod and we would drive to the beautiful curved Nice-style promenade along the Arabian Sea which frames this city by the sea.

It was less than a mile away, and at that time of the morning, with not a soul let alone a car about, it took barely two minutes to get there. Shankar would park the car just where the road curved and Nariman Point, a tongue of land jutting into the sea, began. We knew Nariman Point well and loved it, but now it was as if it had suddenly become a foreign country.

When we, along with the rest of Mumbai, came here every evening to take the sea air, Nariman Point was like an impromptu, fascinating funfair by the sea.

The snake, or mongoose, charmer trying to entice us to watch as he played on his flute and coaxed the snake, or mongoose, to emerge from a basket that he held between his legs.

An urchin doing a handstand then running after us asking for baksheesh.

The blind beggar, walking with the support of a young boy and piteously crying, "Please give me money, good sir, please give to this blind man, god will bless you with much more, he will give you a thousand blessings." If it was a woman he would say, "God will bless you with children." How he knew to vary the cries I do not know, but it seemed to lend credence to Shankar's theory that the beggar was not really blind but was pretending to be so in order to generate sympathy.

And the vendors with their mouthwatering food:

The *channawallah* selling "*Garam, garam channa*", hot, hot, chickpeas.

The *narielwallah*, coconut seller, offering lovely, succulent coconuts whose water we would sip with a straw before he would break the husk with a single, powerful stroke of his knife and offer us pieces of hard, white coconut.

We normally came here just as the sun was setting, trying to capture the all-too-brief twilight which marks the indecent haste with which darkness descends and the light fades in the tropics. But now, surrounded by what seemed like everlasting darkness, the funfair and the wonder seemed to belong to another world. It is a "*morubhumi*," said Baba, desert, and we felt we had suddenly been marooned. At that hour ours was the only car, we were the only people, and it was so quiet we could hear the sea gently lapping against the shore.

The moment Shankar had parked Ma would turn to Baba and say, "Tea?" Baba would nod and Chokra would jump out to fetch the thermos to serve tea for Baba.

Then just as it started to grow light, providing the first intimation that the sun was about to emerge, Ma would ask Chokra to bring the hamper of food and breakfast would commence. Normally at home we had what Baba called an English breakfast. Next to moving his bowels, he considered having a hearty breakfast as the most important thing in the morning. His analogy was that just as the train driver needs to fill a railway engine with coal in order to start it, so to start the day we had to fill ourselves with food, and this meant porridge, toast and eggs. I did not much care for porridge, and as Ma insisted on giving us water-poached eggs I developed an antipathy to their runny, unappetizing nature.

But for our breakfast by Nariman Point we had omelettes or hard-boiled eggs and to go with them, French toast, which Ma called "egg bread", rich parathas smeared with ghee and a spicy vegetable curry. And I was not forced to drink milk but could have ice cream soda.

Ma would time the serving of breakfast so that by the time we finished it was about 7, the sun was almost up, and our adventure could be brought to an end. By this time, matching the slow lifting of the darkness we could see increasing signs of life. The odd *nari-elwallah* or *channawallah*, or the *panwallah*, selling betel nuts, would appear. Then the first walkers. Middle-aged men, and sometimes women, would slowly emerge from the houses opposite Marine Drive and other nearby homes. As the number of such morning walkers increased, and the sun finally emerged from what had looked like the forbidding depths of the Arabian Sea, Ma would say, "Shankar, let us go home." Our adventure was over.

The fifteenth of January had dawned, we had been out of the house on the first day of Posh and the travel gods had been appeased. Now nothing was beyond us.

I cannot remember how often we made such first Posh, January 15 trips to Marine Drive, but after a time Ma decided there was a simpler way of appeasing the travel gods. And here Ma made much of the extraordinary nature of our flat.

This was part of a house which was physically and inseparably linked with two other houses and in turn part of a nine-building complex which stretched from one end of the street to the other. Sailor Building was attached to Darya Building, the Sea Building. You could go from one building to another without leaving the block by using internal staircases.

We occupied the entire second floor of this block of three houses although a part of it was Baba's office, and there was also a "godown", Indian English for storeroom.

This was the most fascinating room, which both attracted and terrified me. It was at the far end of the flat. To approach it we had to go through our kitchen, then past Baba's office and down a short flight of stairs. By the time we had done all that we had somehow turned 90 degrees and were no longer on the street which housed our bedroom and living rooms. The windows in the godown room overlooked a small side street and the room was actually not part of Sailor Building but of Darya Building.

During the day we used this godown room regularly; indeed, it had a bathroom where some of us took our daily baths. The servants used the bathroom to wash our clothes and then hung them up to dry in this room. Many years later, when my friend Munir saw the washing hung out to dry, he christened the room "Dhobi Ghat", Washerman's Room.

We never slept in the room and Ma decided that this meant it was not really part of our flat and would be an ideal place to use to keep the travel gods happy on the night of 14 January. If we slept there on the night of 14 January, then come sunrise on 15 January, we could claim with great justification that we had been out of the house on the first day of Posh.

* * *

So, one January 14 evening Ma announced that once we had finished dinner, we would sleep not in our beds but in the godown. The servants had already organized mattresses and beds for the purpose. However, we had to make sure that whatever happened we could not go back to that part of the flat that Ma considered our normal home until the sun had risen on the morning of January 15. Ma drew her own boundary line where she declared our flat ended. This was at the door which separated the kitchen and the flat we lived in from the Baba's office. The only problem with this was that it put the kitchen out of bounds until daybreak. Ma got round this by making sure we had enough food with us in the godown room. Her particular concern was Baba. He loved tea at all times of the day or night, and so Ma got the cook to put in the little primus stove which normally accompanied us on long trips in the godown room, along with a kettle, milk, sugar and other essentials to last till the morning. The fact that the primus stove was with us made us feel we were really on a journey.

Ma's new edict meant we no longer had to wake up at 4 in the morning of 15 January. We could sleep until 7 and then, as soon as the sun rose, Ma would say, "Now we can return home." Then, as if leading her flock back, Ma would climb up the small steps from the godown room that took us into Baba's office and walk through his office into the kitchen, feeling that once again the travel gods had been appeased.

The godown room also came in useful when some of the other injunctions of the travel gods had to be obeyed. Dadu had also told Ma that it was bad to arrive on a Tuesday or Saturday or leave home on a Thursday. I am not sure why Tuesday was considered unlucky. In any case that was not the only day Ma was suspicious of.

Ma regarded Saturday as a day of great dread, the day of Shani, the divine personification of the planet Saturn. So if a visitor arrived on a Tuesday or Saturday, bad things associated with that day came with him into our home.

The injunction against going away on Thursday was the exact opposite of this. In contrast to Tuesday and Saturday, Thursday is perhaps the most wonderful day of the week for Hindus. It is the day of the goddess Lakshmi, the goddess who promises wealth on earth and is so popular with the materialistic Hindus.

One of Ma's great rituals was worshipping Lakshmi on Thursday. She would get up early on a Thursday morning, wear a freshly washed sari, not eat anything, not even sip water, and vanish into the prayer room. Then, after some time we would be ushered in and asked to cover our whole body except our head. Then Ma would sprinkle water on our heads, claiming it was from the holy Ganges. It came from the Arabian Sea—but we didn't mind. Nor did we heed her muttering unintelligible Sanskrit verses because we knew at the end of it, we would get delectable sweets. It explains why Hinduism is the only major polytheistic religion to survive: because it ends its prayers by offering devotees the most mouthwatering food of any religion.

Look after a devotee's stomach and there is no danger of loss of faith.

But just as somebody arriving on Tuesday or Saturday might bring with them bad luck associated with that day, so someone leaving on Thursday might be taking away the wealth Lakshmi might give in answer to the prayers.

Ma's solution for both situations was, again, to use the godown room. Guests arriving on a Tuesday or Saturday, or Baba leaving for business on a Thursday, slept in the godown room. The guests had no idea of the exact status of the room in Ma's world, but while the outside world might think Baba was travelling on a Thursday, Ma was confident that the travel gods would appreciate that having slept in the godown room on Wednesday night, Baba had actually left home not on a Thursday but on a very neutral day like Wednesday. So none of the wealth Lakshmi had given us as a result of Ma's prayers on a Thursday would therefore leave our house.

If appeasing the travel gods was important for Ma, then so were a whole host of other injunctions which she imposed on us and which defined our life.

They were very precise when it came to food.

The outside world may think India a dirty country, but Indians have a very developed sense of personal hygiene. When we sipped water from a bottle or a can, we never touched it with our lips as it would make it *atto*, contaminated, and therefore unusable by anybody else. It is something I have never seen anyone in the west able to do.

But even here Ma had her own rules of *atto* which was quite remarkable. In Ma's world it was very easy to make any kind of food *atto*. This could be done simply by taking the spoon that had been used to serve, say, the vegetable curry and dipping it into the bowl for the fish or meat curry. All the different foods had to have their own dedicated spoons, and if the vegetable or fish or meat spoons were somehow put in bowls not meant for them, then that according to Ma had contaminated the bowl.

Atto had it most severe application when it came to our own spoons. If I was eating with a spoon and felt I needed a bit more dahl then I could not just dip my spoon in the dahl bowl, for that would make the whole dahl bowl *atto*. It was when we forgot Ma's horror of *atto* that an unexceptional meal would suddenly become one of high drama. As my spoon was about to dip into, say, the dahl, Ma would shout in panic, "Oh! God What are you doing? You are going to make all the dahl *atto*. Do you realize people cannot eat, and you waste food in this way. What am I going to do with this dahl, it is *atto*. You must use the dahl spoon." And if her shout had come just a little too late, it meant the whole bowl of dahl would have to be thrown away or given away to servants or the sweeper woman, who, coming from the untouchable caste, was in a sense *atto* personified.

Ma's most remarkable food custom was to develop the theory that while there was nothing wrong with a second helping, three helpings was a sin; here her concern was not that we would eat too much but that by doing so we would somehow offend the food gods. So, if we were being served rice, then while it would be all right to be served two spoonfuls, if we were served three Ma would say, "No three helpings, that is three enemies, you must have four."

I never asked Ma why she thought three helpings amounted to three enemies, yet when she took us to the temple we were made to circle it three times for good luck. Nor did we inquire how she knew the gods of travel had such rapport with the goddess of wealth that should Baba travel on a Thursday without spending Wednesday night in the godown room, then the wealth the goddess had given us would disappear.

Certainly, I have never been able to look on January 15 without thinking of travelling, and my emotions about the number three remain terribly mixed.

Ma and her world had marked me in a way that all my Jesuit education could not eradicate.

13

AMERICA OVERTAKES BRITAIN

In 1958 Harold Macmillan became the first serving British Prime Minister ever to visit India, no previous resident of No. 10 having felt it necessary to do so. The Etonian stayed at the home of the Harrovian Jawaharlal Nehru and in order to make him feel at home Nehru's cook tried to serve European food, which proved disastrous. "Nehru's food was uneatable ... like a bad boarding house." But Macmillan was delighted that all the Indian institutions were a legacy of British rule: "The Army is British, the parliament and 'democratic' system is ours—and so is much of the ordinary way of living." However, what he missed out was that the Indians were moving away from the style of higher education the British had left behind.

A few months after Macmillan's visit, the first students were admitted to the Indian Institute of Technology (IIT) in Powai, a suburb an hour's drive from Flora Fountain. The IITs were modelled on the Massachusetts Institute of Technology, MIT, and the California Institute of Technology. To get admitted you had to sit an entrance examination. However, you could only sit for that after completing your first year at a college.

My generation accepted Nehru's idea that India should industrialise like the west. He had described the factories and steel plants being built as the new temples of India. A male student who did well at school was expected to become a priest of this new temple by getting an engineering degree. I did well at school and my career path was set.

The ideal choice was St. Xavier's College, part of the same Jesuit organisation that ran our school and the smartest and most elegant of Mumbai's colleges. For that, I needed more than 70 per cent of the marks in my Secondary School Certificate exams in the summer of 1964.

As Baba had done for the exams that Didi and Chordi sat, he made sure I was well prepared. Having worked hard in the weeks leading up to the exam, Baba said I should rest the day before. I would be sitting seven exams in a week, and I should not be tired. That evening our family went for a relaxing evening walk along Marine Drive. When we returned, Baba carefully filled the pens I would take to the examination hall. I could not risk running out of ink during the three-hour exam.

Around ten in the evening before the results were made public, Baba received a call from a friend of his who worked at the *Times of India*. He had in front of him the results which were to be printed in the next day's papers. This was a well-established ritual. In the past he had rung Baba to tell him the results of Didi and Chordi's SSC and graduation examinations.

It was just as well Baba had that call, for the next day's newspaper did not print the results. A few hours before Baba's friend had rung, Nehru died. The result was that the *Times of India*, which until then had religiously published the SSC results, could not accommodate both the results and the passing of Nehru. They chose to ditch the results and have never published them since.

I was in bed with jaundice, so that morning Chordi went to my school to get the detailed results. I had scored over 70 per cent, and she made sure I applied for St. Xavier's—and I got in.

At the end of the first year, I sat the IIT entrance exam. I went to a crammer which specialised in IIT examinations. Baba felt he had an ace up his sleeve. Brigadier Bose was head of the IIT and, while he was no relation, he was Baba's friend who often came to our house with his wife for high tea.

A few days before the results were due, Baba went to see him. Brigadier Bose echoed what the padre at St. Xavier's school had said: that I had no aptitude for engineering but should study English. I had done very well in English. If IIT provided an English degree, there would be no question I would be admitted, but my marks in the science subjects did not match the high standards IIT required. Not even he could use his power as head to get me in. I decided to carry on with my degree in Physics and Maths at St. Xavier's. But over the next three years what gave me the greatest pleasure was taking part in something that was meant to be the preserve of the arts students.

* * *

Quite by chance I discovered I enjoyed debating and was quite good at it. Soon I was the leading debater of St. Xavier's. I won the Mody Trophy, the most prestigious prize given the best debater, "for three years in succession", which nobody else had ever managed.

Not all my debating skills could always overcome prejudice, and on one occasion I experienced the most blatant discrimination I have ever suffered when a competition was held to decide who would represent Mumbai University at the prestigious all-India debating competition in Delhi. The subject was whether the United Nations had proved a worthwhile organisation. At the end of it, the professor judging the competition said I was the best.But one debater, a Parsee, who had often represented the university, had not taken part. And this professor, a large, blowsy Parsee woman, said that in his absence I could not be chosen. She would get him an opportunity to come and speak on the subject. However, he would do so only in her presence. Later I learnt that the professor had chosen her fellow Parsee. However, a few months later, a Jew judged my speaking skills to be so excellent that he gave me a much greater prize. What made it even more delightful was that this was most unexpected.

14

CRICKET, ISRAEL AND A NEW WORLD

One Sunday in the summer of 1968 I took part in an elocution competition organised by the Junior Jaycees, another American import, of which I was the Founder President. I was reluctant to enter the competition and got up so late I very nearly missed it. I spoke on cricket, and I quoted J.M. Barrie's famous line that "cricket is a gift of the gods." What I did not know was that in the audience sat the Israeli consul general in Mumbai, who was using the elocution competition to choose a delegate for the Youth City the Israeli government was holding in Haifa. A year after the six-day war, Israel was keen to convince the youth of the world it wanted peace.

I don't know what he knew of cricket, or Barrie, but he interviewed me, asked me a few questions about the youth revolt then sweeping the west, and decided I was the ideal man to represent India.

However, travelling to Israel was not easy. India recognised Israel but, worried by the Arab boycott of the country, did not have an embassy there and did not allow Israel to have an embassy in Delhi. (Israel only had a consul general in Mumbai.) I required a special Indian passport valid only for Israel. And this could only be issued by India's external affairs ministry in Delhi. I only received it days before I travelled. Baba gave me some pounds from the store of sterling he had secreted away in his safe. No member of my immediate family had ever been abroad. I had only ever been away from Mumbai on my own for a few days with my friends Munir and Ramesh to Matheran and Pune. This was only the second time I had flown. Now I was on a TWA flight, and with no direct flights to

Israel from India, heading for Beirut, where I changed planes for Tel Aviv. I arrived at Ben Gurion airport with a sign saying Shalom, peace, on the terminal and made to feel a VIP. A car awaited me to drive me to Haifa.

* * *

I arrived at the hilltop in Haifa where the Youth City was spread out over several acres of green fields to find the Israelis had assembled all the youth of the world, except those from the Arab countries: Americans—North and South—, Africans and Asians. I had never seen such a range of skin colours and variety of clothes and national dresses. The problem was the tall, large African wearing colourful African robes who the Israelis had appointed Mayor of the Youth City was not up to the job. They decided to hold an election for president of the Youth City. Helmut, a blonde German, seemed a shoo-in. But the other Indian delegate, a fellow Bengali from Delhi, had other ideas.

He came up to me, said I should stand for election and sketched out what my winning strategy would be. The youth from the Third-World countries, Asia, Africa, South America, far outnumbered the Europeans and the Americans. Even if a majority of these whites voted for their fellow white, my Bengali friend was sure he could get the Third World to vote for me. I had never been good at student elections but, thinking I had nothing to lose, decided to give it a go.

Soon after the vote closed the Israelis gathered Helmut and me in a room to announce the results. Helmut, confident he would win, walked in with a swagger and came and sat next to me. The Israeli official read out the results. I had easily beaten Helmut. The Third World had swamped the old European and American world. As the results were read out, Helmut's face reddened with anger. He did not congratulate me and nor did he speak to me again. The Israelis very were pleased and I could only marvel at my fellow Bengali. A Maoist, who always carried the *Little Red Book* with him, he did not care for bourgeois democracy, but knew how to organise winning election campaigns.

* * *

The first few days as president was hard work as I had to get up at five every morning and wake up the Youth City. But then the Israelis took us round the country. I suddenly found I was a celebrity. We met some very distinguished Israelis, and as president of the Youth City I had to respond to their speeches.

In a large blue box in my study are a few pictures of the Youth City. One is of Miriam Eshkol, the wife of Levi Eshkol, the Prime Minister, smiling as she receives a gift from a Japanese lady in a white kimono. I am also sitting on the dais smiling. The other picture shows me with Zalman Shazar, the President of Israel, at his house. I am speaking and the President and his wife are listening. The speeches of the Israeli President and officials all carried the same message: tell your people we want peace, *shalom*. I tried to mix my thanks to the Israelis with a few jokes, some of them at their expense, which seemed to go down well. They were also impressed I was dressed in my white Nehru jacket and black trousers. As we left the Israeli President's house, one of the Israeli officials accompanying us pointed to some of the young Europeans who were dressed in shorts. "They have no respect. They come to our President's house in shorts." Pakistan's *Dawn* newspaper often spoke of the Hindu-Jewish-communist conspiracy, trying to foment anti-Indian feelings in Muslim countries. My Israel trip could be seen as a Hindu-Jewish-cricket conspiracy.

* * *

The Youth City was an instant introduction to the very different world of the youth of Europe and America which none of my reading about flower power and love-ins had prepared me for. My very first evening in Haifa I was shocked to see young white men and women openly kissing and cuddling each other. Initially, I thought they must be girlfriends and boyfriends of long standing. I soon discovered they had only just met. I was also taken by the beauty of many Israeli women, but when I mentioned it to one Israeli male, he said they would not be interested in me. They were good Jewish girls who were looking for Jewish husbands, and their eyes were on Jews from other parts of the world. It was the last night at the Youth City that was to bring into sharp focus the divide between Indians and European youth.

During our travels round Israel my Bengali friend had become infatuated with a German girl who loved to hear him talk of Mao and his *Little Red Book*. My Bengali friend fell in love with her. But as we gathered on the last evening for a farewell party, he saw her kissing and cuddling a white boy. When he summoned up the courage to ask her why, she made it clear her interest in the *Little Red Book* did not mean she wanted to go to bed with him. As he told me this story he was in tears, and it was clear that the great Helmsman could ignite revolutions, but not make a German fall in love with a Bengali.

More shocking still was a very attractive Greek girl with whom I was hoping to develop a relationship. She showed me a necklace: "That boy gave me this. What have you got for me?" Since I had nothing, it was clear our relationship was going nowhere. My angst was soothed by a blonde Norwegian girl, who could not have been sweeter as we talked during that Haifa night. We exchanged addresses and promised to keep in touch.

While the British did not mix much, the leader of the British group, a tall, thin, blonde man from the British Council, had a self-deprecatory wit and could also be waspish saying, "The Irish girls only come to Britain for sex or abortion. They cannot get either in their country. You should see the boats that arrive in Liverpool from Ireland."

Michael, a Jewish boy from Golders Green, who, like me, was overweight, was keen to be friends, and so was a spotty girl from Ilford and a large blowsy one from Shepherd's Bush. We exchanged addresses. However, as I left Israel I was not sure I would ever see them. I wanted to go abroad to study, but America was my goal.

15

OUR AMERICAN CONTRADICTIONS

I had grown up listening to how good British universities were. Many of Baba's friends had degrees from Glasgow and Edinburgh but we spoke of going to MIT, Caltech, Chicago, Harvard, Yale and Columbia. Oxbridge and the LSE apart, we did not feel British universities could match these great American ones.

Our attitude to America was, however, contradictory.

A Madras Brahmin, on reading John O'Hara's *From the Terrace*, had told V.S. Naipaul, "You couldn't get a well-bred Englishman writing this sort of tosh," a view that echoed our feelings towards American literature. The one American poet who suddenly became popular was Robert Frost. His poem "Stopping by Woods on a Snowy Evening" was found by Nehru's bedside when he died. We had never heard of Frost, but the fact Nehru admired him made us think he was worth noting.

America was the land of self-help books, Dale Carnegie's *How to Win Friends and Influence People* or Alfred Tack's book on selling, which was one of the few Baba had read diligently. We subscribed to the *Reader's Digest*. And a school friend suddenly turned out to be a salesman for *Time* magazine and even got Baba to subscribe. But while I noted down difficult words from it in a notebook, I saw it as a magazine of information, not for the sort of high-class writing to be found in British papers.

There were aspects of America we wanted to ape. Our most popular singer was a young man who sang in English and cleverly converted the places in Woodie Guthrie's famous song "This land is your land", to "This land is your land, from the Arabian Sea to the Bay of Bengal." It gave us a great thrill to put on an American play changing Brooklyn to Bhendi Bazaar and Bronx to Dadar, well-known Mumbai localities. When a young American researcher came to our school all geared up to answer questions on burning issues like Vietnam and the race riots, all she was asked about was dating and whether it was really true that boys owned cars and could just drive off to distant parts of the country accompanied by their beautiful blonde girlfriends. Whenever we held a seminar on improving education in India, we called it a "teach-in"; a friend of mine sponsored a beat group named after an American one, we called rupees "bucks", "Hi" was a common greeting, and we were always having "drags" from other people's cigarettes.

* * *

I often went to an office of Mumbai University which had copious literature about American universities. I loved browsing through them and fantasing about going to study in these faraway exotic looking places.

I spent many a Sunday answering fulsome American questionnaires. I sat the American SAT exams. And while these, with their multiple-choice questions, were different from the English-style exams of writing essays I was used to, I did well enough to secure admission to some good American universities. I even secured a partial scholarship in a couple, but I could not get all the foreign exchange I needed to go to America. That left Britain the only choice. But to get to Britain, Baba had to lie, and I had to become a smuggler.

16

TO BRITAIN WITH £800 IN MY UNDERWEAR

In the 60s India's severe foreign-exchange shortage meant to travel abroad Indians needed the Reserve Bank to approve Form P, without which no airline would issue tickets. You only got £2 (about £32 today) in foreign exchange. For a business trip, or study at approved institutions, the bank would sanction more, but studying Industrial Engineering at Loughborough University did not qualify.

Had I got into Oxbridge I would have got foreign exchange as Indians still clung to British class distinctions. For Loughborough I had to get a sponsor

That is when Baba approached Bhanu. Baba had kept in touch with him when in the early 60s he decided to return to Liverpool. After Dadu died, Baba and Chordi made sure he got all the money due to him.

Baba made it clear there would be no financial burden on Bhanu. This was meant to deceive British visa officials. Bhanu readily agreed and I went off to get my British visa. I had to have a medical test including a blood test, and then an interview with a visa official, housed in the same office where I had often gone to read the British papers. But this time I went past the library I knew so well into a small office to meet a female visa official. Trying to show off, I asked her if the 4.50 from Paddington still ran, having read Agatha Christie's Miss Marple story of that name. She said sniffily, "I am not responsible for train times in England." I thought I had blown my chances. But to my great relief I got the visa.

Baba obtained the £800 (£12,250 in today's money) for my first year at Loughborough from a Muslim trader whose store sold Baba's rain coats and other products.

Baba had underwear with extra-large inside pockets made and on the day of the travel showed me how to stuff the money in the pockets. He also told me it was only after the aircraft had left Indian airspace was I to go to the toilet, undress, take out the money and put it in the large leather wallet that he now gave me.

As he said these words Ma came in with some flowers and a packet of sweets. She had just returned from the temple, having offered prayers to Lakshmi. Now Ma presented one of the flowers to me. "Take one and put it in your pocket. It has been blessed by Ma Lakshmi. If there is any problem, take it out and hold it in your hand, and Lakshmi *Mata* will look after you." With that she also pressed one of the sweets blessed by the priest into my mouth.

So, with £800 tucked in my underpants, and a flower from goddess Lakshmi in my top pocket I set off for England.

17

THE BROWN MAN WITH A TRUSTWORTHY FACE

On the Sunday before I arrived in London, David Frost interviewed Enoch Powell. It was just over six months since Powell had made his infamous "Rivers of Blood" speech, in which he feared that immigration of coloured people was "like watching a nation busily engaged in heaping up its own funeral pyre … As I look ahead, I am filled with foreboding; like the Roman, I seem to see 'the River Tiber foaming with much blood.'" A middle-aged white man had told Powell that "In this country in fifteen or twenty years' time the black man will have the whip hand over the white man."

The confident assumption was that Frost would do to Powell what he had done to Emil Savundra, whose television exposure by Frost led to his disgrace. I arrived to find Frost's failure to destroy Powell—some felt Powell had emerged enhanced from the interview—was the subject of much comment in the papers and animated conversation in the Loughborough common room and the students' union. I arrived in London on a cold and wet day in January 1969 wearing a three-piece suit, under which I had woolly long johns but with the bottom ends visible underneath my trousers. I also had a large overcoat and did not remotely look like the black man who one day would take over Britain. When I met Bhanu *Kaku* a few days later he took one look at the overcoat and gave me one of his coats, and I discarded the one I had lugged from India. I had been booked to stay in a hotel costing £3 (£55 today) a night, but a friend of a friend of Baba who met me found me a cheaper one in Russell Square.

When I asked the elderly English lady owner whether the room had an attached bathroom, she snapped.

"Attached? Attached to what?"

My friend intervened, "He means ensuite."

"Ensuite for this price. Next thing you will be asking for the Savoy", and she laughed. "There is a loo at the end of the corridor."

It was my turn to look puzzled as I had not heard the word *loo* before.

My friend whispered, "She means bathroom," and hurried me away.

My friend took me for dinner, and I was glad I did not wear the dinner jacket which Deans, a tailor near Mumbai's Regal Cinema had made. Its walls were covered with pictures dating back to the 20s, showing white men wearing dinner jackets. The owner very proudly said his shop had been making dinner jackets for "sahibs" for decades. Baba, who took me to Deans, felt I should have one because he knew Englishmen dressed for dinner. But in the restaurant, had I worn one then on my first night in London, I would have been taken for another Soma. My newfound friend very generously offered to take me round London. I could not wait to get to Piccadilly Circus, Leicester Square and Soho.

Having devoured *Time*'s cover story describing London as "The Swinging City", I had imagined London to be the world capital of free love. Now it offered paid love. The narrow, twisting streets of Soho had doorbells with little signs saying "Louise, French Model", or "Marie, French Singer", which I learnt were the names of prostitutes. Small shops had a window plastered with advertisements reading "Dorothy, strict Governess" and next to it a telephone number. And when I eagerly stepped into my first red telephone box, pictures of which I had seen so often, I found such advertisements next to the phone. A decade earlier Philip Roth, on his first visit to London, had, after taking in the Rosetta Stone and the Elgin Marbles, headed for Soho and a prostitute. Later I was to learn that one of my favourite writers, V.S. Naipaul, also visited prostitutes. Unlike Roth, I did not, and I have occasionally wondered whether if I had, would I have become a novelist like Roth?

* * *

As I returned to my hotel, the words of Half Pant rang in my ears. Nanu had given him the name as he wore shorts, which Indians call

"half pants". Worn by servants, they are a sign of poverty. Half Pant
was not poor and he was wearing them because he wanted to behave
as the English had done in India. He had lived in England during the
war and much admired the spirit of the Londoners during the Blitz.
He would carry in his pocket a napkin, spoon and fork. When he
came to visit us and was offered something to eat, he would take
them out, and then, arranging the napkin carefully on his lap, eat
using the spoon and fork. Every now and again he would wipe his
mouth with the napkin. This, he reminded us, was how the English
ate as opposed to the Indians, whose habit of eating with their fingers he considered dirty.

Despite this, he warned us about a trap English mothers set for
Indian men who went to England. "You know when you get to
London, you will hire a room, what the English call a 'bedsit'. Your
landlady will be a frumpy old woman, nothing much to look at, but
in your bedsit, hiding in your closet will be her nubile daughter. The
moment you open the closet door she will jump out and trap you.
You will end up marrying her. Beware of her. I would not mind if
our boys married daughters of earls and knights. But they marry
daughters of women who are like Rani there." As he spoke, he
would point to Rani, who was then in a sari rolled up to her knees,
bending down to sweep the floor. "They bring these English Ranis
back and they behave as if they are members of the British royalty.
That is what I cannot stand. Have fun with them while you are there
but leave them in your bedsit when you return."

But when I opened the closet of my room no nubile English rose
jumped out. Instead, I was assailed by a musty smell which suggested it had not been cleaned for some time. There was a daughter
at breakfast the next day, and much as I would have liked to have
been trapped by her, the frosty looks I received immediately convinced me that she would never have thought of hiding in the
closet. I quickly looked away, almost embarrassed I had harboured
any such thoughts.

I could not, though, look away when at the next table I saw a man
buttering the toast. Ma always buttered the toast so lightly that it
was difficult to make out if it had been buttered. When we complained, she would loudly remind us that Bhai could not afford to
buy milk. What was more important: a lavish spread of butter on

toast or milk for Bhai? Now this man was spreading what seemed like enough butter to keep Bhai in milk for a month. I very nearly jumped up and went to hold his hand and say, "You can't do that." Then I realised where I was and cast another sly look at the daughter. Her frosty looks had not changed. Perhaps, I thought, it would all be different in Loughborough.

* * *

It was, but not as I had imagined. At the end of my first week I realised there was no Soma. The clothes I had discarded every day were still there in a heap in a corner of my room. I had to take them to something called a launderette. I also learnt that that many in Britain used a language which even *Just William*'s William Brown would have found foreign. "Dinner" was served at midday. The main evening meal was called "tea", served between 5.30 and 6.30 pm. And the British at home had a very different pattern of drinking to the one in the Raj. There, as the sun set the bearer served whisky, and after an hour or two of drinking there would be dinner.

At Loughborough, it was after tea that the students headed for the pub, where they mainly drank beer, whereas for the Raj beer after sunset was lower-class behaviour. I realised an Indian went to bed with his stomach full of food, an Englishman staggered into bed with his bladder full of booze.

Garlic was taboo and belching disgusting. Soon after my arrival in Loughborough, a friend and I had a meal with some garlic in it. The friend I was with said, "Good food, but you know I will not be able to get laid tonight."

Why, I asked, unable to understand the link between garlic and sex. "Can't you see? I am stinking with garlic. Which girl will come near me? If I go to the dance floor, I shall have to go round with a handkerchief round my face saying, 'sorry', 'sorry', and 'sorry.'"

I was on the point of telling him that every morning my father ate a clove of garlic because the doctor had said this was good for his heart, then thought it would only make me sound even weirder than I already appeared.

I had been brought up to believe that in India a loud belch after a meal was considered a good sign. Whenever Mr Mukherjee of

Baculia House came to our home for dinner he would belch loudly after the meal, and Ma took it as a compliment. But when I belched after one meal a fellow student who I had got to like jumped up as if I had offered him violence: "Oh! God! How disgusting! Do you have no manners?"

Later that night I found him staggering back to Rutherford Students Hall, where we lived, clearly the worse for drink. Just as he got to the door, he was sick. Then, unable to support himself, he just passed out sprawling amidst his own vomit. The next day when he saw me, he said with a huge grin, "You won't believe what happened. I got really smashed last night, completely legless, it was wonderful." *Legless* was a new word for me, and I learnt it was considered a sign of virility to get legless at least once a week.

In India getting drunk was not a badge of honour but a mark of shame. At our parties at home, if somebody got drunk and started misbehaving, he would be quickly shepherded away by the servants.

People in India did drink, get drunk, even go blind or die, but these were poor, uneducated people trying to illegally brew liquor and producing poisonous concoctions. Their deaths made brief paragraphs in the *Times of India*, and we were made to feel pity for them. In reporting such stories, the paper always struck a high moral tone about the dangers of drink for the uneducated poor. That those seeking higher education—something much prized in India—should glory in getting drunk was a revolutionary idea for me.

But the British love for the potato, which formed part of almost every meal, did give me a reputation as a wit. The subject of food came up for discussion at one of our students' union meetings, and I said, "Why are we always being served so much potato? I thought it was the staple diet of the Irish, not the English." This brought the house down. I realised the Irish were the Sikhs of India; any reference to them was bound to produce laughter.

However, what came as a shock was the difference between India and England about which sex you could be publicly intimate with. In India I had never seen men and women hold hands, let alone kiss openly, but for men to hold other men's hands, without suggesting they were homosexual, was very common. This caused me major embarrassment on my first night at Loughborough. Taken by the concern being shown by a male student to explain things to me, I touched his hand as I would have done to a male friend in India. He shrank in horror, quickly walked away, fearing I was gay, and never spoke to me afterwards.

* * *

I didn't know if any Loughborough students had been on the great October demonstration against the Vietnam war in central London, and keen to find out how they felt about such issues one evening I went to a meeting of the Socialist Society, "Soc Soc" for short. A group of people had gathered in one of the smaller lecture rooms round a large table, and when I entered a serious looking young man with a beard was holding forth with a pint glass of beer in his hand. I was immediately impressed with him.

His name was Ian Pyper. He was a final-year student studying Humanities. On the plane from India, I had bought a bottle of Martini, heavily influenced by the advertisements for Martinis in *Time*, *Life* and James Bond drinking it. So, when Ian came up to my room, I offered him one and, while it was not shaken as Bond would want it, it was a large glass of Martini, which surprised him. Maybe because of this we struck up a friendship, and soon we were performing little mimes when Ian and I joked about writing to the Queen to withdraw the grant of university status to Loughborough. Ian pointed out that Loughborough was still run very much like a college with a very strong Welsh Mafia.

A few evenings later, after another Martini, with elections due for president of the students' union, Ian said, "Why don't you stand?" I had been in England for just six weeks. I had no desire to make myself look ridiculous. But Ian was persistent and persuasive. He had tickled my vanity. I consented.

By now I had established a certain reputation in my class. When one of our professors, who often initiated discussions during his lecture which went beyond industrial engineering, had once spoken on the subject of God, I had been severe with him. I had also questioned him when he discussed recession, saying surely the solution was to follow Keynes and print money to get the economy going. At the end of the lecture one of the students came up and congratulated me.

On the day of the elections there was snow. I had never seen snow before. I rushed out with my arms outstretched as I watched the snowflakes fall all round me, thin wispy bits of paper, cold and immediately liable to disintegrate. I felt as if a giant wastepaper basket filled with small bits of paper had been emptied up in the heavens. But as I revelled in the snow, I thought this could not help my election prospects as surely few would bother to vote. To my surprise, I won easily.

Later, Ian told me that a young female student had said, "I voted for that man because he seems honest. From his face I feel he will not run away with the cash." She could not have known many non-whites—there were probably, including me, only about a dozen—but she was clearly happy to let this "coloured" man have the whip hand, albeit only over the students' union. How very different to the then attitude of the Royal Family. Two months later the Queen's Keeper of the Privy Purse (equivalent to chief financial officer) Lord Tron would tell a Home Office civil servant that "It was not, in fact, the practice to appoint coloured immigrants or foreigners" to certain roles within the royal household.

Now, after less than two months in this country, I had suddenly acquired tremendous prestige and influence. The doorkeepers and watchmen would wish me "Sir" every time I walked past. At that stage presidents of the union did not get a sabbatical as they do now, but I was still delighted to discover that the whole machinery of the college union, albeit limited, was now open to me. I had a room, telephone, and a secretary, who was the sort of English civil servant I had often seen portrayed in movies, a long tweed coat over one arm and a pipe in the other hand. I even got complimentary tickets to see Peter Fonda's *Easy Rider*.

The students' union vice president, Nirj Deva, from Sri Lanka, was a follower of the Moral Rearmament movement, and at my first executive meeting he suggested we should all keep silent and switch on the short-wave radio in the sky through which God would address us, a common belief among MRA followers. I swept the idea away, saying it was not on the agenda. More interesting was that he was a passionate supporter of British rule in Sri Lanka and would become a Conservative MEP.

* * *

It didn't take me long to discover that Loughborough students lived up to Mick Jagger's jibe in his "Street Fighting Man", that London could never be a revolutionary city.

For Loughborough students the most important question was whether the Saturday night dances would help find them somebody to go to bed with. The university only had a sprinkling of female students and this was the only opportunity to meet the opposite sex. It attracted students from the teacher training college next door, which was almost wholly female. Gandhi had learnt dancing when he came to London. I had taken lessons on how to do the waltz and foxtrot from Goan ladies before I left Mumbai. I had only been a few minutes at the first Saturday night dance to realise why they were called "cattle market dances". This was no place for waltz, but a ritual that through music drove humans together like cattle.

As the strobe lights created patterns on the floor and the band gyrated on the stage, groups of girls mainly from the teacher training college took to the dance floor. They formed a circle, put their handbags on the floor and started dancing amongst themselves. A group of men, nearly all from the university, having watched them for some time, collectively walked towards them and, without a word being exchanged, started dancing with them. Three quick numbers would be followed by a slow one. Time for the arm of the boy to circle round the waist of the girl, just fondling the small of her back, his chest pressed tight to her breast. In the darkness, not aware of each other's names, or even what they really looked like, they would passionately embrace. Then during a break for drinks heavy petting would start.

If things worked out, then by the end of the evening the budding male technologists had found a bed mate for the night from the aspirant teachers. Some of the female students from the teacher training college were said to keep a scoreboard in their rooms about how many times they had slept with students from Loughborough. The job of the students' union dance secretaries was to book pop groups to which you could dance. One term, when the dance secretary booked a band difficult to dance to, there was a move for a vote of no-confidence in him.

No amount of Soc Soc rhetoric had managed to get the students worked up about the napalm bombing of the Vietnamese by the

Americans. But when the authorities proposed even the few female students should live in a special hall with a watchman and curfew hours, the campus erupted. I sat up all night drawing up a memorandum which I got the university to accept and made sure the proposal was shelved.

There was more talk of revolution when, at the end of the term, I went to the National Union of Students conference in Liverpool, presided over by Jack Straw, the NUS President. But even here what really excited the students were the dances in the evening. A black student friend at Loughborough had told me that his way of getting girls was to go up to them and ask, "Would you like a fuck." With that, he smiled: "You may get your face slapped, but every now and again you will get a 'yes'." Much as I was attracted to the beautiful women there, I could not summon the courage to do what he suggested. Instead, walking down an alleyway, I found myself being followed by a middle-aged white man. While he did not say he would like to fuck me, his intentions were clear. I was shocked and could not hurry away quickly enough.

* * *

In all this, race had played no part except on two occasions. Early in my term as president, I was invited to give a speech to a women's group in Loughborough about university life. At the end of it, the chairwoman, a kindly Englishwoman, who wore large pearls and had a very florid hat, said:

> That was a wonderful speech. How well you speak English. It shows that you have made good use of your years in this country and the education we have given you. I hope you will put it good use when you go back to your country, young man. Your country needs people like you to bring them up from their terrible poverty. Our job is to produce educated people like you. But we cannot have them living here. No more immigrants. This is such a small island, and we are already so overcrowded.

Some months later I spoke at another function on the day Tom Mboya, one of the charismatic leaders of the Kenyan struggle against British rule, was assassinated. One of the elderly gentlemen there commented this showed that it was not easy for these African countries to learn to rule themselves. Independence had come too early.

These references to the empire surprised me, for whenever I had raised the subject my professors had told me the British no longer gave it any thought. In the fifty years I have lived here I have heard this often, yet every now and again I meet someone who proves that the empire has not been forgotten, even by people born long after it had ended. If anything in recent years there seems to be much more written about the great achievements of the empire with any criticism seen as not nuanced enough, if not "wokery".

18

TOILETS, WATER AND BENGALIS

Not long after I was elected President of the Students' Union I received a message to contact a certain gentleman at Herbert Morris, the largest local factory in town. There had been some trouble with their workmen from the subcontinent and they wanted somebody from their native lands to come and help. This was my first visit to the town since my arrival and my first to a factory site in England. I had recently seen the film of D.H. Lawrence's novel *Women in Love*, and had been shocked to see a naked Glenda Jackson in it, the first time I had seen a naked woman on screen. As I made my way to the factory there were no naked women to be seen but it seemed Lawrence had visited the place before he wrote his novel. The same narrow twisting cobbled streets leading to the immense factory gate. On either side of the gate were council houses, their doors almost starting from the pavement, roofed with those peculiarly slanting English tiled roofs and packed next to one another with common walls. Some of them even had outside loos.

It was sanitation problems that had brought me to the factory. I arrived to find a group of workers from what is now Bangladesh assembled to meet me. The foreman, a short, thickset, white man whose hands were constantly in the pockets of his white, soiled, apron, was clearly embarrassed to talk about the problem. He praised the men, who had been working for Herbert Morris for many years, for being industrious and never having caused any trouble. He paused, took out his hands from his apron, rubbed them together and then, almost in a whisper, said, "You see, it is the loos. I mean, the loos are in such a condition now that the sweepers refuse to clean them. Well, as you must understand, one uses toilet paper in the loos. I realise some of the Bengalis were not accustomed to using toilet paper. They use water. As long as they keep it clean, it does not matter. But nowadays in the loos, the sewage is found all over the place. Not just in the bowl but all over the floor. It had caused a tremendous problem. Could you help by talking to these people in their native tongue?"

The Bengali they spoke was the Sylheti dialect, alien to my Bengali and I realised that, like the foreman, I would have language problems. But we could still understand each other and as I explained the problem the workers nodded their heads. Then a tall, well-built man, said, "Sir, we have been working here for many years. We know the customs of these people. It is true we do not use toilet paper, but we prefer to use water." He promptly turned back to his machine and from somewhere behind it brought out a bottle of water. "We all have our own arrangements," he said, "we can assure you we have done nothing of the sort that has been alleged. We do not know who has done it." I emphasised to them the need to be very careful in their habits and manners and they all shook their heads in agreement. I translated what the workers had said to the foreman, who put some questions through me to them. It was agreed that I would write out a notice in Bengali which would be pinned to the notice board.

As I was about to leave, the tall worker, who had acted as the spokesman for the group, touched me on the arm and said, "Sir, we have been honoured by your visit. Will you please come and have dinner with us?" "Yes," I said, "I would love to have dinner with you," and I took down his address. I said I would contact him, and we would fix a day. Sometime later I got a friend of mine to write out a notice in Bengali. I forwarded this to Herbert Morris and in return I received a cheque for £5, handsome remuneration for the work I had done. Much as I wanted authentic Indian food I never contacted the man. I could not imagine dining even with Shankar at his home and I am ashamed to say wedded to Mumbai's Downton Abbey world I saw them as servants. I did not want to know them, let alone explore the difficult journey those Bengalis had made or understand how they had come to terms with this very different world.

A few weeks later on my first visit to Glasgow I saw on the Saturday night men openly urinating in the streets and thought for a moment that I was back in Mumbai.

That summer the writer Jeremy Seabrook, interviewing whites in Blackburn for his book *City Close-Up* was often told a story of "Packie Stan". A white woman who lived in a terraced house was awakened one night by a noise in her bedroom in the space between the roof and rafters. Her husband found that in the loft a Pakistani was sleeping on a mattress. He was not the only one. There were Pakistanis sleeping on mattresses the whole length of the street having gained access through the one Pakistani household at the end of the street. This allowed them freedom to wander the space between roof and rafters. But every story teller told him he had heard it from a friend who claimed to know the woman and her husband. Seabrook could never find the woman and her husband. "Packie Stan" was a nasty person and he alleged racial discrimination when offered £14 by the Social Security Office. He got so violent that the terrified assistant gave him £20. The police were called but did nothing. All the whites told Seabrook they were not "racialists" (the term for racists then) but, echoing what Powell had said in speech, the Race Relations Act had made the non-whites into a privileged class.[1]

Re-reading the book it seems the classic case of "we are here because you were there." Blackburn, like many Lancashire towns, was built on the fortune made by selling factory-produced textile goods to India. In 1931 Gandhi visited Blackburn to explain how this was exploitation and why he wanted Indians to make their own garments. Now Blackburn saw people from the sub-continent in their midst as exploitation.

19

MICK THE COLOURED IRISHMAN

In the summer of 1969, as part of my work experience I went to work at what was then the biggest engineering firm in Leicester. I got accommodation with a couple who said they were accustomed to having coloured students. Why, "only the other year" they had somebody from Nigeria, and "he was ever so sweet." The husband was a research worker, the wife a dutiful housewife, and the arrangement was that I would be given breakfast and dinner during the week and two full meals over the weekend.

However, I soon upset the wife. I came back from work and, feeling hungry, opened the fridge and ate something that was there. What followed was a scene from Goldilocks and the Three Bears. When the wife returned and found it was not there, she looked puzzled: "Who has eaten it?" When I confessed, she thundered, "In this country you do not eat other people's food. That is very bad manners." I have never felt so humiliated and could not explain that in India far from leading to a rebuke, it would have been welcomed as a guest showing appreciation of food.

The night before I started work the Americans landed on the moon. By now I was getting used to gathering round television to watch historic events. I had watched Concorde's first test flight and a few weeks earlier Prince Charles' investiture as Prince of Wales, But this was different. David Frost hosted a programme which was meant to keep us awake till 4 in the morning, when the Americans were supposed to land. Ken Dodd and his Diddymen entertained us, and in between his jokes Armstrong stepped on the moon. As a newcomer to television all this felt to me like a magic show. The reality of life hit me when, after a couple of hours sleep, I went off for my first day of work.

* * *

The factory was some distance from this house and the only way to get there was on foot. I had dressed carefully, wearing my best tweed jacket and tie and a neatly pressed pair of trousers. My first problem was finding *The Guardian* as not many newsagents stocked it. But I finally located it and, with it rolled up under my arm, I arrived at the factory gates, little realising how utterly stupid I looked.

My interview had been with one of the executives and when I reported to him, he referred me to the foreman, a short, stubby figure wearing a large white apron. His face was flushed red and he looked like an overripe beetroot. He escorted me to the shed where I was supposed to work. I had arrived when the men were having their first tea break. I realised that my name would present problems, so I suggested to the foreman that he call me "Mick". As he introduced me to his fellow workers, he said, "Well, this is Mick. He is going to be working with us from today." A large, fat, chesty man wearing a blue apron looked hard at me and then said, "Bloody hell, we've now got a coloured Irishman, have we?" At this everyone laughed.

My job was simple. I was to operate one of a long line of lathes, chopping off a part of a steel rod to a very exact measurement. It required precision yet—after the few initial movements of the lathe—no particular skill or application. The process was repetitive and incredibly boring. In fact, within a few hours I felt like a zombie. I could not imagine doing this work day in, day out. Round about me the fat worker and the others did work which was not very dissimilar and equally boring. To relieve their boredom, they devised simple, childish games. The fat man loved throwing empty cigarette packets at other workers which made him feel as if he was really doing something very useful.

But much as I tried to fit in, I remained an object of intense curiosity and suspicion, not least because of my clothes.

The fat man asked me a day or two after I had joined, "'Ere, why do you wear these funny clothes? Why can't you be like us? Wear some proper clothes." I represented the world they scorned, the world of gaffers, a word I learnt meant "bosses". When I finally became a journalist and started reporting football, I learnt this is what footballers called their managers. These workers, many of whom had cars and were earning a fair bit of money, just could not identify with the world of the gaffers. This was the world of the suit and the tie, the world of *The Guardian* and *The Times*.

One day a worker came up to me and began examining my copy of *The Guardian*. He turned the pages over and then told me in a voice that was incredulous: "Why do you read this paper? This is not a real newspaper. Where's the racing? [In those days *The Guardian*, still espousing the anti-gambling beliefs of the Scott family, didn't carry a race card, only selections from its racing correspondent Richard Baerlin.] Why don't you read a proper paper like the *Daily Mirror*? Here look at this paper, this is a real one."

He thrust a copy of the *Daily Mirror* towards me. It had several pages on racing, including race cards. All the workers seemed to be reading it. In all the years I had seen the yellow bound overseas editions of the paper in the offices of the British Deputy High Commissioner in Mumbai I had never imagined it could be the most popular paper in England. I had always assumed that was either *The Times* or *The Guardian*. Now I learnt that the *Daily Mirror* sold more than five million copies. The workers' reaction to what I read made me realise that it was not only my colour that set me apart. I was the archetypal character in an Osbert Lancaster pocket cartoon, the brown man in a suit carrying *The Guardian* arriving for his first day's work in a factory, the male version of Mrs Rajagojollibarmi.

As I flicked through the *Mirror*, my fellow worker said, "You have a funny name, you read a funny paper, but whatever you do, do not bring your funny food here. It smells and we cannot stand it."

And though the hours of work were from 8 to 5 with 45 minutes for lunch and two breaks for tea—one in the morning and one in the evening—I soon found that nearly everybody there did a 12-hour day. In fact, if one did not do a 12-hour day there was great moral indignation, and everybody worked half days on Saturday and Sunday up to 12. The shift that the workers really prized was the night shift, where they could work the whole night and have the day off. Anybody who deviated from the set procedure was ostracised.

This happened when, after two weeks of work, I had to go up to Liverpool to visit Bhanu *Kaku*. This meant I would not be working overtime on Saturday and Sunday. The worker who had called me a "coloured" Mick considered it a great betrayal: "You're not going to get very far if you don't work overtime like the rest of us." When I returned, I found I had been relegated. I was no longer working on lathes; I had been assigned to another part of the factory to help an Indian sweep the floor. Neither of us had much to do. This work was infinitely more boring then working on the lathes since for long stretches of time there was nothing at all to do. Once, having swept that section of the shop floor, and with nothing else to do, I started reading *The Guardian*. One of the more experienced workers came along and said, "You're not supposed to read the paper while you're working." I replied, "Well, I have finished my work and there is nothing else I've got to do." His reply was revealing: "If you have nothing else to do, you must look busy. Just keep idling away with your broom. Never give the impression you have nothing to do."

* * *

Every morning I'd leave the house at 6, arrive at the factory gate at 7, take my card from the stack near the clock and clock in. Then I'd change my clothes and put on the apron. After that, slowly, gingerly, I would busy myself with the day's work. At 9 there was a first break when ladies came along pushing trollies of rolls, sandwiches and tea or coffee. This was normally a 10- or 15-minute break, and I looked forward to it. In fact, once we started at 7 the only way I could continue with my work was to concentrate on the morning tea break. There were moments during this long 2-hour period when, for minutes on end, I would simply stare at the clock, urging it to go faster and faster. Life was subdivided into hours and then minutes and then seconds. I could not bear to think of the whole day. The tea break at 9 was the peak of ambition. If I could reach that and still be in one piece, then I was alright. The lunch break was at 12, and once the tea break was over we would dally as long as possible and then think of the next 3-hour gap that would take us to 12 o'clock and lunch. Slowly, oh so agonisingly slowly, the hours would tick by.

Some moments before 12 I would stop work to prepare for the lunch break. It involved washing one's hands, taking off the apron and getting ready to leave the factory. Round about the factory there was no suitable place to eat though there was a general grocery store where one could get things to eat. The lunch break went so quickly. I hardly seemed to finish a page or two of *The Guardian* before it was over. Now we were in the second part of the day. Yet it was still a very long day.

I would be working overtime till 7 in the evening and there was no way I could think that far ahead. My next point of concentration was the afternoon tea break at 3. Another 3-hour stretch. Only after that was over could I even begin to entertain thoughts of going home. At 5 the factory would stop for the day. But I normally worked overtime and 5 did not offer any release. So, I would have to again concentrate for another two hours, every now and again stealing a glance at the clock to make sure that time had not stood still. This was how I survived those six weeks. By dividing the whole day into manageable segments of two to three hours. Beyond that I was just not capable of thinking.

Where the work is so terribly boring, the only thought is of escape. It was a remarkable sight just before 5 in the evening to see the workers prepare to go home. Some fifteen minutes before that, they would stop their work and queue up in the toilets to wash their hands—though the liquid soap used for washing their hands was so awful I don't think very much was achieved. Then they would return to their place of work and start discarding their aprons and putting on their ordinary clothes. This would take another few minutes. After that they were like animals on the leash prowling to break free, and they could not wait to get away. Slowly, a few minutes before 5 o'clock they would start drifting towards the factory gate, and at 5 there would be a huge crowd at the gate waiting for those doors to open and freedom to come. It was an eloquent commentary on factory society. The moment the doors opened these people would just rush out and get into their cars, wait for buses or just walk away.

The men had no illusions about factory work, but that was the price to be paid for putting food on the table. I, who had gone there with no idea of what it was like, emerged from it quite shaken. Even today, years later when the pain of just standing at one place for hours on end has gone, I cannot imagine how I suffered six weeks of twelve hours a day of work. The result was that this, my first summer in England, so very different to the unbearably hot summers in India, passed me by.

Here I was, president of my students' union, reading *The Guardian* and still with some hopes that the workers, who all voted Labour and were union members, could become revolutionaries. But I could not even connect with them. For some of them I did not even exist. Once, as we were coming out of the factory, a worker was backing his car. A middle-aged lady shouted, "You better be careful, you may run over this gentleman!" meaning me. He said, "Oh, him? He doesn't matter, does he?"

But then neither could I connect with the Indians who worked in that Leicester factory. They were almost wholly from rural Punjab. They had lived and worked in England for many years, yet they barely knew a few words of English. They certainly did not mix with their fellow white workers and, apart from regularly paying their union dues, they didn't seem to have any connection with the union supposedly representing all the workers. They did their menial jobs and collected their wages, and at the end of the day's work you could see them gather in front of a large van and go home. One worker with whom I worked for some time spoke proudly of his television set and his house. But there was no indication they felt they were part of the country or had any links with the majority white community.

But there was one worker from Punjab who I did get to know although I could not help him fulfil his great dream.

20

THE SIKH'S FUTILE SEARCH
FOR AN ENGLISH GIRLFRIEND

The Indian I did get to know opened a door on immigrant life which was revealing. He was a tall Sikh who took a shine to me. One Friday evening he asked me whether I had had any Indian food in the local Indian restaurants. When I said I hadn't, he said, "Come home with me, my wife will cook you real Indian food, not the rubbish these restaurants serve their white customers."

As we walked away from the factory, he said we would drop in for a few minutes at a friend's house. "*Bohat mouj, maja ayega*," he said in Hindi, meaning, "We shall have lots of fun." With that he winked at me, suggesting he was going to be up to some naughtiness.

After a few minutes walking down various alleyways, he stopped outside a terraced house. There was an empty milk bottle outside and a cat snoozing on the window ledge. The door was opened by a middle-aged Englishman. We were shown to the sitting room. The Sikh asked me to wait, saying he had some business with the man. Although it was high summer and the sun was fairly beating down outside, the heavy curtains were drawn. The room, lit by a small lamp in a corner, looked gloomy and dank. The whole house had a stale, musty smell which I found nauseating. On the far side of the room there was a television set. It was showing the sitcom *Till Death Do Us Part*.

Soon the Englishman returned alone. He smiled, said nothing and we silently watched television. I tried to make polite conversation. This was a few days after the moon landing, but when I mentioned Armstrong's giant step for mankind, he mumbled something inaudible and fell silent.

After some time, the Sikh came down and told me in Hindi, "*Mai inki bibi ko toka hu*", I have just fucked his wife. "*Tik hai, woh janta hai, unki bibi ko maine panch pounds diya.*" It's all right. He knows. I paid his wife £5.

As we got out of the house he said, "This is where I come once a week after work. I have an arrangement with the man and his wife. She is very good, provides a very good service. What you need is good Indian food; it will give you the appetite for it." With that, he thumped my back so hard I nearly stumbled.

He took me to his home, where his wife, dressed in salwar kameez, had dinner ready. The Sikh was keen to know what his wife had cooked. It was a sumptuous North Indian spread: parathas, dal, rice, vegetables, lamb and raita. She did not look docile and submissive; she looked me in the eye. But, like many Indian women, she didn't eat with us but served us while we ate.

The Sikh fairly tore into his food, tearing up the parathas with his fingers and making loud clucking noises as he ate. As he did so, his wife asked him in Punjabi what his day in the factory was like. "Tough, tough," he said in English, then, slipping into Punjabi, he said a man needs to work otherwise how would his wife have money for food. All this while he never looked at his wife, only his food, almost talking into his food as he spoke to his wife.

After the meal was over the Sikh said to me, "Whenever you want Indian food, come home, don't go to those Indian restaurants. They're only for these ignorant whites. Let them eat that rubbish."

During the six weeks I stayed in Leicester, I increasingly spent time with him. The Sikh's great ambition was to acquire an English girlfriend. I found this rather strange, for his wife was charming and attractive. The Sikh had a child and had no desire to forsake them. The marriage was a good one. His father-in-law was well connected in India, had property in Delhi, and, I surmised (though he did not tell me this), had paid a very handsome dowry. The Sikh did not regret having married. Marriage was merely a form. Everybody had to get married. Now he wanted some of the excitement and the joys of English life. Not once on our journeys did his wife accompany us, nor did she even want to. We visited discotheques where the Sikh would gaze at the crowd of attractive English girls with a sense of eager anticipation. He did not know how to approach them. He assumed that because I was a university student and spoke English well I should be able to find him one. To my regret, I never succeeded in introducing him to an English girl who he would not have to pay a fiver for sex.

On one of our first forays to explore nightlife in Leicester the Sikh took me to an area peopled predominantly by Indians. Here, in the pubs, you couldn't see an English face, except the battered one of the barmaid. What a sight! A crowd of Gujaratis, their shirt collars obscuring their jacket collars, tieless, enjoying a pint of beer. Sad, tragic faces in this dark, gloomy English pub. They looked lost. The chatter of voices, the sounds, the noise proclaimed India. Only the furnishing and the environment were English. In a sense, they were doing what many people in England feared they would do and what Mrs Thatcher a few years later would call "swamping" Britain. They had taken a very English setting and recreated a little India within it. In this crowd of Indian men there was not a single Indian woman.

I left Leicester convinced the Asian immigrants would always remain outsiders. But Britain, as it has often done, would surprise me.

21

NOT QUITE MAGICAL LONDON

In that summer of 1969, as every summer, the Leicester factory closed down for two weeks. A few days before the onset of this factory version of the school summer holidays, I told one of my fellow workers, an elderly Englishman, that I was planning to go to London for my holidays. He was amazed. Though he was very nearly 60, he had been to London only once, at the height of the Depression. London was a strange unreal world for him; it existed in the newspapers; it was there on the television screens. In everyday life it meant nothing. Another worker, a housewife, had a daughter who had established a reputation as a member of a pop group. She often came back from London, and as her mother retold her stories, there was in her voice a feeling of incredulity. Neither of them had any desire to go to London. I had been coming to London from Loughborough whenever I could and had many stories of London but thought it best not to tell them as I felt it would make me seem even more alien to them: the foreigner who knew and loved London. That people in England did not know and value their great capital city was a shock. A greater shock was to discover there were many in London who did not share Samuel Johnson's view that if you are tired of London, you are tired of life.

I had got a job with Kensington and Chelsea council distributing electoral forms to make sure the persons registered on the rolls were still living in the addresses given on the forms. At £12 a week it provided me enough money to survive. After the grind of the Leicester factory, this job was exciting, and the freedom was unbelievable. I could keep any hours I liked.

What I had not anticipated was that Kensington and Chelsea, one of the richest boroughs in England, also had areas like Ladbroke

Grove and North Kensington, even Notting Hill Gate, far removed from what it is now, which were poor and rundown, strong immigrant areas with significant West Indian communities. Many streets had boarded-up houses where no visitor from any public authority was welcome. Five years into Harold Wilson's Labour government, with a price and wages freeze, his "the white heat of technology" election-winning promise had not produced much heat, let alone transformed Britain. I found in these poor areas a cynicism and a hatred for the political system that was quite remarkable. "They are all the same, aren't they? Bloody politicians!" was a common refrain. Many of the residents were even reluctant to open their doors, thinking I might be a salesman for washing powder or an even more undesirable consumer product.

But the greatest surprise was to discover that, even though I was not a British citizen, I could vote in British elections, as could citizens of seventy-two countries, which included all Commonwealth citizens, British Overseas Territories and British Crown Dependencies.

More than fifty years later, this voting privilege has not been removed. Even during the Brexit debate, when much was made of who could vote in the referendum, this issue of non-citizens from the former empire voting was not discussed, not even by Nigel Farage. The empire for the British had become like the ghost of Hamlet's father.

* * *

The whole issue of race would take a very different form for me when, towards the end of the summer, I decided that engineering was not for me and that I would become a chartered accountant and live in London.

We had no shortage of chartered accountants in the family. Tuluda and Amalda were chartered accountants. But I had never been attracted to the profession. It was not that I suddenly found the profession attractive but thought as an articled clerk I could earn enough to eke out a living and find time to fulfil my dream of becoming a writer. At least, with an accountancy qualification I would not starve.

Eventually, after many interviews, Myrus Smith and Walker offered me articleship at what seemed the princely annual salary of

£700. The thought of getting my first regular pay packet was intoxicating. And the office was located at the bottom of Fleet Street, whose newspaper offices I walked past, hoping one day to work there.

As I was leaving his office Walker, wearing a three-piece suit, his hair balding and rather unkempt, his thumbs hooked in the pockets of his waistcoat, asked, "Have you found lodgings in London?" I replied "No." He advised, "Well, I hope you will live in an area where there are not too many Indians. The trouble with Indians is that they tend to congregate together." Then he added, "Oh, by the way, you can get a student edition of *The Times*." I hoped Half Pant would be proved right and I would find a bedsit with a nubile English woman in the closet. Little did I realise that, being an Indian, even to get a bedsit would be very difficult.

* * *

A stranger in a foreign land always has a heightened sense of awareness, but wherever I looked in those days the spotlight seemed to be on my Indian origin. In London, the great metropolitan centre of the imagined world I had created in Mumbai, where I had hoped to stand out for what I thought and wrote, I was more often singled out for the colour of my skin.

I first realised this when, on coming down from Loughborough, I found a small hotel in Paddington for £1 a day. One night I sat in the TV room watching a new sitcom featuring Spike Milligan playing an Indian and constantly saying "Goodness gracious me". Before the programme had started, I was just one of the many hotel guests in the room. By the time it finished I was acutely aware that, being the only brown person there, everyone was looking at me, almost wishing I would open my mouth and confirm that Milligan had got the accent right. Among my fellow guests were a young white South African couple, and as they passed I could hear the man mimic Milligan's Indian accent; the minced South African accent overladen with the supposed Indian one sounded hideous, but his blonde female companion found it hilarious.

Following Walker's advice, I turned to *The Times* to look for accommodation. The hunt for a flat always started with a very friendly telephone conversation at the end of which I would be invited to have a look at the property. But the moment I rang the doorbell, the lady who opened the door (it was generally a lady, and rather an old one, at that) would invariably say, "I am sorry, I have just let the flat." After many such rejections, I began to wonder if it would be better to warn the landlady I was from India. So, when one day I saw an attractive advertisement in *The Times* about a place in Hampstead, after the landlady said she would be delighted for me to come and have a look, I added, "Oh, by the way, I am an Indian." For a few seconds there was silence, and then I heard, "I am dreadfully sorry, but my husband would not like that."

I did eventually find a place where being Indian was not a problem as the landlady was Indian.

* * *

In the months that followed, I lived in various parts of London ranging from Brent to Crouch Hill to Golders Green to Earl's Court, and realised London was a collection of distinct villages. But I could never find the right village. It was only after I had moved from the *Times* to the *New Statesman* I found in the village of Clapham Common, then poor and downtrodden, a bedsit I could afford.

The two-storied house in Clapham was owned by a woman whose main income came from renting out rooms—and selective breeding of cats. My landlady broadcast her liberalism and often borrowed my copy of the *New Statesman*. She was unmarried, but as a result of an infatuation many years ago she had a son who was about 12 or 13 years old and a fervent Liverpool supporter. She had written a 2000-page epic poem on the ancient Egyptians which she lent me but which I never got round to reading.

It was a large room with a few rings for cooking, a gas heater and a very primitive wardrobe, which was nothing more than a curtain behind which some bars had been erected. I had to put coins in the gas heater to get it going and make sure I had a store of coins every night by my bed to start the heater in the morning. If I forgot to have the coins ready, then getting dressed the next morning meant leaving my warm bed for a room so frosty it felt like I had suddenly been transported to the Arctic. But the room was only £5 a week.

Even that was a strain on my finances. Despite training to become an accountant, I had been so inept with my own money that I was in desperate financial trouble.

The first sign of my financial troubles came when I received a letter from Midland Bank which returned a cheque I had issued on which was written "refer to drawer". The phrase mystified me. When I checked with the bank, I realised it meant I was overdrawn, and the bank would not honour my cheques. At the end of every month, I was almost £30 overdrawn. With a monthly take home salary of £48 this left me £18 to survive the month, 37 pence less than the average weekly wage in 1970. To do that, I could only spend 10 bob, 50p, a day (£7.07 in today's money) and this included fares. I was at the mercy of the Midland Bank Fleet Street. Fortunately this was still an era where you could meet real people and this real bank manager proved very understanding.

I had got into trouble squandering the money I had got in my underwear trying to impress young English ladies. After one of them I was trying to bed sniffed at the Angus Steak House, I took my dates to restaurants I could not afford. But despite this show of what I thought was sophistication, they were not impressed.

* * *

Then, in the summer of 1970 I decided to write a modern-day version of H. V. Morton's best-selling *In Search of England*, where he had described his journeys round the country in his bull-nosed Morris car in 1926. I bought a second-hand Mini and set out to explore the heart of England.

Having seen the film *Genevieve*, and being fascinated by Arthur and Lancelot, I drove to Salisbury to explore Camelot, having heard of the excavations, but no prose flowed. The streets of Birmingham were full of Urdu and Punjabi signs, and in Wolverhampton, Powell's constituency, I ran into the back of a jeep. The town hall was packed with Sikh women. Shrewsbury, birthplace of Robert Clive, the man without whom I would not have been in England, had a museum about the great empire builder. I saw small boys playing football outside the museum and thought they might find it interesting to talk to a man from India about Clive from India. But while they all knew about Shrewsbury United, they knew nothing about Clive or India and cared even less.

I had to earn money and one Saturday found a job cleaning a recently constructed building. The foreman asked me to clean the loos. This was worse than the Leicester factory and I could not wait for 5 o'clock to come. The building would be occupied by Arthur Andersen LLP. In 2001, when the firm collapsed in the wake of the Enron scandal, I felt a curious sense of satisfaction.

Having read that great writers produced their best work in garrets, I decided to spend my evenings and Saturdays writing a novel. I had read Cyril Connolly's *Enemies of Promise* and was sure there was a novel in me that would set the world alight. I decided to go for the New English Library prize of £3000 to the writer of a first novel of originality, and every evening, in between inserting coins in the gas fire, I abandoned my Foulks Lynch correspondence course in accountancy, sat in front of the rickety table and began pounding away. Lying in bed, I could plot a whole novel, but when I read the pages I had typed it was clear I dare not show it to anyone. It was no better when I entered play competitions by the BBC, or writing prizes offered by different magazines. In all of them, I failed.

I did get my name in print when the Indian government, having failed to stop the BBC screening Louis Malle's series of films on India, threw the BBC out. In *The Guardian* an Indian journalist had fulminated against the west for always being anti-Indian. I wrote a letter saying that Indians should grow up and not react hysterically to such criticism. *The Guardian* published it, and I could hardly contain my excitement. I cut it out and kept it near me, prizing it as much as my cheque book, although it made no difference to my overdraft.

22

DON'T RING US, WE WILL RING YOU

I still hankered after becoming a journalist, and when Cardiff University announced it would have a course in journalism, the first British university to run one, I took the overnight bus to Cardiff and was thrilled to be interviewed by Tom Hopkinson, the Director of the Centre for Journalism. Having read James Cameron describing his great editorship of the *Picture Post*, I felt I knew him. Eager to show off, I did what Indians call "*maska lagoa*", butter him up. But far from endearing me to him, my tactic turned Hopkinson off and he dismissed me as a voluble Indian who could never become a journalist.

Things seemed more encouraging when I applied for a journalist's job in a magazine and was invited to have lunch with the editor. We met at a swish restaurant near the Embankment. I was getting ready to leave the lunch and feeling very pleased when the editor said, "Don't ring us, we will ring you." Never having heard the expression, I assumed I would soon get a call to say I had got the job. I walked back to Myrus Smith and Walker with a spring in my step. A few days later, not having heard, I rang, but instead of warmly greeting me, the editor said in a stern voice, "I told you, don't ring us, we will ring you. Please don't ring us again." I learnt this was yet another subtle use of language by the British which sounded like a yes but meant a firm no.

I should have been warned when a show called "Oh! Calcutta" opened. I thought it would make an ideal *New Statesman* essay. But it had nothing to do with the city of my birth. It was, as its creator Kenneth Tynan said, an "experiment in elegant erotica" and the title a pun on the French for "what an arse you have!" I never wrote the essay.

To make my misery complete, not long after I received a letter from the lovely Norwegian woman I had met in Israel. She told me her Jewish faith meant she could never see a future with me. That lunchtime I walked up and down the Embankment feeling bereft.

* * *

And even when faith was not involved, my colour remained a problem. A young lady who I thought I was getting on very well with said to me at the end of the evening, "I cannot have a relationship with you. I want white babies." She lived near St John's Wood, and as I walked past Lord's I thought of the fantasy I had when growing up. Batting for Oxford in the varsity match, hitting a six over the roof of the pavilion, which had not been done since the end of the nineteenth century, and a blonde in the grandstand swooning with love for me.

The question of race had now so damaged my confidence that a little over a year after I had made speeches in front of the president of Israel, happy to project my Indianness, in London I now tried to deny it. Instead of admitting I was a recent immigrant who had come to this country as a graduate aged 21, I would pretend I had been born here, or educated from a young age. I could never carry it off, and many evenings would end with me consumed by self-hate.

I turned to writers I had never read before like James Baldwin, Eldridge Cleaver, Frantz Fanon to understand the black experience.

My only English friend was Michael, who I had kept in touch since we had met in Israel, and I got to know him well. I learnt that just as Ma never served a milk-based sweet if we had meat, neither did the Jews. I had given him a book on India and he had given me a Bible. He explained that Sabbath in a Jewish home meant all activities came to an end on a Friday evening. But on Saturday evening, with Sabbath over, there was much to enjoy. He took me to a hall near Euston filled with young Jewish men and women. This was London's version of the Loughborough cattle market dance. At first it felt promising. But soon I ran into a problem. I was a goy, a Gentile, none of the Jewish girls were interested in dancing with me. They were looking for husbands and I could never have qualified. My consolation was that on the way back we would stop at a café and eat falafel.

* * *

Worse still, at Myrus Smith and Walker, was the office manager Mr Horscroft. He was about 45, a Christian Scientist, had never married, and lived with his mother. My only job was "casting", adding whole columns of figures written out in large ledgers. I had to do it manually, and whenever I committed a mistake, he made me feel inferior. He would never accept that he could make a mistake. I was the only one who made mistakes. Work became such a misery I could not approach anything with confidence. I hated Horscroft, hated accountancy, and worse still, in the middle of the winter of 1970 the power engineers went on strike. The power in my Clapham bedsit, just when I thought the novel was coming, would suddenly go off. I had never experienced power cuts in Mumbai. Now London felt more like the capital of a Third World country.

But then Myrus Smith and Walker merged with a larger firm. The Indian ghetto that Walker had warned me to avoid was at work to prove my salvation.

23

RACE, CULTURE, RELIGION AND CLASS

Our new office was in a lane just off Fleet Street, and I was suddenly transported from looking at a white man all day to an almost completely non-white world, peopled by articled clerks from the non-white empire.

What united us was we all felt alien: even David, the honorary white amongst us, was a working-class man who had stopped studying accountancy. His prospects in the firm not being promising, he felt nothing in common with our partners, who were all white. I got to know and like him and we started playing tennis together.

Perhaps the mood of this group was best expressed on that day in March 1971 when Muhammad Ali lost his comeback bout to Joe Frazier.

By losing to Frazier, Ali had dealt us a mortal blow, almost as if he had personally decided to cripple us. For all of us Muhammad Ali was a symbol of our racial plight. Ali was representing us and, had he won, we would have walked 10 feet taller.

That morning we gathered in our little room shocked and bewildered. We did not say much to each other. We just could not explain what had happened or why. It was as if there had been some personal tragedy in our family, and for days after we could discuss nothing but how Muhammad Ali had lost. In my final year at St. Xavier's, when Floyd Patterson, a black American, had fought Ingemar Johansson, a Swedish boxer, all of us wanted Johansson to win. Now, after two years in England, I instinctively identified with people of colour.

* * *

Yet colour was not everything, as my relationship with Javed Ahmed, my fellow articled clerk, showed.

He was from Lahore in Pakistan, and one of his first stories was of going to the edge of the city and seeing how far the Indian tanks had come during the 1965 war between the two countries over Kashmir. I thought it best not tell him how, as Indian forces approached Lahore, Russi Karanjia, editor of *Blitz*, had pictured Indian generals getting their dinner jackets ready to dine in the Lahore club once they captured the city. The early days of the war saw Indians make rapid progress on that front, and such a possibility did not seem wholly fantastic. I also did not own up to Javed about being a coward when, one Saturday night, air-raid sirens sounded all over Mumbai and we cowered under our beds in fear of a Pakistani bombing attack which never materialised. Javed, who called me "Indiana", thought all Indians were Hindus and therefore despicable—something which revolted my secular conscience about India being a nation for all religions.

Javed had tried and failed to pass himself off as a Mexican using his own version of an American accent. It made Javed feel an utter fool and realise he could not conceal he was a Pakistani.

When we first met, we circled around one another warily, like two fighters in a ring waiting to land the first decisive punch. But what brought us together was that the white, English world could scarcely distinguish between Indian and West Indian, let alone between Javed and me, and to them we were both "Pakis", which had taken over from "wog" as the standard racist insult for all people with brown skin. Our friendship seemed to be prospering when, suddenly, Pakistan unleashed its terrible repression of Bangladesh in the spring of 1971.

I was appalled that Javed not only supported this brutal military action by the largely Western Pakistan army but despised the Bengalis. In my fading Bengali memory, where ideas of a *sonar*, golden, Bengal still resonated, the Pakistani action was a heinous crime. We nearly came to blows when the Pakistani opening batsman Aftab Gul suggested this was all an Indian conspiracy and the Bangladeshis were Indians in disguise. I felt avenged when that summer the Pakistani cricket team failed to beat England, while India won. Javed felt events were conspiring in my favour.

He was convinced of this when, in December 1971, India and Pakistan went to war. While his High Commission told him almost every day how they had shot down hundreds of Indian planes while all Pakistani planes returned safely, British news media told a very different story. He was no longer the cool Mexican with his supposedly neat American accent.

The Indians had shrewdly allowed western correspondents to report the war. I gloried in one *Daily Mirror* front-page story of their correspondent writing about riding atop Mrs Gandhi's tanks as they liberated East Pakistan and created Bangladesh. But as these and other dispatches filled the media, Javed began to believe in a great conspiracy embracing the BBC and all of Fleet Street, with me playing the central part in it. When the BBC showed the fall of the Bangladeshi town of Jashore, he dismissed the pictures as those of a carefully camouflaged suburb of Kolkata. By the end of the war our relationship was in tatters.

At this stage we were working together trying to unravel a particularly difficult account. I would call out the figures from a ledger and he had to say "yes" in confirmation. Those were the only words he addressed to me during the war.

Our friendship only recovered because of an Iranian, illustrating that culture can be stronger than religion.

* * *

The Iranian, the junior in the office, would try to endear himself to Javed by referring to him as "my Muslim brother". While the Bangladesh war raged, Javed inclined to his Muslim brother. But soon the cultural bonds that still tie Indians and Pakistanis began to reassert themselves.

It was the Iranian's poor English, which Javed made malicious fun of, that brought Javed and me back together. The Iranian had failed his first accountancy exams because, asked to write in the general paper about how the English waterways system helped the transportation of goods, he had written about the London Stock Exchange. He had mugged up on it, and not understanding what the word *waterways* meant had taken it to refer to the London Stock Exchange.

The Iranian's failure to properly pronounce English words drove Javed mad. Asked by Javed to bring a jam doughnut from Dunkin'

Donuts, he came back with a jam tart, the shop assistant unable to understand the Iranian. The breaking point came when Javed asked him to get the *London Evening Standard* edition with the code number 7RR, which would carry the latest cricket scores. He brought an edition containing the lunchtime scores, which we already knew. Javed turned on him saying, "You are useless. You don't know the difference between the English waterways and the stock exchange or the difference between lunch and close-of-play scores." Even liberal applications of "my Muslim brother" did not mollify Javed. Our relationship improved.

Months later, Javed, tired of repeatedly failing his accountancy examinations, decided to return to Lahore. His parents had arranged a girl for him. His father wanted him to look after the family business. "Bye-bye, Indiana," he said as we parted. "You are not too bad." It was the highest compliment he had ever paid me.

I knew I would one day return to India, but wondered if, before I did, I would ever find the England I had dreamt about in the Deputy High Commissioner's library. Then, the *Times* and the *New Statesmen* having failed, a listings magazine gave me the key to the door.

24

TIME OUT AND THE ENGLAND OF MY DREAMS

"Now is a good time to get into a workshop: most of the ones we list are just starting up again after the summer break."

This notice was in the "Workshops" section of the "Theatre Fringe Spaces/Events" of *Time Out* in September 1971. By this time, after nearly two years in London I knew nobody outside my office apart from Michael.

The first workshop listed was Cockpit Workshops, which ran a number of events. The Indians had just won their first ever cricket Test and series in England after forty years of trying, the first Indian celebration I had since arriving, albeit only in sport. A week after that triumph, I decided to give the Cockpit Theatre Company, which met every Tuesday and Friday at 7.30 pm, a try. Little did I know what a life-changing moment that would be.

* * *

We met in a large room which had no furniture. Standing in the middle was Janet Mokades, who ran Cockpit Theatre Company and was planning to put on a play over Christmas. She sat us down on the floor and got us to tell a bit about ourselves. Later Janet would tell me that my stories enchanted the group. This is despite her telling me I told cricket stories—and Janet has no interest in cricket or sport in general. Maybe I told the story of Bella, the elephant from Chessington Zoo, parading round the Oval as India won, or an Indian off-spinner named Venkataraghavan being called by the British media "Rent-a-wagon". I do remember I got the group to laugh as I told some of my stories.

Janet was like nobody I had ever met before. She possessed an intellectual rigour that was quite the most formidable I had ever encountered, combined with an irresistible urge to explore new avenues. Much as I feared her intellect, I was enchanted by her beauty and the warmth with which she welcomed me.

When, after the session, we went to the pub opposite, I soon realised that India was not a strange world for Janet. She had read Tagore and seen Satyajit Ray's Apu films. Indeed, when she first met the man who would become her husband, she thought he was from Kashmir, only to discover he was a sabra, a Jew from Israel. I could see why she might have been confused as Yehuda did not look like a white Ashkenazi Jew, which Janet was. He was as brown as I was and had this wonderful ability to strike up friendships instantly, welcoming me as his Asian brother. Much the most impressive thing about him was that he was a contrarian.

I believed in the story told by Israelis that when the Arabs invaded Israel, following the creation of the Jewish state, the Arabs in Israel were not driven out by Israel. They had left of their own accord as they wanted to return with the conquering Arab armies. But when Israel defeated the Arabs, they could not and became refugees. Yehuda, brought up in a kibbutz, had been in the Israeli army and I expected him to flesh out this story. Instead, he laughed and said, "Are you mad? Do you think people voluntarily leave their homes? They were driven out by the Israelis." He then told me a wonderful tale of how stories are made up.

> There was this Arab in a village having his afternoon nap. Children started playing near him and disturbing him. He decided to make up a story to get rid of them. He said to them, "Why don't you go to Musa at the end of the village. His daughter is getting married. He is giving sweets." The children ran down the street. The Arab started dozing again. A few minutes later he woke up and said to himself, "Musa is giving away sweets. What am I doing here sleeping? I better go and get some." Remember people come to believe their own fictions.

I left Cockpit that Tuesday evening convinced that the English world I had imagined in the library of the British Deputy High Commissioner was not a complete fantasy. What was truly significant about the evening was that, despite being the only person of colour in the group, I was not made to feel an alien. In fact, the difference was something they cherished.

Life outside the office acquired a meaning. Tuesday and Thursday evenings became magical evenings. Having thought *Look Back in Anger* could not be matched, Janet showed me new theatre worlds that challenged and surpassed John Osborne's epic play.

Our first play was Bertolt Brecht's *The Good Person of Szechwan*, where I played one of the gods. I had not heard of Brecht and knew nothing about epic theatre. My only appearance on stage had been in a school play, which had ended with my class hooting and convincing me I could not act. But now, filled as I was with confidence by Janet's direction, nobody mocked my performance as a god.

Our spring production was *The Bedbug* by the Russian playwright Vladimir Mayakovsky, a Marxist who, unable to cope with Stalin's rule, killed himself. Our summer production, *America Hurrah*, a satirical play, portrayed the 1960s counterculture. In the years that followed there were many other new theatrical avenues Janet made us explore. The one I treasured most was when I played the unscrupulous doctor in John Arden's *The Workhouse Donkey*, a rumbustious story of small-town corruption in Barnsley in the 1930s.

Our amateur productions were ahead of mainstream drama, which is still discussing if brown and black people can play white characters. I played white characters without anyone commenting about it. In *The Workhouse Donkey* my problem was not that I had daughters who were white, but that I could not sing. Janet helped me mask it. In *America Hurrah* Cynthia, a black South African, played my wife and we had a blonde son. The *Financial Times* reviewer did not think anything of a non-white couple having a blond son. He was more worried that as amateurs we could not quite convey the complexity of the play.

Janet's family soon became a surrogate family. Her father, who Janet called "Pop", had believed he was a Jew assimilated in Germany, but Hitler's rise forced him find a new home in Britain. He had a miraculous escape when he had managed to get away from a camp for Jewish refugees who were about to be sent on a ship to Canada, the ship then being sunk by German U-boats in the Atlantic. A successful businessman, he always made me feel very special. I knew that after watching my performance he would always have something very complimentary to say. In almost the same way Indians create instant families, I called him "Pop". It meant much to me when some years later he would present me with a copy of the German Nobel Prize winner Heinrich Boll's novel *Group Portrait with Lady* inscribed "to our great friend with deep affection."

Not having had a friend in England for three years, now every evening at Cockpit introduced me to a new one. *America Hurrah* introduced me to Rose Streatfield, who had just come back from America to work as a theatrical agent and whose family welcomed me with great warmth.

There was Judy, who had a lovely flat in Chelsea and with whom I went to see my first match at Stamford Bridge. Mark, another aspiring actor, introduced me to the music of David Bowie and Lou Reed. Neil was expansive on stage, but in the pub very much the careful civil servant who never bought a round of drinks as it would cost him more money. Roy, like Neil a civil servant, shared a flat with me. This in time would generate stories that, as we came home from Sainsburys, he would follow behind me carrying the shopping, as if I was treating him like Soma. I do not ever remember doing that and Roy never complained.

* * *

The writing door also opened. I met a young English woman who was keen to publish a literary magazine. She had gathered together an interesting mix of people, including an American woman who I got involved with. We would sit in the English woman's flat in Finchley Road planning issues which would break free from what we thought of as the stilted world of the *Times Literary Supplement*. I reviewed Winston Churchill's *Frontiers and Wars* and Franz Kafka's *The Trial*. I knew there was no money to be made, but to get review copies from publishers made me feel I had arrived in the literary world. What pleased me most was that my newfound English friend did not think that because I was an Indian, I could not possibly write about Kafka and must be confined to the intellectual ghetto of the subcontinent.

Josie, my new landlady, was also part of this welcoming new English world, becoming almost a mother figure as she let me have the run of the flat in a large old Victorian house in Brixton, just down the road from the Roxy cinema. For the first time in England, I felt I had a place I could call home. Josie had just come back from Nigeria with horror stories of being badly beaten by thugs. She often spoke of her son-in-law, Michael Dean, then a presenter of the BBC television show *Late-Night Line Up*, although I never met him.

Josie turned on its head Noel Coward's famous line, "She married in haste and repented in Brixton". She found love in Brixton with a black boyfriend and tried to find love for me by matching me up with one of the many beautiful girls she worked with in the perfume counter of Selfridges. Josie also became friendly with a white girl whose husband was a black band leader, and we often went to the local pub to savour a marvellous multicultural atmosphere.

* * *

Multiculturalism was not a word I dared mention in front of my next landlady in West Hampstead. With Chordi due to arrive in London, I had to find a flatlet and found one on top of a corner house in West Hampstead. The elderly lady did not mind that I was Indian or that we would be cooking Indian food—although she did not herself eat it. We quickly agreed a deal, but just before I left, the old lady piped up: "I hope just because you are an Indian, that you do not support the Labour party. You know, Mr Churchill would have given India independence if he had come back to power in 1945." This, given Churchill's well-known views on India, was rewriting history on a grand scale. But, desperate for a flatlet, I mumbled something and was very relieved when the old lady did not change her mind. However, sometime later when I told her that one of the plays I had been in was reviewed in the *Guardian*, she said it must also be in the *Daily Telegraph* and was most surprised it was not. I was glad as it was a play whose revolutionary message would have convinced her I was a secret Labour voter.

But for all our political differences, the landlady took a shine to Chordi, giving her tickets for the Chelsea Flower Show and also advising her on how to keep the flat clean. Soon my landlady and I had much to celebrate because we had a Tory government.

Early in 1972, just as Chordi arrived, Edward Heath's chancellor Anthony Barber, going for growth, generated the first modern property boom. Having bought her house for £5,000, the old lady found it was now worth £40,000. She eventually retired to the country a very rich woman. For her, it was a just reward for all those decades of voting for the Tories. Despite feeling a sense of despair when Harold Wilson had been unexpectedly defeated in 1970, I also benefited from the Tory government. Heath's liberalisation of broadcasting opened the doors of journalism for me.

25

ENGLAND GIVES, INDIA TAKES AWAY

In October 1973 the Heath government broke the radio monopoly of the BBC and London Broadcasting Corporation (LBC) started broadcasting from studios in Gough Square. But while its launch was brilliantly timed—the Yom Kippur war between Egypt and Israel broke out just then—I didn't think it would have any impact on my life. Seven months later it did. Quite dramatically.

By then I had qualified as a chartered accountant, having passed all my three accountancy examinations the first time. I no longer had to worry about cleaning loos on a Saturday to make ends meet. Now I earned enough money from my accountancy work to take my girlfriend to the Savoy for dinner.

That summer the Indian cricket team were the season's first tourists. I decided to ride on their back to become a journalist. I knew I stood no chance of landing my dream job of being a commentator on BBC's *Test Match Special* and sitting alongside my hero John Arlott. From a call box near Fleet Street, I rang Ian Marshall, the LBC sports editor. I knew nothing about him but had worked out my pitch. I told him the Indians were the best cricket team in the world, having beaten England both in England and in India, and the West Indies in the Caribbean. Then I bluffed, telling Ian I knew everything about Indian cricket and would be the ideal man to cover this important series. Ian, to my amazement, agreed. India's opening match was against Hampshire at Southampton, and he asked me to cover it. It could not have been more ideal. The three-day match was starting on a Saturday so I did not even have to take time off from work.

I walked into the press box and thought I was in heaven. There on the front row sat John Arlott. I eagerly went up to him and

151

started telling him how he was my inspiration. Arlott smiled and listened politely, and I am sure was pleased when I finally left him in peace. LBC had hired a phone for me, and not long after the match started, they rang me. I had carefully written out what I wanted to say, trying to mix what I hoped would be a few witty phrases with a summary of the state of the match. I broadcast several times that day, and while LBC found my name difficult, and called me "Richard Rose", at the end Ian asked me whether the following Saturday I could cover India's next match, against Yorkshire at Bradford.

* * *

The first Test was at Manchester: walking into the ground at Old Trafford was like being in the shadow of the gods. The place where Ranji had made his Test debut, becoming the first Indian to play for England, and the home of Lancashire cricket, which I had read so much about in the writings of Neville Cardus. And in the press box was Ritchie Benaud, whom I had seen as a schoolboy when he was captaining Australia against India in 1959. He was now the leading BBC television commentator. I so wanted to talk to him about his great cricket exploits, but all I could summon up the courage to mutter as he passed by was that the Indian attack was not as good as the great Australian side he led. He smiled, and looking at the score said, "They are not doing badly."

The journalists in the press box were often as fascinating as the cricket. Basil Easterbrook, who wrote for the Thompson Press, liked collecting bars of soap from hotels he stayed in and also from the press box toilets and arranged them on his desk in a row. Some years later he was mugged in London and after that carried a gun which he flourished in the press box.

Making his debut, like me, as cricket correspondent was Laurie Mumford from the *London Evening News*. He had spent most of his time as a sub on the sports desk, and in middle age, on the retirement of E.M. Wellings, suddenly found himself made cricket correspondent. Laurie stood out because he had very prominent front teeth and also because he knew little about cricket or life in general. In the winter he had covered England's tour of the West Indies but was worried about how many shirts, trousers and underwear he should take to cover a three-month tour. He had assumed he could not get his clothes washed in the Caribbean. When he asked Alex Bannister, the cricket correspondent of the *Daily Mail*, Bannister explained there were indeed facilities to have clothes washed in the West Indies. This was his first home series.

One evening we went on a pub crawl where he got very friendly with a woman, brought her back to the hotel, and the next morning drooled about how wonderful her "titties" were. He loved to claim his reporting was better than his rival John Thicknesse on the *Evening Standard*. "Thickers", a Harrovian and established cricket writer, could not abide the idea that an East End boy who did not have much education could claim to report cricket better than a public-school boy like him.

What touched me was how easily these men, who had reported cricket for years, accepted me and often asked my advice about Indian cricketers. All India Radio had a commentary team, and emboldened by the fact Ian had appointed me LBC cricket cor-respondent, I asked the man in charge whether I could do any commentary for him. He looked at me and said he would like some perfume for his wife from Harrods. I could not ever imagine Ian asking me anything like that. Indeed, I did not even know if he had a wife.

Only one Englishman expressed doubts that I could possibly cover cricket for the British media. He was Alf Dubs, who later became a Labour baron. He wondered if being Indian I could be objective when reporting on India versus England. I did not know that Dubs was a Czech Jew, who had at the age of 6 been brought to this country on the Kindertransport. That one immigrant could not understand another immigrant adjusting to his adopted land seems strange. I was grateful LBC did not think that.

* * *

What was marvellous was being paid to travel up and down the country that summer reporting cricket, even if matches in the north meant coming back to London on the milk train, stopping at all stations, and arriving bleary-eyed through lack of sleep. But this was more than compensated for by the wonderful mix of people I met, including a truly English rose in Derby who turned out to know a great deal of cricket.

Just as fascinating was learning the art of getting a tape ready for broadcast. Cardiff may not have considered me good enough for their journalism course, but LBC was behaving in the classic tradition of British journalism by giving me on-job training. And having got my foot on the journalism ladder, I found I could climb to other levels.

* * *

I had always wanted to write a book on a cricket season in the way John Arlott had done for many years, and I wrote off to various publishers suggesting such a book. I did not expect any replies, but all of them replied, even if it was a no. However, one of them, Leslie Frewin, to my great surprise invited me to his office for a chat. He told me that books on a cricket season, even those written by Arlott, do not sell. What cricket readers like were biographies, and he suggested I write a biography. We discussed various names, and then he said I should write one on Keith Miller. "Now that is a name who will appeal to readers, and what's more, his appeal goes beyond cricket." Frewin offered me an advance of £500. I could hardly believe that barely a few months after my first broadcast I had a publisher willing to be pay me an advance.

I had seen Miller play in India. But with Miller and quite a few sources being located in Australia, I knew it would not be easy. What was astonishing was how helpful everyone was. Despite my having been in the press box only a few months, my fellow journalists responded willingly. Basil Easterbrook told me the inside story of how he had ghosted Miller's book. The book didn't mention Easterbrook's name, perpetuating the myth Miller wrote all his own copy.

"Gubby" Allen, the supremo of Lord's, entertained me in his house. Trevor Bailey was just as generous with his time. The only man who refused to help was Denis Compton. Despite their rivalry, Miller and Compton had been great friends, and I suggested he and I meet for lunch. He refused indignantly: "You guys talk to us players, write books that make a lot of money, and we get nothing." But since I couldn't pay him, nothing further happened. Miller himself was very sweet. While he said he could not remember, he put no obstacles in my path. Even Donald Bradman, widely considered the greatest cricketer ever, replied to my letter, although he did not say much.

* * *

The person I really wanted to meet was Neville Cardus. I feared a knight of the realm approaching his 86th birthday would have little time for a novice journalist. Instead, Cardus invited me to his flat on Baker Street, where we met on a mild winter day in late February 1975. We had a leisurely lunch at his favourite restaurant, the London Steak House, and then strolled back to his sparsely furnished basement flat. Cardus had spent some time in Australia, and he and Miller had lived in the same block of Sydney flats. He could not have been more helpful, even mimicking an Australian accent. As the afternoon turned to evening, he relived his favourite Miller moments. He gave no hint of how lonely he was and how he feared destitution. As we parted, Cardus spontaneously offered to write the preface for my book; we arranged to meet again. Exactly a week later I tuned to my favourite early-morning programme, Radio 4's *Today*. It was one of the first items on the news: Sir Neville Cardus was dead. The preface was never written.

Emboldened, I now deluged publishers with ideas for cricket books which, I assured them, would shake up the cricket world. They were all willing to meet me. Ursula Owen of Barrie & Jenkins nicely explained why my cricket book idea exploring the wider social and political issues would not work.

William Miller and John Boothe, who had set up Quartet, were also very welcoming and introduced me to an agent who read one of my writings and immediately said, "This is ideal for the *New Statesman*." As he spoke, I stood by the bar of the Duke of York in Goodge Street and felt an indescribable sense of inner giddiness of' joy that the magazine I had first read in the Deputy High Commissioner's office would publish my work. They didn't, but I discussed various book ideas with William and John, ranging from history through biography.

England, without anyone asking for perfumes from Harrods, had opened the doors of journalism. Because I was the only son of Hindu parents, India was about to take away what England had so freely given.

26

FAREWELL TO ENGLAND

I knew I had a year left in England and I decided to make the most of it. I was like the man who knows he has to die, but who also knows he has some time before it happens. I had seen nothing of Europe, apart from a visit to Paris with Baba and Ma.

In the summer of 1974 I had my very own grand tour of Europe, armed with Foyle's *Europe On £10 A Day* and accompanied by Francis, a tall American girl from Arizona—blue eyes, fair hair. She could not have been more different from Amy from Cedar Rapids, whom I had met while we were both waiting at the Home Office headquarters in Holborn renewing our visas. Amy, a virgin, had fallen in love with me. There was never any danger of that with Francis, who at our first meeting said she did not want a relationship, although by the evening we were in bed. She had come to Europe for "intellectual masturbation", and as we crossed Europe by train I became aware of the enormous difference between us. Being American, Francis had a Eurail pass; as an Indian I was not entitled to one. And while her American passport meant visa-free travel, I had to get a visa for every country. Every immigration officer looked at me as if I wanted to settle in their country. Years later, when I interviewed Narayana Murthy, Rishi Sunak's father-in-law, he told me similar stories about his journeys in Europe on an Indian passport at the same time.

* * *

I returned to do things I had not done before. I acquired and discarded girlfriends and wrote a play Cockpit put on. It was called *The Black Man's Burden*, and was about the untold story of the empire.

We toured the play round the South of England. It was returning from one such trip, sitting on the top deck of the bus right in front, peering through a decrepit Kensington, that Neil, sitting next to me, questioned why I should be going back to India. "After all," he said, "you are one of the most integrated persons I know, a wonderful example of multiracialism."

A few days before I left England, Janet and Neil along with other Cockpit friends organised a farewell, and in the private seclusion of a room high above Hampstead and looking down on television aerials and green fields, the noise of traffic a very distant, almost pleasant sound, Neil recited this poem:

For now Mihir Bose goes,
For he is one of those
Who chose to pose
A short span as immigrant
and student of our mores,
Customs and womanhood.
Now he departs
With many memories
Of marvellous mammaries
Of Dark Probings
Of Fair forms.
All well he did pursue
His curious investigations.
First,
As we see him as a writer,
Full of fine flights of fancy,
Humorous and passionate by turn.
And then a grave accountant,
Studying columns by the hour
Swapping perks for—nay I jest.
Next comes the superman,
Tennis, hockey, cricket,
And some indoor games.
Pursuing some, he contemplates others
Played with intermittently achieved success and no ruin.
And then reporter, radio mouthpiece to a million
Of Bengali Public-School opinion.

Not least, I say, the Actor,
A man to play a God, Soldier,
And three times doctors,
If I be not now misunderstood.
But most of all we must recall
The Host, the genial splendours
Of those ne'er forgotten feasts
That turned the land,
That runneth through West Hampstead
Into a heart, the core, the very underbelly of the swinging scene.
Many strange incidents obscene I could recall,
Bob, Roy, Ruth, Linda and
Then Roy again.
You will one day smilingly recount them all,
But now I fear that I have spoken too long
And 'tis time to end my song.
I now have only this to say:
Bon Voyage and be not long away.

I was moved. What I did not tell Neil was why I was going back and how much I hated the idea.

* * *

However, still nourishing hopes I could be a journalist, a few weeks before I left I rang Peter Roberts, foreign manager of the *Sunday Times*, and he invited me to lunch in a restaurant which he said was favoured by all the newspaper's writers and editors. As we ate, William Shawcross walked down the steps into the restaurant, and Peter said, "That is the next editor of the *Sunday Times*." By the end of the lunch Peter had arranged for me to have a retainer as a stringer in India, and that every week I would get an airmail edition of the paper, which made me feel I would be like the character in the Somerset Maugham short story who, stuck in a remote colony, always read *The Times*.

A few days before I left London, I bought a portable electric typewriter from a shop in Marble Arch, on which I planned to type my biography of Keith Miller, thereby keeping my hopes of being a writer alive.

But even as I lugged it round on my own continental tour, Copenhagen, Paris, the overnight train to Nice, Milan and Rome, from where I flew back to Mumbai, I did not know if I would ever see Europe again. And whether I had been living under an illusion.

One evening at the Duke of York, Brian, a partner of William Miller and John Boothe's, had suggested that, unlike one of their partners, who was half-Indian and therefore truly English, I could never be English and would always be an Indian. I was upset and argued I could be but could not convince him. Now, as Shankar met me at Santa Cruz airport and the sights and smells of Flora Fountain returned, I felt Brian was right. I was an Indian who for a time had fantasised I could be part of England. The fantasy was over. You can for a time mask your roots, but you cannot shed them.

A few days later I was in Kolkata. On the wall I fixed the present my friends from Cockpit Theatre had given me, a large painting of an eighteenth-century ship and embossed on the frame the words "East Indian Shipping Company".

As I looked at it every day, I felt that while I had bid goodbye to England, the empire would always be with me.

27

BILAYTER MOHO

A month after I returned to India, Neil wrote to me:

> So, I envy you the warmth of the Bombay sun, but not the foetid
> smells of public defecation. I also envy you your firm roots in a tra-
> ditional culture together with your ability to hop, leap, step, jump,
> nay, somersault between cultures. Robert Clive began as a clerk too.
> This comforts me in a strange way. I too wish to span cultures, but
> which one? I have studied Yoga; should I go to India? I admire
> Chairman Mao; does the People's Republic call me? I am besotted
> with Gallic venture, France, then? I like Spanish dancing, Hungarian
> music, American folk singers, Middle Eastern belly dancers, Jewish
> directors and the English language. Where is my destiny?

Yet Neil and I, despite being equals on the Cockpit stage, were not
on the same level playing field when it came to the wider world. I
was from a culture whose world had been remade by Neil's ancestors, which for centuries had been told that it was deficient, an
opinion now being echoed by writers of Indian origin. V.S. Naipaul
had almost followed me to India, arriving two months after my
return, and the title of the book he wrote as a result of his travels,
India: A Wounded Civilisation, perfectly summed up this view. It was
one of the great ironies of the postcolonial world that the sharpest
critics of the book were English people who felt he had missed
some of the nuances of India. In those early months in India I felt
so wretched about having to return that my sympathies lay more
with Naipaul.

I replied to Neil quickly, angrily, incoherently, saying I could not
span cultures, I could not leapfrog between civilisations. What I did

not tell him is that within weeks of being in Kolkata I was desperately looking for ways to help me return to Neil's world. I wrote piteous letters to friends in London, rang some of them, asking was there any way I could get back to London. Could they help me find a job? I was mortified they couldn't help. I felt the ache of not being in England every time I turned to the sports pages of *The Statesman*. There was news of the first cricket World Cup being staged in England. I thought, had I not been the dutiful Hindu son, had I been as adventurous as some of Neil's ancestors, I could have been at that very moment broadcasting on the World Cup for LBC.

Neil, no imperialist, had invoked the image of Clive, who had returned from India with so much loot, a total of £63 million in today's money, that this very Indian word became part of the English language. I was returning with a qualification which could be translated into wealth. Clive came to be known as Clive of India. I, too, had a name associated with the country of my sojourn, *Bilayat Ferot*, "England returned".

* * *

I returned to find Baba and Ma had a wonderful gift for me, converting the top floor of the New Alipore house into a large spacious flat which had a bedroom with an ensuite bathroom. Ma, who had accompanied me from Mumbai, organised a servant for me. The servant called her Ma, and I became "*Dadababu*", older brother, although he had children of his own and was considerably older than me. As often happened, Ma soon tired of the servant and there was a high turnover of older men who also called me Dadababu. I finally found one, Hemanta, who had been described as a "fairly splendid fellow"; what set him apart from all the other servants was he had actually worked for a memsahib, a real English woman. That made him specially qualified to work for a Bilayat Ferot. I paid him £4 a month and food and lodging, which was considered rather generous, and in return he washed my clothes, polished my shoes, made my bed, kept the house clean and made sure I had clean clothes every morning. Every morning as I left the house to go to Batliboi, he followed behind me carrying my briefcase to the car. Had I been a "pukka", a real sahib, a chauffeur would have been there opening the car door, but I insisted on driving my Ambassador, something my fellow partners felt was rather strange, but it gave me a sense of freedom.

This much-talked about unchanging India was very evident in New Alipore and its surrounds. The street I lived in had no name and my house was identified with a number given when the land had been divided into plots. Just past Boromashi's house there was still the fence that marked the end of New Alipore and the start of Behala, and beyond that the pond which I had first seen when Baba had bought the plot of land twenty years ago. Pigs still roamed round the pond and local children swam in its filth. Every now and again a man with a Samsonite briefcase would emerge and, just before he came over the fence, he would pause, put his briefcase down, and have a pee. As friends strolled by, they would turn round and, without pausing, discuss the day's news with him. Then he would pick up his briefcase and feel he was a man ready to enter the wider world of commerce.

I was also back in the world of peons. On my desk was a buzzer, and the moment I pressed it a peon who wore a brown uniform appeared and brought me tea, coffee, food, and carried files from my office to another office. My attempt to abolish it quickly proved a dismal failure. One day, while doing the internal audit at the Jute Corporation, I asked one of the articled clerks to get me a file. He dutifully trotted off but returned a few minutes later without the file, saying it was on its way. When I asked the reason for the delay, he said, "Sir, the department which has the document is waiting for its peon whose job it is to ferry these things, and the moment the peon is available we shall get the document."

"But why didn't you get it yourself?"

He looked at me as if I had uttered an obscenity. "But, Sir, if I do that, I shall have no respect in this organisation. It is the job of the peon to carry books."

And Indians just could not get rid of what the Raj had left behind, even those institutions which had cruelly excluded them.

* * *

Soon after my arrival Amalda and Didi took me one Sunday morning to the Bengal Club. During the Raj, this, the greatest British club of

India, did not allow Indians as members. It was only years after the Raj ended, with too few British left in Kolkata to finance running the club, that Indians were finally admitted as members. Yet Indians felt no bitterness, let alone any desire to wipe out the British memory. Members pointed with great pride to a plaque at the entrance reminding visitors that Thomas Babington Macaulay had stayed here, despite Macaulay's well-advertised contempt for Indian culture.

They maintained all the club's traditions, including the Friday buffet when, having deposited the weekly letter home on a "home-bound" steamer, the sahibs repaired to their clubs and had a large, carefree lunch. Amalda's friends spoke lovingly of how the Friday buffet lunch was the best meal the club provided and I had to sample it.

After independence you would have expected the Calcutta Club to become the top club in the city given that it had been set up after the Viceroy, Lord Minto, was unable to take an Indian the British had knighted for dinner at the Bengal, and it had Indian and white members. But while Amalda and his friends were also members of the Calcutta Club, they, like the British, saw the Bengal as the place for the real *burra*, top sahibs.

All this was part of *Bilayater Moho*, fascination for England. This was astonishingly demonstrated when, in the summer of 1977, Janet and Yehuda visited me in Kolkata with an empty box of chocolates. Just before they left England, Janet had been given the box by a young Indian girl as a present for relatives in Kolkata. Janet and Yehuda had consumed them, thinking that by the time they reached Kolkata the chocolates would melt in the heat of India. Yet they wanted to visit the girl's relations. I suggested they buy chocolates from Flurry's, the city's best cake and chocolate shop, and put them in the box and pretend they were from England.

It worked a treat. The relatives oohed and aahed over the chocolates, exclaiming how nothing like this could be found in Kolkata.

Bilayater Moho extended beyond chocolates.

In Batliboi, the senior partner, Victor Viccajee, the archetypal Parsee, loved western music and refused to accept the Indian numbering system for large numbers. Unlike the rest of the world, Indians do not use millions and billions. Indians call 100,000 one lakh. A hundred lakhs is one crore. A rich Indian is not a millionaire but a *crorepati*. But Viccajee, who did the firm's accounts, used millions. The result was that, when the accounts were submitted to the Indian tax authorities, they had to be restated in lakhs and crores.

For me as *Bilayat Ferot* and qualified as a member of the English Institute of Chartered Accountants, I was automatically a member of the Indian Institute, in contrast to the English institute which did not accept Indian accountancy qualifications. My British credentials could not be doubted. I could cross the divide. My Parsee partners could not be more welcoming: For them I was the honorary Englishman.

* * *

A new class of Indians had emerged whom in a *New Society* article in 1977 I called "Middle Indians": "those who have reaped all the benefits from India's uneven post-independence development, the ones who have never had it so good and are quite determined to enjoy it, whatever the West might say."

This was a Middle India which contained many of those I and my school friends at St. Xavier's had mocked for not knowing English. They ensured their children were educated in an English school, but their children called them *"Daddyji"* and *"Mummyji"*. *"Ji"* denotes respect, making the very English "Daddy" and "Mummy" now rather comforting. There was also a growing confidence among young Indians in using the Indian languages. Unlike my generation of Indians, who would not have dreamt of ever using Hindi words, I found even Indians, who had a convent English education, used some characteristic Hindi words like *yaar*, meaning "mate" or "pal", or *maha*, "great", producing a sentence like *"Are, yaar*, that was a *maha* disco", "Well, mate, that was a great disco". But having benefited from India's democracy, Middle India much preferred dictatorship.

* * *

Two months after I returned on 25 June 1975, for the only time since independence, India became a dictatorship. Mrs Gandhi, faced with losing power, imposed emergency rule—arresting politicians and censoring the press.

That evening I went to the Kolkata Telegraph office to cable a story to the *Sunday Times*. As I handed my copy to one of the clerks, he turned to his colleague and said, "You know. I thought George Telegraph [a well-known football team] played quite well yesterday."

Perhaps the telex operator was worried that expressing an opinion could be dangerous, for afterwards a policeman came round to Boromashi's house to ask about me and why I had sent a telex to the *Sunday Times*. They did not follow it up, but within days of Mrs Gandhi becoming the dictator the country I had grown up in had dramatically changed. Now Indians seemed afraid of their shadows. Almost overnight, a society which endlessly talked about politics now talked of everything else but politics. Unable to report politics, *The Statesman* devoted its front page to a murder mystery. And what generated most excitement was which member of the Calcutta Club had stolen the editorial pages of the London *Times*, which carried a main article on the underground resistance to Mrs Gandhi's emergency rule and an editorial. The club committee could not blackball the member as it had been done by the censor at Kolkata airport and he was not a member. Soon after the censor stopped *The Times* from entering the country.

Middle India liked posters put up after the emergency that said Indians should talk less and work more. They did not see the emergency as a loss of freedom. When I spoke to a Middle Indian he, sitting in his garden sipping the Scotch his bearer had just served, laughed and said, "Killed free speech? Why, I have been saying what I like. People who come here can talk freely." As he did so, he waved his arm round his well-manicured lawn, the work of his gardener, clearly showing the area of free speech that mattered to him.

* * *

In stark contrast to England, in the land of my birth the media world was closed to me. In business my family contacts made life easy, in the media I had no "pull". After much effort I did manage to secure a meeting with Aveek Sarkar, the editor-in-chief of one of Kolkata's greatest papers, the *Anandabazar Patrika*. As I waited outside his office, a bearer asked me for a card, and when I said I didn't have one, he looked at me as if to suggest "How could a man without a card expect to see Sarkar Sahib?" I had to write my name on a piece of paper. When the great man deigned to see me, he treated me with such disdain before dismissing me from his presence that I felt I had soiled his world by merely daring to try and see him. As I left his office, I thought of the kindness and courtesy with which Anthony Howard had received me.

And while Britain could accept the idea you did not have to be an academic historian to write a book on history, Indians could not. In 1976 William Miller and John Booth commissioned me to write a biography of Subhas Bose. His nephew, Sisir Bose, who had helped him escape from India during the war to secure the help of Hitler and Japan to fight the British, had set up a museum in honour of his revered uncle. We had a pleasant enough meeting, but when the librarian showed me some classified British documents about Bose, Sisir Bose was furious and said I was not entitled to see them. Yet they were listed as part of the material available at the library and had been seen by an American academic. The documents themselves were copies of the originals in the India Office Library in London. I could gain access to them in London. While researching the biography I was to discover that in India many shared Sisir Bose's view that authoring historical books was the prerogative of academic scholars, and if they were foreign scholars, that made them even more welcome. For me, a journalist and an Indian, to aspire to such a status was outrageous.

* * *

Every evening I would come home, stand on the veranda of my flat and gaze out at the main road connecting New Alipore to the city. By then, the road, which during the day roared with traffic, was falling silent and I would be reminded of how, growing up, I had done the same when looking across Flora Fountain. Then, having read *Vanity Fair*, I imagined myself to be Dobbin going to England to marry Amelia. Now I had left behind Deborah in London when I returned to India, and I knew there would be no reunion.

My only solace was sitting at my portable typewriter and tapping away at the biography of Keith Miller, a copy of Norman Mailer's biography of Marilyn Monroe by my side. This feeling of being a writer was reinforced when, in 1976, I entered an essay competition organised by *Accountancy*, the magazine of the English Institute of Chartered Accountants. My essay did not win but merited high praise, and soon I was writing for the magazine.

This came in useful when I returned to England in good time not to squander the wonderful present John Crombie had given me. I could not tell my parents or my partners that I needed to renew my indefinite leave to remain in the UK. My partners would wonder about my commitment to Batliboi. Baba and Ma would doubt how much of a good Hindu boy I was. I lied, saying I had to be in England for the *Accountancy* prize-giving ceremony to be held in the autumn of 1976. The Air India plane bringing me back was horrendously late, but this was more than made up for when the immigration officer at Heathrow looked at the stamp saying "indefinite leave to remain" and said with a smile, "Welcome home, Sir." He was probably being ironic. I could not have cared less. I beamed with pleasure.

* * *

The "homecoming" was soured when I learnt that Frewin, the publisher who had commissioned my Keith Miller biography, had gone bust. Worse still, William Miller and John Boothe had run into financial problems and Quartet had had to be rescued by Naim Attallah, a Palestinian businessman. However, both William and John were just as welcoming and eager for me to write a biography of Subhas Bose.

While Mrs Gandhi showed every sign she saw her son Sanjay as her successor and the next dictator of India, British media were eager for news from India. David McKie of the *Guardian*, aware of the perils of reporting from India, gave me his home address, where I could always send copy I would not want Mrs Gandhi's censors to see. The *Sunday Times* put me on a retainer of £100 a month, £850 in today's money. On my return, Mrs Gandhi declared an election would be held and I was confident I would be able to write quite a bit for the *Sunday Times*. But all such hopes crashed when Ian Jack, who had flown out to cover the election, wrote an article in which he reported that some people in Delhi had been speculating the reason Sanjay had such a hold on his mother was because they slept together. An outraged Mrs Gandhi banned the *Sunday Times*. However, other English media outlets kept alive my journalistic hopes.

I covered England's cricket tour of India in the winter of 1976 for LBC by travelling up and down the country, though this meant lying to my partners that this was for Batliboi work. And, while the Indian media world remained closed, England's cricket success, under the captaincy of Tony Greig, opened more doors for me in the English media.

Paul Barker, editor of *New Society*, to my great delight published an article in which I had called Greig "the Clive of cricket". It astonished his staff because he had never before published a cricket article. Soon he commissioned me to write other pieces, including one on the sad, forlorn Anglo-Indian community, who had been abandoned by the British when they left India. It was disturbing to hear their young girls were falling prey to Muslim men. Emboldened by this, I bombarded other journals. I could not fulfil my desire to get the *New Statesman* to accept any of my ideas, but the *Spectator* did, and after Mrs Gandhi's fall the *Sunday Times* was once again being allowed into the country. But here again my Indianness became a problem with my fellow Indians.

I had persuaded the *Sunday Times* to carry an article on Kamala Das, whose book *My Story*, which claimed to reveal the secret sex life of upper-class Indians, had become a bestseller. But Das, the wife of a director of the Reserve Bank of India, refused to believe an Indian could be writing for the *Sunday Times*. She thought I was Pritish Nandy, a well-known poet and literary figure, playing a practical joke, and to test I was speaking the truth asked me to name the editor of the paper. It turned out she herself had confused *The Times* with the *Sunday Times*, and we eventually met. She came over as the classic Indian housewife, getting her servants to produce tea and biscuits.

Das should have been grateful to me. My article made such a huge impression on Naim Attallah that he published her book in Britain. But she never thanked me, and some years later confessed that much of what she had written about upper-class sex life in India was invention.

The contrast between Indian and British attitudes was provided by Jennifer Kendal, sister of Felicity, who was married to Shashi Kapoor of the famous Indian Kapoor acting clan. Theirs was one of the great romances of Bollywood: the English daughter of the manager of a touring company, which put on Shakespeare plays in India after independence, falling in love with a son of Bollywood's greatest dynasty. I was keen to write about Jennifer because she was very different to the other stars of the Bollywood film world.

She did not live in Bombay's Bollywood district, extending from Pali Hill out to Juhu, but in Malabar Hill. Unlike other Bollywood stars, she did not feel the need to advertise that she drank the best Scotch: no Black Label whisky, which was the standard tipple for other Indian film stars. The Bollywood film magazines had endless stories about stars and their private lives. Around Jennifer and Shashi there was never any such gossip. They lived a life that made them part of India but kept the frenzy and the *tamasha*, fun and frolics, at bay.

* * *

It was Rose, my friend from Cockpit, who brought me one of the most wonderful publishing gifts. After months of hawking round my Keith Miller book, I was about to sign a contract with an Australian publisher when Mark, Rose's brother, a marketing executive of Allen and Unwin, arrived in India to talk to Indian distributors of his company's books. When I mentioned my Miller manuscript, he expressed interest in seeing it, and when I drove him to the airport for his flight back, he took it with him, promising to show it to his editors. Within weeks they wrote back saying they would like to publish it. Keen as the Australian publishers were, I had no hesitation in choosing Allen and Unwin. They were the publishers of Bertrand Russell and, while he had had no interest in cricket, to be associated even at such a remove with a name I had always revered was exhilarating.

* * *

The winter of 1977 saw me return to Mumbai to run the Batliboi office. My life had come full circle. I was back in Sailor Building in the very bedroom I had grown up in, and nothing much had changed since my youth. Baba still ran his firm with the same staff and Ma had her empire of ghatis. Munir and Ramesh were still there, and in addition to our evening walks we met on Saturday for a meal which soon developed into an institution we called "Saturday nights".

Nirad Chaudhuri has written that only in the Indian subcontinent can a man be made to feel aristocratic quite so easily. What else-where would be a simple journey to the office made me feel like royalty. Every day I would drive up to the covered entrance of the tower block and a tall, uniformed man complete with beard, cap and baton would open the door of my car. Then, from somewhere underneath his armpit, a short little man, more of a boy, one of the peons, would shoot out, grab my briefcase and run in front of me to hold open the lift door. All the while, people in faded beige uniforms, doormen and liftmen, saluted me, murmuring "Salaam", which I acknowledged with the distracted nod of the head I had so often seen Baba employ.

Before I reached my desk I passed the outer office, where a large telex machine clattered away all day. Next to it was another desk with a typewriter and a young lady with long, fluttering eyelashes, ready with notebook to take dictation. In my spacious room there was a sofa where I could seat important clients, and next to my desk a buzzer which would fetch peons eager to do my every bidding.

My mind was on the clock that was ticking away, and I wanted to make sure I got back to England before the two-year indefinite leave to return expired. Back in January 1969 I had had £800 in my underwear. Now I carried the manuscript of my biography of Subhas Bose, along with books and documents needed to complete it, and I happily paid the excess baggage. The thought at the back of my mind was that the books would come in handy should I decide to remain in England. But I was not sure of taking the plunge and abandoning the luxury of life in India. It was in this state of uncer-tainty that I arrived at Heathrow that cold, autumn day in September 1978. To my surprise, the stamp the immigration officer put on my passport made up my mind for me.

28

BACK FOR THE COLONIAL LASH

Those are the words Shiva Naipaul said to me when he invited me home for dinner. The decision to return for the "colonial lash" had been made for me.

I had little reason to expect anything dramatic as the Air India plane finally landed at Heathrow that October evening in 1978. The Indians in front of me in the queue were let through very quickly. But I was kept waiting at the immigration desk. The officer scanned my passport. Instead of picking up the stamp which would mark "RR", he turned to a file of important-looking papers and kept turning the pages back and forth. Suddenly my stomach muscles knotted. He told me my absence away for all but three years clearly indicated I had no desire to live in the UK and could not claim to be a true resident.

So, he now stamped "Leave to enter the United Kingdom is hereby given for six(6) months." I was no longer a returning resident, merely a visitor. But the immigration officer's decision had also thrown down a challenge. Had he reconfirmed my RR, I might, after a month, have gone back to India, content to postpone my literary fantasy. Now the die was cast. The more I looked at the wretched stamp, the more determined I was to fight it, to prove I genuinely wanted to become a writer.

India had begun to provide me with more writing opportunities. I wrote regularly for *Sportsweek*, published by Khalid Ansari, and just before I'd left for London, over drinks on the lawns of the Cricket Club of India, with the band playing and Indians round me recreating the atmosphere of Raj evenings, I had urged Khalid to take on "the Old Lady of Boribander", as the *Times of India* is known because its offices are in Boribander. But he demurred, saying he wouldn't have the resources. In that case, I said, why not the evening paper, the *Evening News of India*, a dreadful rag? I outlined what could be done. From London I sent Khalid a detailed editorial plan for the new paper, organised syndicating rights of articles from the British press and wrote for it. It led to the birth of *Mid-Day*. But I knew a return to India would still mean I'd be a chartered accountant who, in his spare time, wrote.

I cajoled the Home Office to restore my indefinite leave to remain in this country, marshalling as many voices as I could, including the *Sunday Times*, in support. On 6 November 1978, within days of the Home Office returning my right to live in this country, I wrote to my partners and Baba and Ma. I should really have met them face to face. But I felt a journey back to India so soon after being told I could remain here for good would jeopardise the right I'd regained after such a struggle. I've also never found it easy to have face-to-face confrontations, preferring letters.

To my sweet, unsuspecting partners, addressing them as "Gentlemen", I wrote,

> I have been feeling uneasy about my life and career for some time. It is only now, at the age of 31, that I realise I have done nothing. If I should die tomorrow, who will remember me? Nobody except a few generous relatives who have put up with my appalling behaviour and a few kind friends. This may sound grandiloquent nonsense for me. But I do believe that if I take writing seriously I can leave some work behind that future generations will find useful. As an accountant I have nothing to offer.

William Miller reading the letter would say, "Rather theatrical, I think. Don't you? I suppose you wrote it for posterity to read."

If that was not bad enough, I was even more theatrical in my letter to Baba and Ma:

> I have never made any claim on your wealth and property, and I do not intend to make one now. I would suggest that you publicly disinherit me and make your properties over to your three grandchildren: they are worthier of your affection and love than your son. If it helps you please think your son is dead. Maybe someday another, reincarnated son will be born.

While I said I loved them, I also warned them not to put obstacles in my path, as they'd done through "misguided love", and declared dramatically, "I am not cut out for the Hindu world of business and money. I like money and the comfort it brings, but I cannot openly grasp it as so many Hindu businessmen do so happily."

Rereading it, I cannot believe I could have been so insensitive and caused such pain, but at the time it all seemed to make wonderful sense. But just to show the practical mindset I probably inherited from Ma was still there, I listed a whole range of things I wanted them to send me such as my portable electric typewriter, my books, my stereo system, my files and various boxes of papers and cuttings, some newspapers and cuttings stored in Calcutta, a dictating machine and any warm clothes that might be there. I also wanted the writings I'd done in India, which were stored in a drawer on which rested my stereo system.

The letters were typed by Serena, who I'd met a few days after my arrival back and with whom I had immediately started a relationship, in her father's office, just off the Edgware Road. I can still picture Serena, her skirt riding high, sitting at her desk in front of her new electric typewriter of which she was so proud, where a little golf ball kept pace with her manicured fingers, while next door her father arranged and rearranged his array of dentures. And as the words poured out, Serena murmured her approval, which meant a lot then but now makes me realise the touch of melodrama I showed wasn't confined to Bollywood movies of my youth.

Exile in the Indian tradition comes as a result of failure, misdemeanour or betrayal. Many years later, when a former accountancy colleague came to London he refused to believe I had given up my houseboys, servants, peons, secretary, chauffeur-driven cars and membership of various clubs in the hope of bashing out words for a newspaper. He insisted a partner had conspired against me.

I had read about V.S. Pritchett making his dash for freedom, but Pritchett was twenty and all it required was getting on a train to the Gare du Nord. I was thirty and there was no Mr Hotchkiss waiting for me in London. I had just over £700 in the bank but no prospect of regular income and nowhere to sleep except the sofa in my friend Debu Ghosh's living room. While I was in India I had given Debu's address to Midland Bank. Now he proved very hospitable. Janet and

Yehuda made me feel like the returning prodigal with a sumptuous dinner every Sunday night, and there was Serena. Despite not being very religious Serena would sometimes take me for a Sabbath meal on Friday night. The intonation of Hebrew prayers sounded very like a Brahmin priest chanting. Her family didn't seem to mind this brown goy in their midst.

* * *

What made the risk all the greater was that I was aware some of the high priests of the English media believed I wrote like an Indian trying a bit too hard to convince that I knew the complexities of English life. Six months earlier I'd sent an article comparing media in the west and the Third World to Alexander Chancellor, then editor of the *Spectator*. I'd got to know him when he'd come on a visit to India and he'd said he would welcome articles from me. For four months I heard nothing. Then he replied, saying the article was "a little embarrassing in parts", "You write very much as an Indian (nothing wrong with that) but you seem eager for the English reader to realise that you are as familiar as, if not more familiar than he with the subtleties of English life, English literature etc."

Fortunately, sweet Robin Dunham, who'd been impressed by my essay and ran the prestigious sections devoted to accounts in *Accountancy*, and the magazine's editor didn't share Chancellor's views. I soon got work as a staff writer. There was a certain irony in all this. I'd given up my accountancy partnership to write for the magazine that catered to members of the profession, many of whom were partners.

* * *

LBC also had no problem in accepting my broadcasts on cricket would be intelligible to their English listeners. Here I was lucky. That winter England were touring Australia. LBC couldn't afford to send a correspondent to Australia. I was hired to broadcast on the Tests and make it sound as authentic as possible.

I would come into the LBC studios in Gough Square round about midnight and broadcast every half hour till 8 in the morning, or even later if the Test was being played in Perth and Brisbane. These were the days long before overseas Tests were televised, and all I had to go on were Reuters teleprinter messages for the scores. To make my radio reports sound more authentic I got the numbers of Australian correspondents watching the match and every half hour would ring them to find out what exactly was happening. The Australians, after recovering from their initial surprise—"You mean to say you are calling from London!"—were very friendly and provided me with just the colour I needed to make the listeners feel my reports were not inferior to those by Christopher Martin-Jenkins, who truly was in Australia, and broadcasting for the BBC. Every half hour or so the presenter on LBC would say, "Now we go to Mihir Bose for the latest on the Test." I would read out the report I'd written. While I didn't say I was broadcasting from Australia, many listeners got the impression I was as I realised when, months later, I met some of them.

I felt a huge sense of fulfilment as I emerged early in the morning out into Fleet Street just as the cafés were opening to have a good English breakfast.

* * *

A few months earlier, when Pelé came with his Cosmos team to play an exhibition game in Kolkata, I was one of the radio commentators and had persuaded John Lovesey, sports editor of the *Sunday Times*, to take a piece describing the incredible background to the match. This had seen the local communist government repair local roads in honour of Pelé and more than 100,000 people gather late at night at Kolkata's airport to welcome the man considered the greatest-ever footballer.

I'd never met Lovesey and knew nothing about him, but when I went to see him at his offices he immediately said he would like me to do some match reporting, offering me either football or rugby. The choice was simple: I knew nothing about rugby, the one English sport that hadn't taken off in India. On Saturday 18 November 1978 I went to Stamford Bridge to cover Chelsea v Tottenham.

At this stage—after four years reporting from the press boxes of English cricket grounds—nobody had made any reference to my colour. That day at Stamford Bridge, ten minutes before the start of the first football match I ever covered, my colour made me stand out.

A person tapped me on the back: "Who are you reporting this match for—the *Southall Express?*"

For a moment I thought it was a wind-up from a colleague in the press box—there was another row of press seats behind me—but I turned round to find a man leaning forward from the rows of season-ticket holders, wearing a leather jacket and a smile that was more smirk than grin.

It turned to laughter when I replied, "No, the *Sunday Times.*"

"Cor blimey! Brian Glanville must've changed colour."

It was only after 5 o'clock, when I had returned to the warmth of the pressroom and John, the short, sweet press room steward, had given me a large whisky, that the full import of what the season-ticket holder said struck me.

The more I thought about what the racist had said, the more I realised it could be turned to my advantage. Newspapers then didn't have special sports supplements. The *Sunday Times* reported sports at the back of the paper and limited its reporting to a mere four pages. Brian Glanville, the paper's legendary football correspondent, was allocated some 800 words. None of the other match reporters got more than about 350, which seemed to be an excuse for most of them to tell a few jokes and ignore what happened in the match. One reporter had devoted his entire match report to writing about the number of flags and hospitality boxes round Old Trafford. It made the match reporter a cross between a comic turn and a social reporter, and I was attracted by the genre.

As the 6 o'clock deadline neared, fortified by a second stiff whisky from John, I felt sufficiently bold to lead my report with a recital of the conversation—if you can call it that—with the Chelsea season-ticket holder. Then, desperately searching to find a connection between that and the game I had to report, I went on, "Good London wit also found expression in this London derby. English football is alive and well, if still requiring the help of immigrants." The reference to the "immigrants" was because Tottenham that season had shattered the cosy, insular world of English football by signing two foreigners, Ossie Ardiles, who that summer had helped Argentina win the World Cup, and his teammate Ricky Villa. This was the first time Ardiles had appeared at Stamford Bridge, and Tottenham's purchase of Ardilles and Villa at the beginning of the season was still something of a sensation. Villa was a sub that day, and his name was considered so unfamiliar that as the announcer gave the line-up, he spelled it out.

To my delight, Tottenham won 3–1 and I ended my report by saying that, well as Spurs played, "What they will have to do to get in the *Southall Express*, I don't know."

I'd expected a reaction, a chortle perhaps, even an "Oh", when I dictated the copy, but the lady who took it down said nothing. She was probably exhausted by her efforts to understand how my name was spelled—in the end it was misspelt and appeared in the paper with an imaginary *h* in Bose. When I rang the desk for my check call half an hour later, this time fortified by another whisky in the pub opposite Stamford Bridge, I got no reaction from the man I came to know so well, Stan Levenson, then the football editor of the *Sunday Times*. His first words to me were "You overwrote."

"Sorry?"

"We wanted 350 words, not a novel. But never mind. That's what we have subs for."

"Er," I mumbled, desperate to find out what had happened to the introduction. "I started that way because I thought …"

"Oh, that," he cut in brusquely, "Very funny." Then a sudden "Gotta" and he put the phone down.

That evening I was tortured by the thought the introduction might have been left on the cutting-room floor, and just to make sure it got an audience I narrated the story over dinner to Dominic Allan, who had taken over from me as the LBC cricket correspondent, and his soon-to-be wife.

I stayed the night with them, sleeping on their living room floor. Next morning Dominic burst in with the *Sunday Times*, threw it in my direction and said, "See, they used your intro. I knew you would get colour in somehow, you old racialist." (The word *racist* hadn't then come into use.) We laughed uproariously. Then, it didn't strike me as unusual that Dominic, who wasn't remotely a racist, had pictured me and not the Chelsea season-ticket holder as the person introducing race into this story. He clearly didn't think the Chelsea fan was making an unmistakable reference to the general stereotype of the subcontinental immigrant: Paki, Southall, *Southall Express*. To the season-ticket holder the idea a brown man could write for a mainstream paper was clearly ridiculous. I was also the only non-white in the press box—and that day might've been the only non-white in the stadium. Although only a week later Viv Anderson would make history by becoming the first black player to represent England, this was long before the era of black footballers in English football. The day of my conversation with the Chelsea supporter, needless to say, neither team had a black player.

* * *

It was sometime after this that I had dinner with Shiva Naipaul. I had gone along somewhat fearfully: his wife Jenny was Alexander Chancellor's secretary and would've typed his letter about me writing English like an Indian. I had met Shiva through Alexander when Shiva had come to Mumbai to write an article about the city. The dinner in his house in Maida Vale was the result.

Much of the evening was spent discussing India, which proved a one-way street where every idea of mine about India was dismissed as just the thoughts of an Indian who thinks he is western and can converse with the west. Shiva made it clear I and my fellow Indians couldn't claim such a status. In his essay on Mumbai Shiva had mocked the class of Indians I came from. He shared his brother's view of India. They were summed up in his essay on Bihar, which was called "The Dying State". It was during this not very pleasant dismissal of my views that I told Shiva of my decision to live in England. That is when he responded scornfully about my wanting the colonial lash. I was too embarrassed to tell him I was so keen on the colonial lash I was living in a bedsit down the road from his house where to use the phone on the landing on the ground floor was a major exercise. Nor did I have the courage to narrate the Chelsea season-ticket holder story because he might've seen me as another Indian with a chip on his shoulder.

But, for all his dismissal of India and Indians like me, I found that when it came to food he stuck to some old Hindu customs. Jenny had prepared a fish dish for supper since Shiva didn't eat meat. As we ate, I thought that while I may be the Indian writing Indian

English, trying to pose as a westerner, I didn't have any problem eating meat, even beef. Shiva, of course, could have claimed I'd been so weakened by years under the colonial lash and by struggling to write English that I had abandoned my Hindu beliefs to fit in, whereas he, already a celebrated writer, who would in 1983 be acclaimed along with Salman Rushdie, Martin Amis, William Boyd and Kazuo Ishiguro as "The Best of Young British Novelists", could hold on to them.

29

LOVE AND HATE IN A CHANGING BRITAIN

The first indication of how the racial situation had changed since the early 1970s came one Sunday morning in January 1979 when, having finished my overnight LBC cricket broadcasts, I was walking past the Law Courts to the tube station. I passed a parked car with four white men in it, one of whom beckoned me over. Thinking they were lost, I approached them, only to be met by shouts of "Paki" and very rude gestures and I feared they might attack me. I hurried away as quickly as I could.

In the six years I had lived in this country as a student between 1969 and 1975, the only time I had felt physically threatened had been one night in Brixton by a black man, before his black mate came over and shouted, "Maan, you let him go, maan. He's one of us, maan." Back in 1974 I could return home past midnight after rehearsals at Cockpit, walking down London streets without fear. The years since I had been away had seen the rise of the National Front and the emergence of skinheads, and now I had to worry about white men who might be lying in wait for me.

A year later, a day forever imprinted on my mind, Friday 30 May 1980, I was to meet one of them on the Piccadilly Line. I had just left the offices of the *Sunday Times* thinking of then going the next day to Taunton to report on Somerset v Middlesex, a match that had assumed tremendous significance. The word was that Ian Botham, who played for Somerset, would take over from Mike Brearley as England captain. Brearley was also Middlesex captain, and the prospect of seeing England's present cricket captain against the future one filled me with excitement.

The tube was packed and I was standing holding on to the straps. As the train stopped at Holborn a skinhead, who had been sitting, got up and as he left the train smacked me in the face with his fist as if he was swatting a fly. The force with which he did it made my glasses fly across the compartment. As I bent down to gather them up, the rest of the passengers neither said nor did anything—as if they were in the cinema watching a film.

My experience was something Bhanu *Kaku*, who was visiting from Liverpool, couldn't relate to. One of the first Indian consultants in the UK, he was more concerned that I had kept him waiting for dinner and rebuked me for it.

It was some months after this that this skinhead menace acquired a football face. Twice.

The first was on the evening of 21 March 1981 when, returning from covering Norwich v Arsenal, an Arsenal supporter chased me down the train shouting, '"Coon, Coon, hit the Coon over the head with a baseball bat," a popular football song. The train was packed with Arsenal supporters who, fortunately, didn't take up the invitation. As the "coon" basher caught up with me a black policewoman apprehended him. He turned out to be a chef who didn't find it easy to find work, and when he pleaded guilty in a Norwich court, in the autumn of 1981, was fined £20 for using abusive language and threatening behaviour.

Three weeks after the court hearing, returning on the 19.03 from Nottingham after covering Nottingham Forest v Leeds, my encounter with Chelsea fans made me feel I mightn't survive the night. After young boys had taunted me by calling me "Paki", about ten Chelsea supporters came to my compartment, scattered the contents of my briefcase on the floor, roughed me about and then danced round me debating who did the "wog" belong to. I was grateful for this indecision by the Chelsea mob, for by the time they made up their mind the train had pulled into St. Pancras, British Transport police boarded the train, and the fans, shouting "Old Bill's coming", made a run for it.

That evening I went to the *Sunday Times* office and felt like leaving a note for John Lovesey saying I didn't want to report football anymore. I didn't, and Lovesey's response was to make me realise that Britain is a country of many colours, more of them enchanting rather than depressing. And in Lovesey and his sports department at the *Sunday Times* I had found one very fragrant and colourful bouquet. The week after my escape from the Chelsea mob, Lovesey got Dudley Doust, the sports feature writer, to write a piece about my experiences entitled 'Journey into Terror on the 19.03 from Nottingham'. The joke in the office was that whatever I had suffered at the hands of the Chelsea mob was nothing to what Dudley would put me through. Dudley, an American, brought up in that country's school of journalism, was famous for teasing out details. He must have rung me at least a dozen times, possibly more, in what proved to be a masterpiece of recreation.

However, Lovesey's reaction to my trauma was not matched by the football world. Nobody from Arsenal, Chelsea, the Football League or the Football Association reacted. One football supporter even wrote to me saying I was attacked not because of my race but because I was travelling first class. I realised how very privileged I was to have been spotted by John Lovesey.

* * *

Lovesey brought to sports reporting an originality that was unique in Fleet Street, reflecting his experience of working for the American media. His sports desk brought together some of the best writers and subs from Fleet Street. There was Alan Bromley from the *Daily Mail*, the best subeditor I have ever worked with, and Stan Levenson, the football editor, whose weekly job was to be the sports editor of the *Morning Star*. In one of those great contradictions which can make Britain so fascinating, this communist party paper had in the immediate post-war years a race tipster who was the best in Fleet Street. The story went that people who worked in the City would hide the paper under the *Financial Times* to read his tips. Under Stan, the *Star* had developed a superb sports desk which was a nursery for many journalists who then went on to work for the *Sunday Times* and other papers.

In many ways the most amazing man was Brian Glanville. Brian, who ran his own football team called Chelsea Casuals, had spent many years in Italy in the 1950s. While there he had written for *Sport and Pastime*, produced by *The Hindu*, one of India's leading papers. The £5 an article he got from *The Hindu* had kept him going in Italy. I had grown up in India reading Brian's football pieces and now to work with him was a joy and a revelation.

Brian, who is Jewish, speaking in his public-school, upper-class accent, loved regaling the press box with Jewish jokes, proving the old adage that the Jews can make fun of their community in the way nobody else can. He would write out his match report by hand and, as he dictated his copy over the phone, would cross out the words he had read out so his copy was exactly the length required. For him a good football match was if he finished filing his copy minutes after the referee blew the final whistle. Brian's most remarkable contribution to English football reporting was bringing Italy to football press boxes. He still maintained his Italian connections. At the end of the match, having filed his copy for the *Sunday Times*, he could be heard speaking Italian on the phone while dictating a match report to an Italian paper. As part of his mission of educating us about Italian football he would often talk of *catenaccio*, the unique Italian defensive system of playing the game, and did it so successfully that even those of us who knew not a word of Italian, let alone anything about Italian football, understood what it meant.

What made Brian stand out was his refusal to accept the major change that came over football reporting in the 1970s. After a game managers held a press conference. The result was that what they said was now considered more important, and a match report was no longer a description of a match but more often the manager's view of it. But Brian, who rarely ever interviewed managers or players, had no time for their post-match views.

Brian believed *Sunday Times* readers wanted his opinion, not managerial spin. He didn't attend the Saturday press conferences. The rest of us did, but, taking our cue from Brian, we loved mocking them as real-life versions of Ron Knee, the fictional manager of *Private Eye's* spoof football team, Neasden United.

Unlike other football correspondents, Brian very seldom travelled outside London to matches. This was the era when Liverpool were supreme, but Brian contended there was no need to go to Anfield; Liverpool would have to come to White Hart Lane, Highbury, Stamford Bridge, Upton Park and other London clubs, and he could just get on his bike to see them there. It meant I was often sent to Anfield, Old Trafford, and other great theatres of English football and sat next to the country's leading football writers, who were bemused that the *Sunday Times* reporter for such an important match was a junior. What baffled them even more was that I was a brown man.

Contrary to what I had been told, I found little evidence of the fabled warmth and friendliness of the North, although my experiences were nothing compared to the black players then emerging in the game. They had horrendous experience of racial abuse which, if it happened today, would probably see those teams forced to play in empty stadiums. At some northern grounds black players would have to run in at half-time with their shirts over their head because father and son were leaning over the barrier and spitting at them. English football was changing, reflecting changes in the wider society.

* * *

In the England I had come to in the 1960s, football, work and home formed a neatly symmetrical pattern. All matches, apart from Cup replays, started at 3 pm on a Saturday. The supporter worked in the factory till lunchtime, then went to the pub, and just before kick-off, the football stadium. Then, after the final whistle had blown, he'd pick up the pink 'un, the evening paper selling outside the ground which carried the match reports, and walk home. There the missus would have the tea ready. The factory, pub, football ground and home were all within walking distance of each other. Contrary to myths that have since been pedalled, football watching wasn't a family affair and was very sexist. Fathers took sons, but certainly not wives and daughters.

But by the time I had covered my first match for the *Sunday Times*, in 1978, this world had disappeared and, astonishingly, English football had turned on its head the American idea of bussing. This is where black kids were bussed to prosperous white neighbourhoods to provide them with a decent education. In football on match days it was this country's whites who travelled back to grim inner city areas their parents had worked hard to leave, to watch twenty-two men kick a round ball in a decrepit stadium. Yet the brown and black people who now lived in the homes the parents of these whites had vacated took no interest at all in the game, despite the ground being a couple of minutes' walk away. The sight of this returning white army, which could often be violent, was so worrying that they often welcomed them by boarding up their doors and windows. Every Saturday I would be part of this white "invasion", and as the odd non-white wonder what a Martian would think of England should they suddenly arrive.

This had struck me on my first visit to Villa Park, one of English football's most historic grounds. The Asian kids who swarmed round my car saying they would look after it had no interest in football or Villa, no plans to go to the match, and they were strangers to the uniformly white crowds streaming in from Birmingham and other parts of the country. To get to Upton Park, then the home of West Ham, I walked through a market which looked like Delhi's Khan Market, but none of the Asian shopkeepers or Asian customers had any interest in football. Upton Park was in the middle of the East End Sikh community, but there were hardly any Sikhs in the ground. They might have been put off by the fact that the National Front was distributing its *Bulldog* magazine outside the ground, as it did at various stadiums. I noticed how the vendor cried out even more loudly as I passed by, "Get your colour supplement."

For me the classic case of the dysfunctional nature of English football was Luton, whose matches I often reported. Jim Pegg, the *Sunday Times* assistant editor, who organised the football match rota, had decided that I was best suited to report the team. The football they played was a delight. However, the nature of their support told a very different and worrying story. The hilly streets round the ground contained inhabitants who were totally alienated from the club and its football. They were Asians, mostly Muslims, and the area boasted three mosques. When Chelsea and Luton were both in the old second division, raids on the mosques formed part of a Saturday afternoon work by some Chelsea supporters. All this gave Saturday afternoon at Luton an almost surreal quality. Bemused Asians, many of them dressed in the traditional Muslim fashion with skullcaps, would watch in incomprehension as coachloads of whites arrived flaunting extravagant hair and clothes styles and often fighting with each other or the police to watch this strange game of football. The area had a few shops and visiting them I felt like I was back in the subcontinent. I would chat to them in my pidgin Urdu, buy a Yorkie bar, and then walk into the Luton ground into an all-white press box and a stadium that was almost wholly white.

What made it even more curious was that this all-white crowd were watching a Luton team that had some of the finest black players in the country, some of whom went on to play for England, and was managed by a Jewish manager, David Pleat, although this wasn't well known. By this time, unlike my first match for the *Sunday Times* in 1978, these whites were often watching mixed teams of blacks and whites, which I found had led to a curious form of differentiated racial abuse: our blacks are good, their blacks are animals. I would find the home team's black players lovingly referred to by their Christian names, while the opposition were greeted with ape-like sounds that old Tarzan films used to feature, interspersed with shouts of "Go back to the trees." If the opposition was being a bit too vigorous, it was almost certain that the big black opposition defender would be the first to be booed or hissed. Some years later I would hear a chairman of a football club tell his opposite number in the middle of a match "Our blacks are better than yours."

Along with this had come two fundamental changes to British life which had a dramatic impact on football. Until well into the 1960s there was little scope for travelling far distances to watch away matches. A Tottenham or an Arsenal supporter would be at their rival's ground every other Saturday and even had season tickets for both clubs. This was sporting rivalry, not the present-day hate-filled enmity. This historic pattern of football watching was revolutionised with the arrival of the motorways and the five-day week. In came the world we now consider normal, fans journeying for several hours to see their team play away from home.

By the time I covered my first match in 1978 this new pattern was well established—and so was hooliganism. When going to football with Judy or John from Cockpit in the early 1970s this was not something I had to worry about. Now an air of menace hung over football matches. There was the forbidding atmosphere at the main railway stations on Saturdays as policemen with dogs patrolled. Away fans were escorted to the ground as if they were contaminated and any contact with home fans lethal. In 1972, when Judy and I went to Stamford Bridge nobody asked me whether I was a home or away fan. Now football fans had to say whether they were home or away supporters. There were separate entrances, seating was segregated, and there were barriers to prevent home and away fans being in contact with each other. English football had reproduced what had historically been done by whites in the Deep South of America to keep the races separate.

But what surprised me was that the media weren't interested in reporting this. In August 1985, with the football season about to start, I wrote a piece for the *Listener* entitled, "We misreport football by ignoring ugliness." I argued that "The media misreport football by ignoring the ugliness or ascribing it to mindless group of 'nutters'".

As it happened, that season marked my return to train travel when reporting matches. I had not taken a train for five years, between 1981 and 1985, as a result of my experiences with the Arsenal fan and the Chelsea mob. In that period, I had driven to all the matches I covered, even if it meant driving back and forth to Swansea in a day and taking the risk of nodding off on the journey back, which at times I did. I checked where teams with well-known hooligan supporters were playing. I arrived at towns three hours before the match, got to the ground even before the stewards had arrived so I could park my car as near the ground as possible. The idea was to make a quick getaway at the end of the match.

* * *

In 1979, when union problems made Thompsons, owners of the *Times* and the *Sunday Times*, close down the paper for a year, I had written to other Fleet Street sports editors looking for work. My post bulged with rejections from the *Evening Standard*, *News of the World*, *Sunday Express*, *Daily Mirror*. Ian Watson, the sports editor of the *Daily Mirror*, wrote the sweetest letter, saying should "we need an extra hand, I will contact you first."

These rejections had come when I wrote asking for cricket work. When I asked for football work, there was astonishment. They might believe as an Indian I could, at a pinch, cover cricket, but a person of Indian origin knowing about football was unheard of. I regularly wrote on cricket for *Time Out* and Peter Ball, the sports editor, provided me generous space, including printing a long diary about England's tour of India in the winter of 1981. But when I asked him about football work, he said, referring to my Indian background, "You cannot possibly know anything about football." I didn't even bother to tell him that Father Fritz had compared us to the Tottenham double team as I felt this would cut no ice.

* * *

However, away from Fleet Street, sports editors, both editors of magazines and publishing firms, were happy to use me. And the country's race situation wasn't as grim as my weekly visit to the football ground suggested. Soon after my return for the colonial lash, Paul Barber had asked me to go to Leicester and report on how the Asians were doing there. I hadn't been back since I was the "coloured Mick" in the summer of 1969. The story of how the city in 1972 had received the Ugandan Asians expelled by Idi Amin was hardly encouraging. When they were allowed into this country by the Heath government, the local council had placed advertisements in the Kampala papers advising them not to come. Leicester, the council said, was overcrowded; there were too many immigrants, and another "flood" would cause enormous problems.

The headline on my first article for *New Society* summed up how things had dramatically changed for the better. It read: "The Asians of Leicester: a story of worldly success". My piece opened with Harbans Singh Ratoo telling me about a fellow Sikh who couldn't write English. Ratoo would write out his home address in English on his letters to India. His Sikh friend, a keen letter writer, would send two or three letters a week to India and couldn't understand why his relations never replied. One day the Sikh invited Ratoo to his home, and when Ratoo arrived at the house he burst out laughing. The Sikh asked Ratoo why. "Don't worry," said Ratoo, "now you will get replies to your letters." The address his Sikh friend had given him was 63 Lackborough Road. In fact, as the street sign showed, it was really 63 Loughborough Road. The Sikh, unable to speak English properly, had mispronounced it. There was no road called Lackborough Road. "In those days if the postman saw Indian names or strange names they couldn't understand, they would just throw away the letter," said Ratoo laughing.

Ratoo could afford to laugh. He had come a long way. He had arrived in Leicester in 1954, and through the 1960s at many a hotel and pub was told, "Shove off, you coloured bastard, we don't serve you lot." When visiting engineering firms in search of business, the receptionist reluctantly took his card only to return it torn in two— the managing director couldn't believe Indians could be engineers. Now Ratoo ran a successful engineering business himself and was planning to open a disco in the city centre—opposite the Grand Hotel where he was once refused admission. He sent his children to public schools and was a prominent member of the city's Labour party.

My second article highlighted how some young Asians felt they were neither part of their parents' world nor accepted by the white world. At his sixth form at Gateway school, if Rajesh mixed with the whites, his Asian friends called him "*gora chamcha*", arse-licker of the whites, but his old white friends dropped him because he had too many Asian friends. In pubs his skin colour stood out, and he would be served last even though he was the first. Rajesh had been stopped by a policeman because he was wearing cream jumpers, tatty jeans and had scruffy hair, which made the "copper" feel he was a hooligan: "You wogs are all the same."

For Kemak Patel, an Asian who had arrived as a child from Kenya, his long hair and scruffy looks made his relations feel he was too western. He had been stopped so often by the police, some fifteen times, that he got to know the policeman, and when he asked what he was hoping to find by all this stop and search, the policeman said, "You never know. One day I'll get lucky." He was well aware of how racist Indians could be. His family might accept him marrying a white girl, but a West Indian would be unacceptable. "We come from Africa, and we regard blacks as inferiors. A cousin of mine says West Indians are beasts." Equally unacceptable would be marriage to a Muslim. "My mother had a relation killed by a Muslim during Hindu-Muslim riots in India, and marrying a Muslim would be the worst thing." He was keen to discover his Indianness, was learning Gujarati, the language of his ancestors, and avidly followed Indian cricket.

* * *

If Leicester was now welcoming Indians, then I found, while researching and writing my biography of Subhas Bose, that the great and the good of England were much more approachable than the great and the good of India. Malcolm Muggeridge, the legendary historian A.J.P. Taylor and the author Christopher Sykes all readily responded to my requests for information. Skyes showed a facet of English character which fascinated me. He had written a biography of Adam von Trott, who had been the main German Foreign Office contact for Bose when he was in Berlin during the war. But he was also opposed to Hitler and was hanged by the Nazis when he took part in the failed plot to kill Hitler. Sykes was sympathetic to Trott. But for Bose he felt contempt, describing his desire to get rid of the British as "irrational hatred". Colin Welch of the *Daily Telegraph* even published a letter in the paper asking for information on Bose, even though most of its readers would have considered Bose a traitor. The Czech-born historian Milan Hauner gave me access to his marvellous thesis on Axis strategy in India during the Second World War, which was later published and is quite the best study of this important but much ignored subject.

My Bose book also brought me in touch with one of the most remarkable Englishman I have ever met. Hugh Toye, a British Army intelligence officer in the Second World War, had interviewed the Indian prisoners of war who, after the British surrender to the Japanese in Singapore, had joined Bose's Indian National Army to fight the British. Hugh should have had every reason to see them as despicable traitors, just as many British writers have done, but he sought to understand them and wrote a fine study about Subhas Bose, *The Springing Tiger*. He also became very friendly with Major Iwaichi Fujiwara. No friendship could have been more remarkable. Fujiwara was a rare, idealistic Japanese intelligence officer who truly wanted to act as liberator of Asians from European colonial rule, unlike his fellow Japanese, for whom "liberation" was a fake slogan to cover up their true aim of taking over from the Europeans as the new and even more brutal colonisers of Asia. Fujiwara's job was to contact Indians in South Asia to work for the Japanese, and he had some success in this. Toye was fascinated by his story. After the war he got in touch with him and unearthed much material on Japanese intelligence work.

Initially, Toye refused me permission to consult his dissertation on Subhas Bose at Oxford called 'Subhas Pasha'. But after he had read my book, he was so impressed that he publicly said it was the best biography on Bose. He also recommended me to the *Times Literary Supplement* to write a review of the Indian National Army, the first time I had written for that august journal. I became a frequent visitor to his home in Wheatley, where he had the greatest treasure trove of material relating to Bose and the Second World War. His unfailing courtesy to my many demands on his time and his absolute mastery of details, even in his 90s, was truly remarkable. As I sat with Hugh in his Wheatley home, I would think back to the time when, as a teenager, I had picked up his *Springing Tiger* on one of the pavement bookstalls of Mumbai and read it. Then I could never have imagined that I would one day be on such intimate terms with its author. An Englishman's home may be his castle, but Hugh proved that these castle doors do open, and strangers are made to feel at home.

The sharp contrast was with the Indian whose books I had also picked up from those Mumbai bookstalls. He was Nirad Chaudhuri, who had worked as secretary to Sarat Bose, Subhas's older brother and financier, settled in Oxford and would have been a wonderful source. But he dismissed me contemptuously, saying he was himself writing about Bose and had no time to talk to me. His memoir is titled *The Autobiography of an Unknown Indian*; now he found another unknown Indian bothering him quite outrageous. Whereas the National Archives in Delhi had treated me with disdain as a journalist, the India Office Library in London could not have been more helpful. The British may have looted India, but they had also left behind the best records on India, and these descendants of the conquerors were happy to share them with the descendants of the people they had conquered. In this contrasting world between India and England, I knew which I preferred.

The sharpest contrast between India and England came when I contacted Lady Diana Cooper while researching another book. She wrote me a handwritten postcard in red ink agreeing to meet me, joking that if it was going to be on television she would want a fee. She asked me to ring her and we arranged to meet at her home overlooking London's Little Venice. In India a lady of her standing would have been surrounded by "chamchas", sycophants, making me grovel before giving access. She lived on her own and could not have been more charming. It was early evening when we met and sitting in her drawing room as the light faded it felt magical.

* * *

This feeling of now being part of the English world was reinforced by my first visit to the tall book-lined offices of Allen and Unwin in Museum Street, just round the corner from the British Library. Walking up the steps I felt I was following in the path of Bertrand Russell. I was aware that the money Allen and Unwin made from his and Tolkien's works was helping subsidise books like mine. To be involved in its production opened up a new, exciting world: approving the cover, the blurb, helping John Newth, the editor, select the pictures, and learning that captions could also be used to tell the story.

And while, Lovesey apart, Fleet Street sports editors had no time for me, my solace was that LBC still valued my cricket broadcasts, and I suddenly got a call which made the 1979 cricket season unexpectedly exciting. It was from Nick Hewer, who then ran a corporate PR firm and was years away from becoming a television star, to have lunch with him and Ted Dexter, a former England captain.

* * *

We met at Giovanni, an Italian restaurant in a little alleyway in Covent Garden. Dexter had persuaded Holts Products, which made car-care products, to sponsor the matches that visiting cricket teams played against the counties, hoping it would revive interest in them. He wanted me to write a preview for each match with notes on the players that could be distributed to the press. At various grounds marquees were set up, where Holts Products entertained their clients by providing lavish lunches and wonderful scones and cakes during teatime. To their great delight, journalists, who at these matches had survived on pork pies and curled up sandwiches, were also invited, and this provided me one of the best lines in any cricket broadcast I have done.

This was when, during lunch in the match between Gloucestershire and the Indians at Bristol, a journalist mistook the bowl of mayonnaise for cream and poured it on his strawberries. I couldn't tell the LBC presenter, who was vastly amused by the story, that this wasn't because the cricket was so exciting but more due to the drinks the journalist had, of which there was always a liberal supply at these lunches. Nick Hewer's PR firm was well aware that journalists needed drinks and ensured that John Arlott, a wine connoisseur, always got a bottle of wine.

It was Arlott's need for wine that made me aware my reporting life had begun when journalism and sports were on the cusp of seminal change and about to enter the modern sports world as we know it. The problem was, this new age was struggling to be born.

Test cricket had a sponsor for the first time, Cornhill, then a little-known insurance company. But the sports editors didn't like mentioning that Cornhill was a sponsor. As one of them told me, "Test cricket has been going for a hundred years, why should we call it Cornhill Tests?" So, to persuade journalists, Cornhill provided lunch and tea to the cricket journalists for the first three days of the Test. They also hired Crawford White, "Chalky", the former cricket correspondent of the *Daily Express*, as their PR man. His duty at lunchtime was to go around the press box pouring out the wine and saying, "Remember lads, it is the Cornhill Tests."

On the first day of the first Test between England and India in Birmingham, as Chalky passed Arlott's desk Arlott asked for another bottle of wine. Chalky refused: "John, you have had a bottle. You have got to do *Test Match Special* and also write your piece for the *Guardian*. I don't think you should have a second bottle." Arlott's response, in that wonderful Hampshire burr of his, was, "If I don't get another bottle, tomorrow's Test will be the Prudential Test." Chalky laughed. What none of us knew was that Arlott meant it.

This was still the age of typewriters and Arlott, like all of us, typed out his report on a portable typewriter. Except Arlott, unlike us, didn't himself dictate his copy to the copy-takers. This was done by Irving Rosenwater, a well-known cricket researcher and writer. Rosenwater wouldn't have dreamt of changing Arlott's copy, and neither would the *Guardian* subs. The result was that Arlott's report in the next day's *Guardian* said this was the Prudential Test. What is more, the *Guardian* ran a "rag-out", a small news item, on the front page mentioning Prudential's name. For want of a nail, the shoe and the battle may or may not have been lost, but that bottle of wine did lead to Prudential becoming the sponsors of cricket. No cricket correspondent of the modern age would have dared do such a thing.

What we didn't know was that we were witnessing the last roar of a journalistic age that was dying. Arlott, following in the footsteps of Neville Cardus, was part of a breed of cricket writers who were essayists, not reporters, whose copy was sacrosanct.

* * *

In keeping with England's nuanced story, in my weekday world of financial reporting, which was my bread and butter, my background and race played no part. Ironically, my sports reporting often elevated me to a status higher than my fellow financial journalists.

30

WE MONEY MEN SEE NO COLOUR

I have never fulfilled my dream of being the *Guardian*'s cricket cor-respondent but it was an advertisement in the "Media" section of the paper that opened up a new and exciting world. The advertisement was placed by James Wootten, who was looking for an editor for a new magazine called *Essex Homes*.

I knew nothing about property and the only place in Essex I had been to was Chelmsford Cricket Ground, to cover cricket. But this did not worry James, who, after a very pleasant chat, offered me not one but two jobs, the second one being editing the *International Fund Guide*, aimed at the rich trying to avoid paying tax by investing in funds in Curaçao in the Netherlands Antilles, Jersey, Guernsey, Grand Cayman and the Isle of Man.

James's office in King's Cross, far removed from the swanky area it has become where even during the day prostitutes and drug deal-ers could be seen wandering around, was next to a pub. He would sit on the first floor with his door open. Often, when I would climb up the stairs to his office, I would find him picking his nose, and, having removed the snot, examining it minutely.

James had a penchant for hiring young women who saw the job as a journalist training school before they moved on to women's magazines. Or, if they were from Canada or the US, a sojourn before they resumed their grand tour of Europe.

* * *

Starting with the first issue of *Essex Homes* in July 1980 I assumed the rest of the country didn't know how to get to Essex and provided a commuter guide about the roads into and around Essex and a map showing the district councils, towns and villages of the county. I also wrote a feature on South Woodham Ferrers which, in the light of Brexit, reads very interestingly. Describing the town centre as mediaeval Europe, I wrote "you may be forgiven for thinking you are in Holland or Southern Germany." Five years after the country had voted to stay in Europe, the people of South Woodham Ferrers felt uneasy about Europe. I reassured them, saying the "town centre represents not another illustration of our supposed loss of sovereignty to the EEC but a bold calculated piece of modern development." The feature had a cartoon showing a travel agent, whose firm was called "European Travel", pointing to a sign marked "South Woodham Ferrers" and saying to a client, "Well, that is the EEC for you. They have even started imposing their continental town centres on us." I couldn't have imagined that thirty-five years later Essex would vote for Brexit.

With inflation at 13 per cent, the worst recession since the war, and over two million unemployed, *Essex Homes* couldn't survive despite James broadening it to cover all the South East and renaming it *Property Guide*. Ironically, its death improved my position. James offered me the editorship of *Pensions*, which examined in great deal the finances of the country's pensions industry. He had always earmarked me for the job and was only waiting to fire the current editor.

* * *

I couldn't have taken over at a better time. The pensions industry was on the brink of a revolution which would not only see some of the most dramatic changes in its history but also provided great scope for campaigning journalism.

* * *

In November 1982, I had an exclusive interview on pensions with Arthur Scargill, who in the summer had taken over from Joe Gormley as President of the National Union of Miners (NUM). He was still two years away from becoming "the enemy within", as Mrs

Thatcher would put it, but was already in dispute with the Coal Board trustees and the professional fund managers about investing in South Africa. It was a reflection of the times that not everyone opposed apartheid, and even those who did wanted to maintain normal relations with the regime.

I also interviewed Mrs Thatcher for *Midday* but this was on the basis of questions submitted to her office and which I suspect was answered by a civil servant.

A month after my meeting Scargill a book called *The Impending Crisis of Old Age: A Challenge to Ingenuity* landed on my desk. Aware Enoch Powell had been Minister of Health, I wrote to him asking him to review it. His secretary replied asking about the fee. Keen to show off that I also had a secretary, I got a lady who did some typing for me to reply. Powell, happy with the fee offered, wrote a two-page review which was both scholarly and very readable.

But while this was Powell, the acceptable thinker, writing for a magazine edited by a brown man, a month later I was made very aware of the effect Powell's views on brown and black immigrants had had on certain sections of the white population.

This had come the night the police saved me from being beaten up by racist Chelsea fans. Before they invaded my compartment, some young boys were taunting me about being a Paki and why like all Pakis I was not called Patel? Then a chubby boy asked, "What do you think of Enoch Powell?" I said, "I understand he is a very fine Greek scholar." I wonder how they would have reacted had I said he had reviewed a book on old age for me. Would they have wondered how could Powell write for a magazine edited by a Paki not called Patel? But what I really missed was interviewing Powell and asking him about the boys' behaviour. His reply would have been revealing.

* * *

If my outsider status was marked by my colour, I was soon to meet someone who was also an outsider but reflected the deeper, more historic, prejudices of the European world which has led to so much evil. Hyman Wolanski was an actuary who proved to be the greatest pensions expert I have ever met. He also provided me with one of the best pensions scoops I ever had.

Hyman would become a friend, a bond strengthened by the fact that he was also a Tottenham Hotspur fan. During the 1987 season Hyman, his two sons and I travelled together to see Tottenham play the semi-final against Watford at Villa Park.

The day promised to be perfect. The sun shone, Hyman and his two sons were ideal companions, and for me watching a football match as a supporter and not as a journalist who had to meet deadlines was liberating. The drive up the M1 was full of laughter. The only time the laughter stopped was when I mentioned I was about to buy an Audi. "I would never own a German car," said Hyman. His Jewish family originally came from Poland and had perished in Auschwitz.

As we were about to park our car outside the Granada Social Club, next door to the main entrance at Villa Park, a group of Watford supporters passed the car and, on seeing my face, started shouting "Paki, Paki", followed by "I'd rather be a dog than a Paki." I was still trying to take all this in when a Watford supporter—he couldn't have been more than 12 years of age—shook his fist in my face: "Where do you think you are—Bangladesh?"

I thought, "It's such a lovely day, such unprovoked anger and what an odd question." At that stage I hadn't visited Bangladesh. And the supporter had only to look around him and realise that if any ground looks like Bangladesh has been transported to England's "green and pleasant land" then it is Villa Park. But Tottenham won 5–1 and I could soon exult at the misery of the Watford fans. The next day I wrote a piece about my experiences in the *London Daily News*, the paper I worked for. A postcard arrived, written in spidery handwriting, with no address and an obviously fictitious name, and read as follows:

Mihir Bose And Friend Hyman,

Your remarks in today's L.D. News re your visit to Villa Park is a bit of claptrap. Have you ever realised Asian and Jewish remarks you make is breeding Nazism all over again. Because we Jews and Asians have taken over again. Remember Germany 1936–1945. Wish you schmocks would shut up. I'm scared for my kids in NW8 and others in NW4, NW11 and other areas.

L. Cohen

That letter showed how race can at times set both Hyman and me apart from the majority white community.

* * *

Quartet had been sufficiently pleased with the success of my Subhas Bose biography to suggest I write another book. This couldn't have been more different: a history of one-day cricket, a subject strangely neglected by cricket writers. I decided to call it *All in a Day* and while writing it I got an insight into how Naim Attallah ran Quartet. His editors were some of the most beautiful young women in London, most of them daughters of famous writers, and my book was edited by Rebecca Fraser, daughter of Antonia Fraser. Rebecca had little interest in cricket, but she was one of the best editors I have ever worked with.

When, in 1979, Dr Anne Smith, head of the English Department at Edinburgh University, set up the *Literary Review*, seeking to create a lively, intelligent literary magazine for people who love reading but shudder at academic and intellectual jargon, I found her very receptive to my ideas. I was soon reviewing books for her, including biographies of Nehru and the writings of V.S. Naipaul.

* * *

Editorship of *Pensions* meant invitations to marvellous lunches hosted by various City fund managers. They were cooked by some of the most beautiful women I have ever met. I later discovered they were daughters of distinguished City men in what felt like the City reinventing the debutante ball. Much as I fancied them they were looking for husbands in the Army and I stood no chance. But the government actuary Edward Johnstone had made me a member of his club the Reform and it was there years later that I found the love of my life. All this marvellous bonhomie suddenly ceased when, in 1982, Argentina invaded the Falklands and Mrs Thatcher sent a task force to liberate it.

Both City executives and journalists, who in the past had never suggested they were interested in the military, suddenly began to display astonishing knowledge about weapons and military strategy.

It was as if the Falklands had ignited a war-like spirit that had long remained dormant.

In some ways it was the sports writers who were most relaxed about the war, and it became common for football match reporters to describe a terrific long-range shot leading to a goal as an "Exocet", the French missile the Argentinians were using.

* * *

In addition to lunch there were occasionally trips abroad. The one I loved was the annual visit to Turin for the Fiat shareholders meeting. Fiat would fly us out for the day and provide a sumptuous lunch followed by a tour of the city. What made the occasion truly memorable was that we met Fiat's founder, Gianni Agnelli. The way the Italians addressed him made me feel Italians had a touch of the Indians: never by his name but very reverentially as *Avvocato*, lawyer. Agnelli presided over the meeting in a masterly fashion. His talent for dealing with awkward questions emerged when he was quizzed by Carol Thatcher, Mrs Thatcher's daughter.

As always, we travelled on a Fiat private jet. I sat opposite Carol. A female Italian MP had bared her breast. Agnelli also was a member of the Italian parliament, and while this had nothing to do with Fiat's annual results, Carol thought she would put him on the spot by asking him about it. Agnelli was neither angry or flustered, but speaking in excellent English defused Carol's potentially explosive grenade with remarkable skill. Even Carol was impressed.

It was another foreign trip that changed my journalistic life. In 1983 Legal and General, having often invited me to their offices for lunches, offered me a press trip to Paris. I cannot recall now why we were going to Paris. On the trip was Roger Hardman, the Deputy and City Editor of *Financial Weekly*. Hardman had just lost his personal finance editor to the *Sunday Times* and asked if I would like to replace her. I instantly agreed.

Legal and General had, quite unwittingly, introduced me to the best and brightest in the land.

31

A FAKE JOURNALISTIC WORLD
OR JUST PLAYING GAMES?

In 1986, two years after I joined *Financial Weekly* the City was revolutionised by Big Bang. Stockbrokers and jobbers sold their companies to large banks, foreign and domestic, and the City was awash with money. The "loadsamoney" era had dawned. This change was matched by the change in how financial journalists operated.

Legendary City editors like Patrick Sergeant at the *Daily Mail*, whose chauffeur carried his rackets on court for a tennis match, had gone. He had made loads of money launching *Euromoney* yet the Sergeant column, which came complete with his picture, was often not written by him. He frankly told me, "Anybody on the outside must have felt that I had written it, but of course my assistants contributed and often wrote most of the column. It carried my name because I took responsibility." In any one year only a third of the 300 stories in the column were written by Sergeant. Neil Collins wrote many of them and acquired the reputation he could write a Sergeant column ever better than Sergeant. Kenneth Fleet at the *Times*, who was taciturn and unemotional—except when discussing his beloved Everton FC—described himself as "the last of the Mohicans" and readily admitted to me his daily column wasn't his own work but carried his name for "homogeneity".

At *Financial Weekly* there was no fake journalism and neither did we benefit from the "Friday-night drop" which provided a bonanza for the Sunday papers. Late on a Friday evening, the PRs would ring their favourite newspaper and give them stories that would duly appear on Sundays. What appeared to be exclusive news dug out by hardworking journalists was often a telephone call from a shrewd public relations man, who often even dictated the story word for word. Then, a company was allowed to tell reporters they were going to bid for another company and no rules stopped reporters from dealing in the shares. Fill your boots lad, was the cry. By the time I came into financial journalism stock exchange rules had made this impossible.

* * *

The sports desks of Fleet Street were also masters in deception. At the *Daily Telegraph* I often shared a by-line with Richard Bright, except there was no such person. He was a name the subs desk had invented. They had added a bit of agency copy to my story but instead of crediting the agency had pretended there was an additional *Telegraph* journalist who had worked on the story. There was also an Italian Richard Bright, Ricardo Luminoso, whose by-line appeared on stories about Italian football lifted from the agencies. But I never shared a by-line with him.

Telegraph always made sure these code names were tailored to the sport. So, Astrid Ingrid reported on winter sports, the assumption being the name would obviously be seen by readers as Scandinavian and therefore knowledgeable about winter sports. Dan Harbles, an anagram for handlebars, was an expert on cycling.

One of these code names, Nelson Clare, did cause me problems. This name had come about one evening when the chief sub searching for one decided to take the second name of one sub Paul Nelson, and the first name of another sub Clare Middleton.

It was on a press trip to Antigua that Nelson Clare created a huge problem for me. The West Indies were playing Australia and the *Daily Telegraph* was using agency copy under the by-line of Nelson Clare. We were guests of the President of the Antiguan Cricket Association and when he realised I was from the *Daily Telegraph* he told me, "I have been reading Nelson Clare's reports. They are marvellous. I want to meet him. Let us go to the press box and I can tell him how well he is reporting the match" As I could not invent a real life Nelson Clare I told the President that I had to meet a friend and when I returned I would introduce him to Nelson. I spent the rest of the day avoiding the President's box and missing out on his hospitality.

A FAKE JOURNALISTIC WORLD OR JUST PLAYING GAMES?

The big divide in financial journalism, as Sir William Rees-Mogg, the magisterial figure who edited the *Times* for fifteen years until 1981, put it to me was between the two main schools of City editors: the share-tippers who, as insiders, thrived in a bull market and the scholarly reporters who came back in favour during a bear market.

But for some City editors scholarly reporting did not mean investigative journalism. Ivan Fallon, then City editor of the *Sunday Times*, advised Lionel Barber, a young reporter on the paper, to cosy up to men of finance. Lionel, who I played cricket with, recalled:

> Forget all this investigative stuff, just get to know a small number of successful businessmen. Make friends with them. Take them to dinner. Get invited to their homes—you'll find some of them, like Tiny Rowland, are great fun to be with.

I never met Tiny Rowland and I doubt Rees-Mogg would have rated my writings as scholarly but *Financial Weekly* did give me scope for investigative journalism.

32

THE LOTUS AMIDST THE MUCK

In India I had grown up seeing the wonderful lotus flower emerge from the muck. But I had no reason to believe that at *Financial Weekly* I would find some of the lotuses of British journalism amidst such muck. Many of them still remain my friends.

The "muck" was that *Financial Weekly* was owned by Robert Maxwell, although then he was courted by the City, financed by the major banks, had made an unsuccessful bid to buy Manchester United and had links to Westminster and the Kremlin. In one of the offices facing the open-plan area where I and most of the staff sat was his Chief of Staff, Peter Jay, a former British ambassador to the US. I never met Maxwell or his daughter Ghislaine, who floated round the office, although long after Maxwell's death I did get to know his sons Ian and Kevin. Maxwell would get an early press copy of *Financial Weekly* to help him fox the stock market on his share dealings.

Tom Lloyd, who had taken over as editor just as I joined, had a light hand on the tiller, surrounded as he was with a great deal of journalistic experience from various media outlets. David Smith had worked for *Now*, James Goldsmith's failed attempt to launch a British-style *Time* magazine, which *Private Eye* mocked as the "*Talbot*"; Nigel Dudley had come from *Middle East Economic Digest*, and Cathy Gunn had been a freelancer for the *Times*. David had this air of total command over news combined with a nice line in deprecatory wit, talking of a badly written feature as a "one phone call feature". Every now and again he would provide nuggets that illuminated the English world. A fervent supporter of Wolverhampton Wanderers, he reminisced about the time when football was played on Christmas Day and men, having opened their Christmas gift, always gloves, would wear them to go to the matches. David not only knew his subject but knew how to explain it lucidly.

Nigel Dudley knew the Middle East well and told me how the Arabs distinguished between whites, who were treated with respect, and those from the subcontinent, who were treated as disposable commodities. As lobby correspondent he would tell us intimate stories about the Westminster scene and every week spoke to Harold Wilson, discussing what he should write in his weekly column. He was also the first one to tell me that John Major, who was then a junior pensions minister, would reach high office. He used his great wit to puncture pomposity, but as he showed when he punched a policeman who had insulted his wife, he could go to war to protect his loved ones. Some years later his eldest son Edward suddenly died one night. For a parent to lose a child must be the most awful grief to bear. Nigel and his wife Helyn showed remarkable fortitude and resolve in coping with it, starting an annual cricket match to honour Edward's memory, and the stoicism with which the pair have put up with other misfortunes is an object lesson in how not to let grief overwhelm our life.

It was Nigel who introduced me to a remarkable Englishman, which also illustrated that while in India "pull" is provided by family connections in Britain it is who you have been to school or university with. It was in the summer of 1985, by which time I was City editor and looking for a City reporter. Nigel suggested Peter Oborne, who had been at Sherborne with him. One Friday I invited Peter to have a drink with me at the City Golf club just off Fleet Street. That summer Australia were touring and we spent the evening discussing cricket. I had a cricket team called the Fleet Street XI made up of Nigel, David and a few others from various newspapers and magazines. Peter was a keen cricketer and had his own team, White City All Stars. That Sunday, we were playing at Marlborough against the Marlborough masters. On Saturday I rang Peter to ask whether he'd be free to play. Peter instantly agreed.

In the match I asked him to bat No. 4, and he hit four fours from the first five balls, a total of nine fours in his 44 and a third of our score of 125. We lost the match heavily, but I had seen enough to convince me he was just the person I wanted on my City staff. I hadn't read anything he had written, but his having worked at Rothschild reassured me. He had told me he had left to write a novel. I felt that while we waited for his novel, he could bring his City knowledge to *Financial Weekly*. I had, not long before that, written an article arguing that when England did well in cricket, shares rose, when they performed badly, shares fell. Now I was trying to match cricketing performances with journalistic ability. I have never made a better choice.

This was Peter's first journalistic job and he did have to be taught what deadlines were; occasionally, with the subs screaming for copy, we would have to tear the paper from his typewriter to stop him writing. But he could certainly write and knew the City. He could also instantly spot a story.

Peter also has a marvellous ability to adapt to any situation and was always sensitive to the environment he was in. When, some years later, I took my Fleet Street XI on a tour of India, he instantly dressed in a Nehru suit. He knew India, having been there as a child while his father was posted as a military attaché. His desire to blend in with India was in stark contrast to many other members of my team. After one match during the tour, the Indians invited us to a musical event where classical Indian music was played. Many of the team members didn't conceal their boredom. I was struck by Peter's annoyance that this was not showing due respect to our hosts.

Peter also introduced me to a great galaxy of his friends, many of whom played for me. This was a neat reversal of my Oval Maidan team which had working class boys like Edwin and Bala. Now Peter was introducing me to the English upper class. When he invited me to his stag night at the Wig and Pen club in Fleet Street there was the sort of scene that suggested we were in P.G. Wodehouse's Drones Club. After dinner, one of Peter's friends, finding striking printers were marching down Fleet Street, started throwing bread rolls at them. Soon, the police who were escorting the printers were at the door of the Wig and Pen, warning us that if we didn't stop we would be arrested. I hadn't thrown a bread roll but felt, should they come in and arrest us, they might make no distinction between those who had and those who hadn't.

The second, even more upper-class, friend Peter introduced me to was William Sitwell. "Sitters", who came on another Indian cricket tour, would himself admit he was no cricketer. He was a man of great wit and charm but did enjoy provoking people, thinking it would all end in a laugh. But sometimes it didn't work, as was dramatically demonstrated in Kolkata. We were wonderfully entertained by Amalda and Didi, taken to the Bengal club, and then wined and dined at their home in the company of some of the most distinguished citizens of Kolkata.

I thought it would be a good idea if I got Sitters to give the thanks on behalf of the group. He decided he would have some fun at the expense of the Indians. Our hotel had a disco called The Pink Elephant. When one of the hotel staff asked Sitters whether he would like to go to it, he replied that that very morning he had his own moment of the pink elephant with his wife. With this Sitters laughed, but I could see the shock on some of our players' faces. His next comment, which had a touch of V.S. Naipaul's writings on India, went down even worse. He pointed out that while the hospitality had been marvellous, on the way to the flat we had passed dreadful filth on the streets. Surely something ought to be done about the dirt by people whose entertainment showed such affluence.

The next day in the coffee shop I found a few members of the team gathered together in earnest discussion. They told me they had been appalled: Sitters had mocked the Indians after enjoying such lavish hospitality. This wasn't how the English behaved. What about the much vaunted English sense of fair play and decency. They asked me to reprimand Sitters. I told them the Indians didn't seem to have been offended and it was best to let it go but I wouldn't ask Sitters to make another speech on behalf of the group. I didn't. Sitters, who was always very charming with me, didn't seem to mind. He even asked me to speak at his wedding. I was careful to make sure I didn't upset his wedding guests.

Peter also introduced me to Martin Rowson, a cartoonist who I had no hesitation in hiring. Right from the start Martin's cartoons were a delight. He always delivered on time and has since graduated from financial cartoons to political ones.

Over the years Peter has always been exceedingly kind to me. I would have loved to have had him as a younger brother, combining as he does many of the qualities of Laxman and Arjun, two of the greatest younger brothers in Hindu mythology, although I realise at times his exuberance and sudden bursts of enthusiasm would have called for great patience.

In some ways the most striking thing was the friendship Peter developed with Jeff Randall, the features editor. Jeff, an Essex boy, educated at Nottingham, couldn't have been more different in class and upbringing to Peter. It may have helped that they were both West Ham supporters, but this was more the classic story of contrasting personalities forming a bond and becoming firm friends.

* * *

I was very impressed with Jeff's ability to build up fabulous contacts in the City providing him many stories. We struck up an instant friendship with Jeff such an integral part of my cricket team that he was once late for an important family gathering. Jeff would always make jokes that I was constantly smoking his cigars, but his sense of humour didn't always go down well with women financial PRs. If he answered a call from one of them for me, he would shout across to me, "A call from another of your floozies", which would prompt the sharp retort "I am not his floozie."

Jeff and I also agreed on who would make a good journalist. The growth of journalism courses since I had failed to get into Cardiff meant *Financial Weekly* received several applications from young journalism graduates. Tom Lloyd and I often disagreed on who among them we should hire, but Jeff almost invariably supported me. It required all our combined pull to persuade Tom that Jason Nisse should be given an opportunity. We were proved right when Jason went on to become business editor of the *Independent*.

At *Financial Weekly*, despite being the only non-white in the newsroom, I was never made aware of my colour. And my Indian origins only came into play once a week, thanks to *Time Out*. Sometime before I got the call from Roger Hardman, I had become *Time Out*'s Indian food critic. This proved a great boon for me and my *Financial Weekly* colleagues. After we had put the paper to bed on a Wednesday night, I would take everyone from our printer to an Indian restaurant, where I was always warmly welcomed and got a good discount on our meal. And over nan, vindaloo, tikka masala and papad we set the world to rights.

* * *

My *Financial Weekly* cricket team introduced me to an English world I had read about but never experienced. George Orwell memorably described the typical English village green cricket match as an occasion where a blacksmith playing in braces is called away mid-innings and, as the light begins to fade, a ball hit for four kills a rabbit on the boundary. I never played with a blacksmith and I never hit a four to kill a rabbit but there were many lovely Sunday afternoon matches at the pristine grounds of high profile banks and investment houses, where the cricket tea was sumptuous and drinks flowed freely. The Bank of England may never have been very helpful to the press but its hospitality at the annual cricket match could not be faulted. Through cricket I also formed lifelong friendships. Richard Heller was quite the most remarkable of them.

Richard combines a love of cricket with an encyclopaedic knowledge. He was so dominant on quizzes on a train journey during an Indian tour that we persuaded him to enter Mastermind. He reached the final where his subject was the life and times of Garry Sobers, arguably the greatest cricketer ever. But in the final Richard flubbed two questions on Sobers and was edged out by the winner, an Oxfordshire vicar. Richard says, "I swear he had help from Above. Having passed several questions he lifted his eyes and suddenly correct answers started to flow from him."

I was aware my English friends would find the exposure to the poverty of India unnerving. What I did not expect was one *Guardian* journalist demanding I arrange matches with those begging on the streets. When I said that was not possible, he called me an "an upper class Indian", who did not want to mix with the poor. I assume his sense of guilt was heightened by the fact that we had been entertained in a Hyderabad club, which had preserved all the traditions of the Raj. Thankfully the rest of the team were in a celebratory mood. Nobody more than Dominic Lawson who had taken five wickets in the match, always a great bowling honour, with me taking the catch for his final wicket. This saw his then wife rush on to the field and kiss him, much to the astonishment of this very puritanical Muslim city.

What most of the English players appreciated was how Indian crowds loved a show. This was exemplified at the Chepauk Stadium in Madras, later renamed Chennai, when we were playing the Tamil Nadu Journalists' Association on the nursery ground while England A were playing India A in the main stadium. Bored by England A the Indian spectators turned to watch us hoping our Englishmen would provide more drama. They were not to be disappointed.

I had brought Peter on to bowl. Richard was fielding on the boundary. One of the batsmen hit a huge skyer in his direction. Richard misjudged the flight of the ball and, in trying to catch it, tipped it over the boundary for a six. Let Richard take up the story:

> I took my cap off, hurled it on the ground and did a dance of self-loathing around it. Peter made a matching gesture and performed a dance of his own, but of pure loathing. The incident did make me the hero of Madras. Every time I touched the ball I was greeted by applause and "wah-wahs".

My cricket tours also brought out the contrast in the hospitality provided, with the Indians generous and the British miserly. As Richard puts it:

> The British High Commission in India did not provide any food or water, never mind fresh lime juice, and we had to send away for them ourselves. Exactly the same happened the following year on our American tour at the match in Washington against the Embassy there. Spending cuts were biting hard in the FCO in those years. I tried to get Questions asked about it in the House of Commons but was frustrated by a stuffy chap in the Table Office.

But it was also at *Financial Weekly* that I experienced one of the greatest tragedies of my life, which still makes me feel I was an uncaring, selfish son and is something I have never got over. It is the price immigrants pay for leaving their homeland.

33

THE UNIVERSAL GRIEF OF MIGRATION

The story of immigration told in the West is that of the poor and hungry arriving, often illegally, with politicians competing with each other to keep these hordes at bay. The story that is not told is the pain the immigrants suffer when they choose to leave their homeland. When the Europeans ruled the world they made much of the sacrifices their fellow Europeans made when leaving their homeland for the colonies.

On my shelves is a copy of *Bound to Exile* which records how the British felt the pain of leaving their country. David Gilmour in *The British in India: A Social History of the Raj* draws the contrast that in Britain people "usually lived near the graves of their relations so could visit them", they had "members of the same family buried together in the same churchyard. Such conditions did not exist in India..."

In my front garden in west London is a portion of Ma's ashes, which I brought back from India, surrounded by the wonderful flowers my wife Caroline grows. Some years earlier it was Baba's death that brought home to me what exile means. I am reminded of this almost every day.

Baba and I never ever discussed the letter I wrote to him about giving up accountancy and settling in Britain. In the years that followed, he came to England and I travelled back to India, but he never mentioned it. However, I could see from his face the long shadow my decision had cast and how it had devastated him. He just did not understand it. All he wanted to do was be near me somehow.

This was vividly brought home to me at Christmas in 1983 when I went to India for a holiday. Baba had retired and gone to live in the

New Alipore house. Throughout his life he had had a hacking cough and always carried a spittoon. He was already a very sick man suffering from emphysema. A few months earlier, he had come close to death but I had not been told of this. It seems that it is an Indian peculiarity that family members are often shielded from news of this kind. The result was that I had planned my trip to India in total ignorance and promised Jim Pegg that, after I had visited my family in Kolkata, we would go on a tour of India which would take in cricket and the Taj Mahal. Jim was to join me in Mumbai.

When I flew back to Mumbai Baba insisted that he and Ma came with me. It was only as we got to Kolkata airport that I began to realise how sick he was. He needed a wheelchair to get on the plane and looked very frail.

The night before I was due to leave Mumbai for my holiday, he came to my room and stood there. His frame, once so sturdy and handsome, now looked like a broken reed. In the half-light where he stood, he seemed ghostly and almost unreal. I felt he wanted to talk but said nothing; indeed neither of us spoke. We should have had so much to say to each other. It was to be the last time we were alone.

The next day, Ma came to bid me goodbye at the airport. As I was about to walk to the departure gate, she broke down and wept uncontrollably. She told me how sorry she was that she and Baba had forced me to come back from England. She said she realised that this had provoked my revolt against Baba. Now she wanted me to return. She was old, Baba was old and he needed to be looked after.

I did not know how to respond. I felt I could not let Jim down. So, after a few meaningless words to Ma I turned away and walked to the waiting aircraft.

A few days later, I heard that Baba had been admitted to a hospital. I should have flown back then. But I was watching my old school mate Sunil Gavaksar score a double hundred against the West Indians which had one of the most fearsome attacks ever seen in cricket and I decided against it. Eventually, having shown Jim the Taj Mahal, that great monument of love, I flew back to London. To my lasting sorrow and shame my worry on the flight back was not Baba's health but that the Sikh in the seat behind me would not allow me to recline my seat and the Pan Am stewardess did nothing.

Over the next few months Baba lay in hospital. Ma was the only member of the family looking after him—with such devotion that the Arab in the bed next to Baba wished he had a wife like that. The Arab would have heard Baba call Ma, *Ogo*, the name Bengali husbands often use for their wives. Ma would have responded with Tripty's *Baba*, Tripty's father, Tripty being my eldest sister. Or maybe KC, Baba's initials. What he would not have known was that all of Baba's property was in Ma's name.

I did not hurry back to Mumbai, worried whether Nigel Lawson, the Chancellor, would in his budget remove the tax relief on pensions. The previous year he had removed the tax relief on insurance policies. The pensions industry whipped up a storm hoping to generate business. He did not. Then, suddenly one morning, I got a call from my cousin Ashok. Baba was dead. I took the first available flight to Mumbai. As I arrived at the hospital, Baba's body lay on a stretcher in the car park being prepared for his final journey to the crematorium. On seeing me, Ma shook him and said, "Wake up, wake up, see who is here. Mihir has flown in from London."

How much I wished Ma's frenzied jerking would bring him back to life. I just hid my face in my Marks and Spencer suit overwhelmed by the thoughts: why had I never taken the chance to tell Baba that, for all our differences, I loved him? And how sorry I was to have caused him any hurt.

And then, half an hour later, I was at the crematorium performing that necessary but grizzly ceremony that falls to all Hindu sons. I took a lighted taper and put it to my father's face. I saw his body explode into a thousand bits. Then I journeyed to the Gateway of India, built to commemorate the arrival of George V, the first British monarch to visit India, to scatter Baba's ashes in the Arabian Sea.

A few days later there was a *sraddha* ceremony. Until then, I as the son could not cut my nails or hair and had to eat vegetarian food. There is sexism in the sraddha ceremony as the number of days to observe mourning before the ceremony is performed is longer for men than women. On the day the ceremony was held I had to wear clean clothes. A priest performed the religious rituals in front of idols to which Ma prayed every day. These were followed by a feast which we ate sitting on the floor. We no longer had to be vegetarians and consumed a variety of food including fish and meat with some of the dishes served being those Baba had loved. My Aryan ancestors believed in an afterlife. But they were also very practical people. So, during the religious service, bed sheets, pillows, blankets are piled in front of the priest. The gesture is meant to say, "This is what the departed will need to have a comfortable sleep in the other world he or she has gone to." In reality the priest collects all the bedding and takes it home, no doubt using it himself to sleep in this world. When Baba's *sraddha* was held, my little niece's clothes including her knickers, which had been in a pile near the sheets and pillows, also got mixed up in this offering to the priest but they were rescued in time.

After the ceremony I should have taken the rest of the ashes to the Ganges and performed the *pindi-daan* ceremony, the homage to Baba's soul and also that of my ancestors. But I didn't. I was in the middle of writing another book. There were any number of journalistic assignments and, if truth be told, I felt numb and guilty. I was convinced that, had I not come to Mumbai from Kolkata the previous Christmas, Baba would have not felt compelled to accompany me. He would probably still have been alive. His desire to be near me, even for a few days, had made him take the totally unnecessary trip which had probably hastened his death. I felt the gods had punished me. I just wanted to nurse my grief in solitude.

And so the years passed. After that I visited India often. But I did not make the trip to the Ganges and bring closure. It was as if there was nothing I could do to make amends.

Then a journalistic assignment to write about a new luxury rail trip from Kolkata to Delhi, with Sir Mark Tully as our guide, took me to Benares and I decided finally to perform the *pindi-daan* ceremony.

There I was on a wintry morning on the banks of the Ganges, trying to hold on to my MCC Panama hat as I bent over the side of the little boat and floated a leaf containing a few balls of very sticky rice on to the river the Hindus consider the holiest in the world. This was the final act of the *pindi-daan* ceremony.

I had waited twenty years to become an MCC member, an honour I craved and treasured. But I had waited even longer, twenty-six years, to pay the homage every Hindu son must offer to his father's soul.

My journey on the boat had come after the *panda* priest had performed a ceremony beside the Ganges. I had to take off my trousers and strip down to my underwear with, as always happens in India, a crowd gathering round to watch. I quickly used a small *gamcha*, or towel, to wrap over my underwear. Then the *panda* and I sat down on the riverbank to perform the *pindi-daan*

He thrust in my hands several rice balls and asked me to name members of my family who had died starting with Baba. Every time I named someone I offered some rice to them, placing the rice ball on a palm leaf in front of me while the priest intoned Sanskrit verses. As the priest mumbled, I had to repeat his words, not knowing what I was saying but keeping up the pretence so essential to the ceremony.

The ritual could not obscure the fact that, beneath it all, the ceremony was a convoluted example of coming to terms with sorrow in an age of migration. Offering mouldy rice to my father may not seem much. In making the offering, I was also acknowledging my origins, something I had taken much pleasure in denying during Baba's lifetime. Now, by offering rice, I was saying that, in the other world Baba now inhabited, he was hungry. Like a dutiful son, I had to feed him.

As I floated the leaf on the Ganges and watched it disappear downstream, a memory of my childhood came floating back. Baba and I are having a meal at home. The servant brings the rice and goes back to the kitchen for the dal, vegetables, meat. But, by the time the servant returns, Baba has finished eating the rice. He was always a quick eater, explaining to me that, as the eldest of several brothers, he wanted to make sure he had his fair share. I have acquired this trait.

So, as the rice floated to whichever Aryan celestial heaven Baba was in, I hoped he would welcome it with the same relish he had the rice the servant had served all those years ago.

Perhaps he would see this as the wheel turning full circle. Baba himself had rebelled against his own father. Like me, he was far from home when his own father died. He never spoke about him. However, from the odd comments he made, I sensed the pain he had caused his father. Now I could only hope that he could feel my pain and forgive me.

And I hoped he would understand how much I wished I could have turned the tide back and have had one brief moment with him to say how much I loved him and how much I had wronged him. That I could not has meant the torment has increased after his passing because I believe that my thoughtless actions may have contributed to his untimely death at the age of seventy-three.

In *The Interpretation of Dreams* Freud wrote that the death of a father is "the most important event, the most poignant loss, of a man's life". That is felt by all. But for the immigrant it is all the greater whether an asylum seeker, economic immigrant or, like me, someone hoping to fulfil the dream of becoming a writer.

34

PLAYING THE WHITE MAN'S GAME

This was what an Indian accused me of for investigating an Indian-run company which had run into severe financial trouble.

Ironically, I had been put on to the story through some Indian contacts who had asked me why given the Fraud Squad was investigating it the British press was not reporting the story? The only answer I could think was that the British press saw this as an Indian story despite the fact that it was taking place in London and affecting UK creditors who had lost huge sums of money. In 1984 that was not an unusual attitude for the financial press, almost wholly white men, to take.

* * *

Tom readily agreed that I should do the story. Justin, the *Financial Weekly's* lawyer, who read articles for libel, took some convincing that my sources were impeccable. Almost as soon as my first story appeared I started getting calls from total strangers offering information. One of them was so secretive that he was dubbed "deep throat" by my colleagues, a jokey reference to the more famous deep throat of Watergate.

In my experience when you break what you think is a great exclusive you are both elated and fearful. Elated because you have beaten your rivals, fearful that they will follow up with better exclusives. To my surprise no one followed up my story or the ones I did for nearly two years after that. I was made to feel I was writing a ghetto story which the nationals could not be bothered about. There were some Indians who felt, as one of them told me, that I was letting the community down and doing the white man's dirty job undercutting the emerging Asian business. Yet white lawyers, representing clients who had lost money, could not wait to read my stories and often used them when writing legal letters seeking to get the money their clients were owed. Perhaps the most curious aspect of this whole saga was the one journalist on a national newspaper who had shown some interest in this story said he could not compete with me as I was an Indian and therefore would have contacts which he, as a white man, could not match.

* * *

Financial journalism is still largely white but such has been the growth of Indian business in this country that journalists, whatever their colour, cannot ignore them. Back in 1984 I could not have imagined that and it illustrates the very special way this country changes often surprising those who doubt its ability to do so.

35

THE UNEXPECTED MAXWELL LEGACY

The *London Daily News* lasted a bare seven months. Yet I am reminded of it every time I open the *Daily Telegraph*. There on its City pages are the "Alex" cartoons of Charles Peattie and Russell Taylor. I had given Peatie and Taylor their first start on the *London Daily News* where I was the City Features Editor.

The failure of the *London Daily News* was a combination of the ineptitude of Robert Maxwell and the ruthless way the Rothermere group made sure the paper was, as Bert Hardy, the *Standard* chief executive, told me, strangled at birth. Having planned it as an evening paper Maxwell suddenly made it into a 24 hour paper. The promotional slogan of the paper was "For the city that never sleeps, the paper that never stops". The result was the staff hardly ever slept.

The previous year Rupert Murdoch had finally made the typewriter redundant in British newsrooms by introducing Atex computers. Writing for the *Sunday Times*, I had become familiar with them. But Maxwell brought in new computer systems and we had a whole new learning process.

The Australian media being far ahead in technology, Maxwell got us a tutor from Australia. This was Amanda Platell, a tall, imposing woman who very expertly guided us through this the new technology. What we didn't know as we obeyed Amanda's instruction was that she would prosper and go on to carve a niche for herself in British publishing and politics, whereas Maxwell's paper was doomed.

On the day Maxwell launched his *London Daily News*, Rothermere relaunched the *London Evening News*, which had merged with the *Standard* eight years earlier but whose title was still owned by the group. The *Evening News* was priced at 10p; Maxwell slashed the price of his *London Daily News* down to 5p.

Despite this circulation fell and rumours began circulating we would be closed. In July 1987 the staff were told there was no truth to the rumours. If anything, extra resources would be provided to ensure we could really compete with the *Evening Standard*.

I went off to Paris and was happily going round one of my favourite cities when I got a message from Jim Levy, the City editor, that "The paper has closed."

* * *

When I returned to London and went to the offices I discovered that some of my colleagues, furious with Maxwell's deception, had taken revenge by carting home some of the computers, telephones and even some of the furniture.

However, I soon profited from the wonderful fellowship among journalists. Margaret Hughes, who had worked under me as personal finance editor, moved to *The Guardian*. I became a regular on the paper's personal finance pages. I also got a column writing on personal finance for the *People*, although the editor felt a name like Mihir Bose may not convince *People* readers to take my financial advice seriously, so I wrote under the pseudonym "David Sterling". Garth Hewitt, editor of *Banking World*, who played cricket for my team, introduced me to the editor of *Director*, the magazine of the Institute of Directors, and I got a column.

Hugh Pym, one of the nicest people I have ever met, helped me get a job on Radio 4's *Financial World Tonight*. I also got a job presenting the BBC World Service equivalent of the Radio 4 evening program, *PM*, to South Asia. This was an exciting time at the World Service, when star journalists who now dominate our screen, like Jeremy Bowen and Lyse Doucet, were finding their feet.

And within weeks, in the autumn of 1987 the stock market crashed spectacularly and Kathy Rooney at Bloomsbury commissioned me to write a book. I wanted to write one on the Hindus, but she felt that wouldn't sell. What would sell was a "quickie" book on the crash, inevitably called *The Crash*.

The Crash's success led to a string of business books. None of these books made my fortune, but they showed that when it comes to money people are willing to open up even to total strangers. At the personal finance desk at the *Daily Mail* Ideal Home Exhibition I was surprised how many people came up to me and told me frankly of their investments, showing me certificates of shareholdings and unit trust investments. They were not worried my real name was Mihir Bose, not David Sterling.

36

HOW MY OUTSIDER STATUS HELPED ME
EXPLORE THE SECRET WORLD OF SPORTS

On 8 February 1994 I was in my room at The Taj Mahal in Mumbai when I received a call from the *Sunday Times* that would eventually lead to a minister in the Blair government calling me a shit and briefing Cheri Blair about London 2012.

I was in India presenting a BBC television programme on Indian cricket, part of a series on BBC 2's *India Week*. Nothing could have been more delightful than to be paid by the BBC to walk down memory lane, filming at the places I knew so well: Oval Maidan, Azad Maidan, Shivaji Park, Kennedy Sea-Face, CCI. I was particularly pleased with my first ever piece to camera in a lane where young boys played gully cricket, bringing back memories of when Hubert and I had done so all those years ago.

The call was from Nick Pitt, the *Sunday Times* deputy sports editor, who said "Chris Nawrat [the sports editor] has been sent home." It suggested Nawrat had been a naughty boy. And he had. Asked by the *Sunday Times* to edit a book on sports for which the publisher had provided money to pay contributors, he had paid them from the *Sunday Times* sports budget. Nawrat always denied any wrongdoing, but by then the editor, Andrew Neil, had had enough.

The son of a Polish father and an English mother, Nawrat revelled in being an outsider. This may be why he had taken to me. There was no knowing what he would do. Once, when we invited him for dinner, a friend offered him a lift home. He immediately asked him, "Would you like me to suck your cock?". He was the first Fleet Street sports editor to have a separate sports section. He accepted my view that sports pages did not cover the growing field of sports business and gave me space to do so including a ground-breaking one on Maxwell's stewardship of Derby County. In 1991, when Tottenham were bought by Alan Sugar and Terry Venables, Chris Nawrat suggested it would be much more interesting to interview Sugar. Then, long before *The Apprentice*, Sugar was only of interest to the City press. It was to produce a memorable quote.

I met Sugar just before the start of the 1991–92 season at his offices in Tottenham. Alan Sugar is two months younger than me, and I asked him whether, like me, he fell in love with Tottenham when they did the double in 1961, winning the league title and the FA Cup, which at that stage no other club in the twentieth century had managed. His reply was, "Double? Is that something in the 1950s?" This quote has been used so often that I wished I could have secured the copyright on those words. While Sugar had been taken to the club by his father, it was his brother who was really a fan and had a season ticket, although, as I often joked with him, Tottenham won the First Division title in the only two seasons he missed, 1951 and 1961.

Nick was ringing to ask me to rush from the warmth of Mumbai to the snows of Lillehammer to cover the Winter Olympics. Three months later, I flew to the States to cover the first ever football World Cup held in North America. However, on my return I realised that after twenty years of writing for the *Sunday Times* I needed fresh pastures.

The question was, where?

I had sometime earlier met Richard Lambert, then editor of the *Financial Times*, and said he should have a specialist sports writer covering sports business and offering myself as the ideal person. Lambert had politely dismissed the idea, claiming his existing staff covered the subject well enough. The FT now has a sports editor. 1995 was another world.

* * *

The only other option was the *Daily Telegraph*. A couple of years earlier I had been interviewed by the then editor, Max Hastings, for the job of the paper's cricket correspondent. I expected a grilling from a man with a reputation of being the most formidable journalist of his era. But Max couldn't have been sweeter and only asked me one question on cricket, about Ian Botham.

I had written for the *Telegraph*, but apart from the odd story on the sports pages they were mainly pieces on the comment pages. When in 1989 Ayatollah Khomeini issued his deadly fatwa on Salman Rushdie for his novel *The Satanic Verses*, I wrote the op-ed piece expressing outrage. And when Mrs Thatcher's government was negotiating with China about handing over Hong Kong, I joined in the debate raging in this country about whether Hong Kong residents should be allowed into Britain after the Chinese took over, arguing they should be. I made the case for Britain moving to an Australian-style points-based system. The op-ed editor particularly liked my suggestion that, with Australia ravaging England in the Ashes series, the country could import players who could bolster the team. The article was so warmly received in Hong Kong that I got a free trip to the colony, organised by the group demanding Britain open its doors to Hong Kong residents.

I rang David Welch, the sports editor. He had just launched a separate sports section, and though it appeared only on Saturdays it marked a major innovation for the media. He had also recruited some very interesting writers. Paul Hayward, who wrote on racing for the *Independent*, had come in as feature writer. Henry Winter, a sub on the *Independent*, had been brought in to write on football.

My pitch to David was that what he lacked was an *Inside Sports* column which looked at sports stories in depth. While sports pages should report what men in shorts did, it was the men in suits who often determined the world in which the men in shorts operated. Keith Perry, his deputy would later tell me that when David told him Mihir Bose was available, Keith replied "Sign him up immediately." This was to prove for me as significant a call as the one I had made to Ian Marshall of *LBC* twenty-one years earlier. David Welch and Keith Perry provided me with a wonderful platform to write about the men in suits—and Keith, like me, a fellow Tottenham supporter, became a great friend.

* * *

I had joined the *Daily Telegraph* at just the right time. Because no sports paper covered sports business and politics stories regularly, let alone in depth, I had an open goal to aim at. However, my first story came from an unexpected source. A few weeks after I joined, in early March 1995 I had quite by accident a meeting in the corridor with Jeremy Deedes, son of the legendary Bill, and the paper's managing editor. He mentioned he had had a chat with Peter Hill-Wood, chairman of Arsenal, who had told him interesting stories about what was going on in the club and, in particular, what had happened to George Graham: "You should talk to him."

The previous month Arsenal had sacked George Graham, one of the club's most successful managers, having had advance information about the Premier League bungs inquiry. It later emerged that Graham had received £425,500 from the Norwegian agent Rune Hauge to sign Pål Lydersen and John Jensen. Graham had insisted he had received an unsolicited "gift", not an illegal bung, from Hauge and as he put it in his autobiography had not cheated anybody.[1] But at this stage none of these details were known. Arsenal, always very secretive, had made a cryptic announcement saying the Premier League inquiry had informed them of "alleged irregularities concerning certain transfers and Mr Graham did not act in the best interests of the club". Graham had called it a "kangaroo court judgement".[2]

Jeremy Deedes gave me Hill-Wood's number and I rang him, fully expecting to be fobbed off. But to my surprise Hill-Wood invited me to Highbury. When we met, he told me the inside story of what had happened with Graham and how several months earlier directors had argued about Graham's future. "We did think of sacking Graham." There was some discussion with lawyers about whether Arsenal should seek to prosecute Graham. "It was our money, and we took counsel's advice," said Hill-Wood. "Counsel waved his arm in the direction of the window and said, 'The police have a lot on their plate.'" With that, Hill-Wood waved his hand round the oak-panelled room, quite the most impressive boardroom in English football. He also told me City brokers Smith New Court had prepared a report about Arsenal floating on the stock market, as their neighbours Tottenham had done, but rejected it. It meant the Archbishop of Canterbury, who owned one share, wouldn't be able to sell his share at a profit on the stock market.

This was old money talking. Hill-Wood, an Etonian, was the third member of his family to be chairman, following in the footsteps of his father and grandfather. And a major shareholder and director was a descendant of the former Lord Mayor of London. This would be the first of many conversations with Hill-Wood, often at his favourite Italian restaurant in Chelsea and even at his home in Kent.

At that stage, with an FA inquiry into Graham going on, there was still much speculation about what would happen to him. Four months later the FA found him guilty of serious misconduct and imposed a world-wide ban of a year. He was also ordered to pay £50,000 as his share of the FA's legal costs which he felt was a fine.[3] My story generated a lot of comment. Thanks to an Etonian I had had a wonderful story for my newly launched *Inside Sport* column.[4]

I had started the column just when British sport—and football in particular—was going through a dramatic change. Money from sponsors and television, which had been small scale when I first started in 1974, was now hugely important and mattered more than what spectators paid for their tickets. It was only three years since the FA had fathered the Premier League by allowing the clubs of the old First Division of English football to break away from the Football League. I found the men—and they were all men—who ran these clubs were happy to spill many a secret, mostly off the record. They painted a picture of what was happening behind the scenes that was fascinating.

My best contact was Peter Robinson, the chief executive of Liverpool, who gave me his private number. Although he managed one of the greatest clubs in the land, he had a keen interest in cricket and we would often talk of it. Maurice Watkins, a lawyer and director of Manchester United, who would also prove an excellent contact and become a great friend, would often joke that Liverpool were famous for coming late to a party and then drinking all the champagne. Peter never bought me champagne but gave me enough stories to earn me many a glass from David Welch, who was always very good at looking after his journalists. I worked out a very useful formula. Whenever there was a major story brewing in the Premier League, or a meeting due to take place, I would ring Peter to find out what was going on. He would give me the details. I would then ring Maurice and quiz him without letting on I had spoken to Peter. He would often be astonished by how much I knew: "You have the agenda papers in front of you, don't you?" he would ask. Maurice, the legal man, was always involved in formulating the rules, and helped fashion football's current transfer system. He would also provide me with the sort of legal details that completed the picture and made it appear as if I had been inside the room when the Premier League discussed the issue.

Just to make sure I observed the standard journalistic formalities, I would ring Mike Lee, head of communications of the Premier League, for a comment. I knew he would issue the standard denial. My story would appear on the day of the meeting and Mike would be furious, all the more so as he was unable to explain to his bosses and other Premier League chairmen how I had got the story. I would follow up my story by ringing Peter and Maurice to find out how the meeting had gone, which would provide me with yet more details, further infuriating Mike. One Premier League chief executive decided the only way to stop me getting stories was to keep secrets from the chairmen. It would lead to his dramatic departure.

This was Peter Leaver, who had given Sam Chisholm and David Chance, former Sky executives, a three-year contract which provided a million upfront each year, plus possible bonuses, to negotiate television rights. The bonus could be either five per cent of any increase in a new television contract or a five per cent stake in a Premier League channel. But he feared the details would be reported by me in the *Daily Telegraph*.[5] So, Lever got the chairmen to sign a confidentially clause before he would tell them the details of the deal, which was extraordinary given the chairmen were the owners of the League and had appointed him. In a stormy meeting of the League, Lever was sacked, leaving, as one chairman told me, blood on the floor. Lever after his departure gave me an exclusive interview in which he said, "The problem was that anything I told the chairmen somehow ended up in your column in the *Daily Telegraph*. We felt we might as well take a four-page advert in the *Daily Telegraph* and publish the entire agenda."[6] Almost a year later Chisholm and Chance took the Premier League to court and won a £12 million payout to settle the court action.[7]

* * *

From the Englishmen in suits to the Europeans in suits running world football and Olympics was a natural transition, although the initial breakthrough came quite by chance in Lausanne in 1998. The International Olympic Committee (IOC) was having its final executive meeting of the year. I happened to be in Lausanne covering a football story and although it was a Saturday, a day off, I decided to pop in to the IOC headquarters in Lausanne. Very few journalists were covering the meeting, which was expected to be a routine one. Then suddenly an elderly Swiss lawyer turned the greatest ever Olympic whistle blower.

Marc Hodler, a senior IOC member, had never before said anything controversial. That Saturday morning, he suddenly came down to the lobby where we journalists were chatting and, to our astonishment, revealed how deeply the Olympics were mired in corruption. Hodler, moving round like a fish in a tank, at times standing in front of the passage that led to the restaurant to which journalists had no access, even in front of the men's toilets, tore away the pretence so studiously maintained that there was no corruption in the Olympic movement. Not only, said Hodler, could IOC members' votes be bought, there were agents specialising in such deals; one agent was himself an IOC member.

I was the only person from the British print media there, and with the Sunday papers not having given it much space, it left the field clear for me to write about it on Monday.

I rang Keith, who was editing the paper, and told him this was the greatest crisis in the Olympic movement. "Bigger than the 1980 Moscow Olympics?" he asked. "Yes," I said. Keith agreed to make space available. The *Daily Telegraph* ran not just the longest piece but the only one which could be by-lined by its own correspondent in Lausanne. And this time I did not share it with Richard Bright.

I was certain the IOC, FIFA, UEFA and other such sports bodies had many stories, particularly about their finances and governance, which needed to be investigated.

I was a double outsider. The British media saw me as a loner, an accountant who was straying into the hallowed world of the sports pages. Abroad there was initial disbelief that a brown man could claim to be British and represent such an august paper as the *Daily Telegraph*. At press conferences I would always slowly say my name and then quite loudly announce that I was from the London *Daily Telegraph*, emphasising London in case they thought it was a *Daily Telegraph* in some third world country. I enjoyed watching the surprise on the faces of these white men. But once they got over their shock I found people within these organisations, many of whom were also outsiders but privy to secrets, very willing to talk to me off the record.

David and Keith were happy for me to go to IOC and FIFA meetings and investigate stories. It would become a joke with the subs at the *Daily Telegraph*, and when I left the paper their leaving present had a mock-up of the front page of the sports section which said "Mihir Bose—man of letters—UEFA, FIFA, WADA, IOC, FA, BALCO, LOCOG, BOA, ODA, etc., etc."

But while such cultivation of the men in suits yielded scoops, it led to a British minister calling me a shit and accusing me of being in the pay of the Germans.

37

I WON'T TALK IN FRONT OF THAT LITTLE SHIT

The words were used by Tony Banks to describe me to Franz Beckenbauer, one of the legends of football, in the lobby of a Luxembourg hotel. He was furious because I was not parroting his widely expressed view that England would win the bid to host the 2006 football World Cup and throws an interesting light on the curious mix of politics and sport which formed a part of the Tony Blair years.

England, having staged the European championships in 1996, had decided to bid for the 2006 World Cup, having only ever staged it once in 1966 when it had also won it. But it faced competition from Germany who wanted to use the World Cup to advertise it had become a united country for the first time since the Second World War. South Africa had an even greater claim. The competition had never been staged in Africa. And with Nelson Mandela, the modern-day living saint, campaigning for the Rainbow Nation how could the world of football resist? With many in the Blair government football fans, Banks was a fervent Chelsea supporter, the FA had government support. But Lennart Johannsson, the large, jowly, avuncular Swede, who was President of UEFA, and who I had got to know well favoured Germany and felt that England should honour the gentlemen's agreement it had with UEFA that should UEFA give England the Euros, England would not bid for the World Cup. Johansson feared an England bid would split Europe and might let in a non-European country, particularly South Africa.

But the FA insisted there was no such gentlemen's agreement and asked UEFA to produce the minutes to prove it existed. This led one UEFA executive telling me, "But 'gentlemen's agreement' means there is nothing written down. 'Gentlemen's agreement' is a British term. Do they not understand their own concept?" Bobby Charlton, one of the bid leaders, even boldly declared there was no such agreement although he had not been privy to the discussions.

I found Banks campaign absurd particularly when, having assiduously courted Jack Warner of Trinidad, then a powerful FIFA vice-president, he with great joy declared that he was joined at the hip with Warner. As I write this Warner has been barred for life by FIFA and is fighting extradition to the United States on multiple corruption charges.

In such sporting contests the reporter is often forced to become a laptop supporter. I was determined to avoid that and set out to cultivate the other bids. I quickly realised that this was not so much a sporting as a political contest shaped by much wider considerations then whether a country had the stadium and facilities to stage the event.

I had had evidence of this in June 1999, just over a year before the vote was to take place. I was in Manchester to cover a World Cup cricket match between India and Pakistan and went to the football Old Trafford, next door to the cricket ground, to chat with Peter Kenyon, chief executive of Manchester United. He was a good contact and told me that in order to get into the good books of FIFA and its President Sepp Blatter, the FA was twisting the arms of Manchester United to take part in the Club World Championship, a new competition to be held in Brazil that Blatter had dreamt up. This would come in the middle of the season and Alex Ferguson, the Manchester United manager, had ruled this out emphatically and that seemed the end of the matter. But Kenyon pointed out such decisions were taken by the Board and the FA were offering two carrots: the season would be extended to accommodate the rearranged fixtures and United would be allowed to field a weakened team in the FA Cup without fear of penalty. United had just won the Champions League, making them kings of European club football, and the FA felt if United went it would please Blatter and he would support England's bid.[1]

This was a sensational story but much to my surprise I found it difficult to convince the *Telegraph's* chief sub that we should run it. Alex Ferguson, he said, is like the leader of a band, football's equivalent of Mick Jagger. If he says Rolling Stones do not tour then they do not tour. I reminded him what many club chairmen and chief executives had told me, in particular Maurice Watkins, that managers, despite being called bosses by their players were employees. If the board took a decision then the manager had to accept it. He agreed to run the piece but said with a mock laugh, "I will give you a blow job if Manchester United go to Rio".

Banks also got involved in the process telling the club that he had been personally informed by three members of the FIFA executive, who had previously said they would vote for England, that they would not do so if United did not go to Rio. When United raised the question of indemnity should they be sued by sponsors for not taking part in the FA Cup, Banks assured them he had spoken to ministers at the highest level and sent a handwritten fax assuring United that the government would meet any loss United suffered. The FA, in an unprecedented move, allowed Manchester United to miss the FA Cup despite the club being the holders.

* * *

Banks did not react to my United story but he did respond when on 19 March 2000, four months before the vote was to take place, I wrote that England faced the prospect of being knocked out early, getting only three votes. I gave the probable votes for the five countries still in the race as Germany 7, South Africa 7, Brazil 4, Morocco 3 and England 3. England's three votes would come from Scotland, which represented the four British home nations on the FIFA executive, the USA and New Zealand. I took care to praise the bid team.[2] But this cut no ice.

A few days later I received a letter from Banks saying my story would have been risible were it not so damaging and suggested that I was in the pay of the South Africans and the Germans who, he added, no doubt would continue to express their gratitude to me. I could have understood if he had said I had been misinformed. But for him to say I had taken bribes was astonishing and I was amazed that a seasoned politician could even think like that.

Banks was still smouldering with anger when a week before the vote he spoke at the UEFA Congress. At the Congress the UEFA members of the FIFA executive sat in the front row. Banks looking at them said, "We have done the arithmetic. If they don't support England, they may not host the World Cup for many years to come." I was staggered that Banks was telling people whose votes he wanted that they could not count. One UEFA delegate expressed sadness that England, a country which they associated with high standards, should indulge in such "blackmail." UEFA had 8 votes in the 24-member FIFA executive and was crucial if England were to get the 13 they required to win. To antagonise UEFA in this way made no sense. In my *Inside Sports* column I described this as "an amazing diplomatic blunder," and that it was "Banks' crass attempt to win votes".

The headline on the column read "Banks blunder leaves bid to fail with no grace".[3]

The bid team was furious and one member of the team who I saw quite by chance, while waiting for a lift, said, in a voice full of contempt, "You will always win the rubbish journalist award of the year". I was struck as to how angry members of the bid team were, not just to me but to members of rival bids. Terry Paine had been part of the 1966 World Cup-winning squad and knew Bobby Charlton well. Having settled in South Africa he was part of their bid team. But he told me very sorrowfully, "Bobby won't speak to me because I am supporting South Africa. I cannot understand it." I was soon to be even more mystified by Banks' behaviour.

The day after my column appeared I was in the lobby of the hotel where the German bid team was staying and seeing Beckenbauer, began to chat with him. Soon after Banks entered the lobby and walked towards Beckenbauer saying, "Franz I want to say about my speech". He then saw me and shouted, "I do not want to speak in front of this little shit," and with that he turned round and stormed out. Der Kaiser looked at me and said, "What have you done to so upset your minister?"

* * *

The vote was to be held in Zurich in FIFA's headquarters and just before I flew out I wrote a preview piece saying, "All the signs are that the bid will end in tears, with England getting between two and four votes" and that, "it would be a fight to stay in the ballot beyond the first round". The piece was headlined: "England's world crashes down."[4]

The piece took up a whole page but there was nervousness in the paper about it. David Welch told me, "I have put the house on you being right that England stand no chance. I hope you are right". So did I.

I arrived in Zurich to find that contrary to most of the media who thought South Africa would edge it Germany were finishing strongly. So much so there could be a dead heat with each country getting 12 votes each with Morocco eliminated in the first round and England eliminated in the second round.

The night before the vote in the bar of the hotel where the FIFA executive members stayed in Zurich I had a chat with Lennart Johansson who was confident Germany would win. The South Africans, realising they could lose, played their great trump card hoping they could stem the German tide.

Early on Thursday morning around 6.30 am Mandela rang Charles Dempsey, a Scot who had migrated to New Zealand. Mandela knew that Dempsey in the first round would support England. But, pleaded Mandela, could Mr Dempsey please vote for South Africa if England was eliminated. While millions would have been delighted to get a call from Mandela Dempsey was upset he had been woken up so early and was fairly brusque with Mandela.

Mandela would not give up. One of the Asian delegates was Thai and Mandela rang the King of Thailand. Another Asian was from Qatar and Mandela was on the phone to the Emir of Qatar. His most dramatic call was to the King of Belgium. One of the executive members was Dr Michael D'Hooghe from Belgium. By the time Mandela called, the FIFA executive had started discussing the bid. But the meeting was interrupted and D'Hooghe was told he must take a call from his King. The call was put through to a private room where the King spoke to his subject. D'Hooghe was respectful but he would not budge from his support for Germany. South Africa's great card had failed.

So it proved as the vote proceeded. Morocco went first. England survived with five votes. However, I had been told that Warner, who controlled three of them, despite being joined at the hip to

Banks, had told him that if England did not get to 6 he would not support them in the second round. He did not. The result was England, having spent £10m and after three and a half years of effort, were eliminated in the second round with only two votes, one from a Scot in Scotland, another from a Scot who had migrated to New Zealand. Friends did make some fun at my expense saying I had got it wrong. Back in March I had predicted England would get three.

In the third and final round Germany with 12 just edged out South Africa with 11. My South African and German contacts told me the inside story of the voting and I could write a very comprehensive piece.

I later learnt that four days before the vote Beckenbauer had met Dempsey in Rotterdam and tried to persuade him to support Germany once England were eliminated. Dempsey refused but agreed to abstain and FIFA then sent a letter to the bidding countries that an abstention would not be considered a valid vote. This meant Germany needed only 12 votes of the 24 votes to win not 13 as would have been the case had all 24 votes counted. Later there were allegations of corruption against Beckenbauer but nothing was ever proven.

This time Banks did not say I was in their pay. Years later he was proposed for membership of the Reform Club. I could have blackballed him but did not.

* * *

In December 2010 I was again in Zurich covering an England bid, this time to host the 2018 World Cup and the former KGB man, Vladimir Putin, proved that when it comes to ruthless deception British politicians are no match. David Cameron had come to Zurich to match Tony Blair getting the 2012 Olympics by bringing football home. Keen to curry favour with FIFA he had entertained Sepp Blatter at No. 10 and even allowed him to hold Cameron's little daughter Florence. He was accompanied by Prince William and David Beckham. With William about to get married much was made that FIFA executive members could be swayed if William invited them to his wedding. I knew the corrupt world of FIFA, which was soon exposed, did not work like that.

I WON'T TALK IN FRONT OF THAT LITTLE SHIT

On the morning of the vote Putin announced he would not come to Zurich because he felt sorry for FIFA in the way the British press had slated the organisation. He did not want to put more pressure on them and allow them to come to their decision in quiet contemplation. An English press colleague announced Putin knew Russia was going to lose and England must now win. I was not so sure but I was in a minority. England with two votes was eliminated in the first round and Russia won. Within minutes we were told Putin would fly in to Zurich and hold a press conference. At the press conference in the front row sat Roman Abramovich, the Russian oligarch who owned Chelsea, looking up at Putin on the podium with admiration. Abramovich had never given a press conference or been seen at one. I asked Putin about a damming report by the Americans describing Russia as a racist country that spied on the world. Putin's minders glowered. Putin looked hard at me, but replying in English, dismissed it as American propaganda. But he broke into a laugh when I asked who would finance the World Cup. Pointing at Abramovich he said, "He has money. He can do it." Abramovich smiled. Putin could not hide his pleasure at beating the west. Cameron left Zurich complaining FIFA executive members had lied to him but this only revealed his naivety.

Interestingly Henry Kissinger, who was keenly interested in football, had supported the USA's bid for the 2022 World Cup but this latter day Metternich was astonished when Qatar snatched the prize. Watching Putin I could not help but think of the time I questioned Kissinger about America's support for Pakistan's genocide in Bangladesh in 1971. Kissinger, advising President Richard Nixon, had called Indians "those sons of bitches" and likened Pakistan President Yahya Khan, the architect of the genocide, to Abraham Lincoln. America supplied weapons to Pakistan and Kissinger even shared secret US intelligence with the Chinese, hoping China would concentrate troops on its Indian border and force the Indians to abandon plans to stop the slaughter. India required the support of the "evil" Soviet empire to veto an American resolution in the Security Council to stop the Indian army liberating Bangladesh. In a final attempt to help the "Pakistani Lincoln", as Indian troops neared Dhaka, the US government despatched the Seventh Fleet to the Bay of Bengal. Some years later Kissinger was in London to promote a book and I asked him at the press conference about this contrast between America and Russia. While Putin had glowered at me Kissinger squirmed and did not answer my question.

38

THE A, B, C, D ROADS CRICKET MURDER

In Mumbai's Churchgate, a ten minute walk from Sailor Building, there are four roads known as A, B, C, D roads. These were the names they were given when this area was reclaimed from the Arabian Sea in the 1930s and nearly a century later they are still known by these names. I know these roads well and it was here in December 2001 I was made aware that writing a cricket story could put my life at risk.

It had begun in April 2000 when the Delhi police released incriminating extracts from the transcripts of conversations showing that Hansie Cronje, captain of the South African cricket team, had conspired with Indian bookmakers to fix matches.

The British media's initial reaction was to believe Cronje who dismissed the story as "absolute rubbish". This surely was the police of a third world country trying to malign a born-again white Christian. The South African government claimed the Delhi police had damaged its relations with India. Bob Woolmer, the South African coach, even told me quite seriously that the Indians had spread this story to cover up for the fact that they had lost the series.

* * *

For me the story had more than a ring of truth in it. A few months before the Cronje story broke I had written in *Wisden* that there was "little sign of this sorry story [of cricket corruption] ever ending. Let alone soon". I had for years been hearing stories from Indian journalists about players in the subcontinent colluding with bookmakers. Vinod Mehta, editor of *Outlook*, an Indian news magazine for which

I wrote, had run many articles on the subject. Soon after the Delhi police story broke I rang Vinod, who I knew well, and he told me, "The Delhi police are very confident of what they have got. But what they have released so far is only the tip of the iceberg and there is a much bigger affair that they are investigating."

One reason the British media had not bothered with the cricket corruption story was that they had not paid much attention to how India was changing. More than fifty years after independence there was now a prosperous Indian middle class of nearly 400 million which no longer worried about hand-outs from the Aid India Club. International companies like Pepsi, Coke, eager to cultivate this growing market were pouring vast sums of money into Indian cricket making it the richest in the world. But the Raj's shadow hung over India as the country had not changed the betting laws it had inherited: legal bets were only allowed on horse race tracks. This had pushed the Indian betting industry into the hands of illegal bookies. They knew the insatiable Indian appetite for betting. The story of the *Mahabharata* was based round betting. The result was illegal bookmakers targeted cricketers.

I had been writing about the rise of Indian cricket's economic power for some years although I could not always get stories past Arthur Wynne-Davies, the *Telegraph* lawyer. He would not allow me to say that Jagmohan Dalmiya, the Kolkata businessman, and the first Asian head of world cricket, who was spearheading India's rise to world cricket dominance, was such a ruthless businessman he could outwit a Jew and a Scot in a business deal. Arthur claimed it would outrage the paper's Jewish and and Scottish readers.

Four days after the Delhi police revelations the entire picture changed. Cronje confessed. The South African government announced that a former judge, Justice Edwin King, would hold a judicial inquiry. I was on a plane to Cape Town.

* * *

Cape Town in winter had so few tourists that I virtually had the hotel to myself. I was also the only journalist from this country covering the King inquiry, thankful the rest of the British sports media was concentrating on the European football championships.

THE A, B, C, D ROADS CRICKET MURDER

I have always found lawyers and accountants are the best sources for scoops. King was assisted by Shamila Batohi, Deputy Director of Public Prosecutions. Over dinner in one of Cape Town's swish restaurants she revealed that Cronje had been offered immunity from criminal prosecution by the South African government provided he told the whole truth to the King Commission.

Much the most explosive story was how, only five months earlier, Cronje had fooled the entire cricket world. Then on the final day of the Test against England, which looked a certain draw with three days washed out by rain, Cronje offered the England captain an astonishing deal. Both sides should forfeit an innings, unprecedented in cricket history and not sanctioned by the laws. Cronje would set a target for England to chase making a match of it. It worked like a treat and England won by two wickets. The press hailed Cronje as a saviour. Now I heard Cronje had done it as part of a bet with an illegal bookie, getting 53,000 rands and a leather jacket for his wife. Cronje said that having been corrupted by Indian bookies he was like an alcoholic who could never refuse a drink, even when he returned to South Africa.

It was strange in that Cape Town winter to hear of how in towns like Nagpur, which I always associated with Daskaku and the tiffin carrier, Cronje had taken money from Indian bookies. I was struck by the extraordinary power of Indian bookies to corrupt a white who would have grown up in a country where Indians were considered inferior and forced to live in Indian townships. What was also striking was many South African cricket fans still saw Cronje as a hero. Three years later when I came back to cover the Cricket World Cup fans held out placards dedicating it to the memory of Cronje.

* * *

My journey to the A, B, C, D roads came when in the winter of 2001 England visited India for a three-Test series. I learnt that some £420 million would be wagered across India for the series. Yet Graham Sharpe of William Hill had told me the entire bookmaking industry in England may might not take more than £100,000 for the series.

An old school friend knew a bookie who lived in the same block of flats in one of the A, B, C, D roads and arranged for me to meet him. The picture painted by the bookie had echoes of illegal betting in Britain before betting shops were licensed in the 60s. Nigel Dudley's grandfather used to ring up bookies and place illegal bets calling himself Smoke 2. The Indian bookie said, "You are 'Mihir' and your account will be called 'Charlie'. Your basic bet is Rs. 200 [£2] that would be one and when you bet you say Charlie one plus three which means that you are really betting Rs 500 [£5] or you can bet one plus eight which is Rs. 1000 or one plus 98 which is Rs. 10,000 [£100]. Whatever you do the bet that will be written down will only be one."

To place a bet you had to hire a betting line which was supplied illegally by telephone workers. On these lines you could hear continuous commentary on the cricket betting. The more expensive the lines the more information you got and for the right amount you could not only hear the constantly changing odds but also what the big punters were betting on.

* * *

It was what this bookie said next that was chilling. That the betting market was controlled by *Dadas*, underworld dons, who were wanted on numerous charges. The week I met him an associate of the underworld don, who had been involved in illegal cricket betting, had been shot dead in what the police called an "encounter," Indian euphemism for the police killing a suspect.

The bookie I was speaking to was very much a small trader and towards the end of our conversation he turned to my contact and said, "This is a very dangerous game and these criminal elements will stop at nothing. There have been 19 murders already." Then with his voice turning very cold he said, "Tell your friend to be careful what he writes".[1] He confessed that he had been threatened and wherever he went was protected by two armed men. My *Telegraph* piece had been headlined 'Murder rife in illegal betting'. A few months later I heard that the bookie in question was shot dead not far from where we had spoken.

Back in the 60s H.R. Keating could write his Inspector Ghote crime novels about a Bombay policeman without ever visiting India.

Now Scotland Yard officials went to India and met India's Central Bureau of Investigations, whose existence they had not known of, and returned full of praise for their work in unmasking cricket corruption. The illegal cricket bookies had, unwittingly, transformed India's image.

* * *

Less than three years later, in April 2004, cricket showed me the frightening face of an evil regime. That regime was Robert Mugabe's Zimbabwe where I had gone after Mugabe had politicised the cricket union. The former captain Heath Streak, and fifteen of his colleagues, all of them white, had rebelled and been replaced by a virtual all-black team. Zimbabwe were playing Sri Lanka and I flew into to Bulawayo the day before the Test. British passport holders do not require a visa and I had been told to lie and pretend I was a tourist. But I told the truth and the immigration officer was very helpful. After charging me 55 dollars he gave me the change in US dollars as Zimbabwean dollars were worthless.

On the way to the hotel we encountered a police roadblock and the driver advised me to hide my notes as police stole money. The driver of the pick-up truck explained it was not safe to put the luggage in the large space available for it as it could be stolen but hid my laptop and small bag under the front seat. Cricket officials were so fearful that one of them would only speak in my hotel room once he had closed the curtains and checked he wasn't being followed. Soon I had reason to be fearful.

I was summoned to the reception of my hotel where waiting for me in the lobby was the head of immigration in Bulawayo and two officials. He confiscated my passport and asked me to report to his office at 7.45 the next morning. He told me he had received orders from on high in Harare that I was to be deported. The authorities felt as a British journalist I might foment trouble between the Zimbabwean authorities and the rebel cricketers. His order was to deport me immediately but with no flights from Bulawayo he had to wait till the morning. He should have taken me to the jail but a kind man he treated me with great courtesy and I was allowed to spend the night in the hotel. I was later told had I been in Harare I would have been jailed.

I could now understand what Hannah Arendt meant about the banality of evil. Around me Sri Lankan cricketers chatted up local women and their extraordinary spinner Muttiah Muralitharan was presented with a birthday cake by a well-wisher.

At 8 am the next morning in a government office I signed an order presented by a Zimbabwean immigration official deporting me from the country. The day before I had arrived, Mugabe in a speech marking 24th anniversary of Zimbabwean independence had berated Tony Blair and mocked Zimbabweans "who are running away to wash the bodies of the elderly in the UK". Yet I met a woman studying for post-graduate qualification who asked me for help getting to the UK and was grateful when I paid for her full English breakfast. On my drive to the airport the immigration official escorting me looked forlornly at advertisements by Air Zimbabwe about flying to London and asked me for help in migrating. I have never felt such relief as my flight for Cape Town took off. In South Africa I had been told Zimbabweans were too timid, having been flattened first by Ian Smith's racist regime and now the iron fist of Mugabe. It was disheartening to see how things had turned sour since I had rejoiced when the Smith regime fell. As I wrote in *The Telegraph*, to see Zimbabweans so submissive "it makes you want to weep." It raised larger questions which went much beyond cricket about the struggles of newly liberated countries. It made me feel proud that India, for all its faults, had avoided taking such a route after it emerged from colonialism.

39

THANK GOODNESS FOR CITIZENS OF NOWHERE

Theresa May mocked the British who claimed to be citizens of the world calling them citizens of nowhere. My writing career would not have prospered without such citizens of nowhere.

I met the first of them, Derek Wyatt, on a cold winter evening in the offices of George Allen & Unwin. A former England rugby international, who later became a Labour MP, he commissioned me to write a book looking at the social side of Indian cricket. The result was *A Maidan View: The Magic of Indian Cricket*. I treasured what John Arlott wrote, "It should be read by everybody concerned with the social setting of cricket wherever it is played". To read such praise from the man I had worshipped since I was a boy made me feel I had finally arrived as a writer.

* * *

Derek then suggested I do a Studs Terkel on cricket. Talk to people involved in the game and let the reader hear their voices. The result was *Cricket Voices*.

Derek's follow up was, probably, the book I least expected to write.

* * *

It was a biography of Michael Grade, who was then head of Channel 4. Grade made it clear he did not want to co-operate and asked me to make it clear it was very much an unauthorised biography.

It resulted in my writing two more books. Irving Scholar, who had recently sold Tottenham to Alan Sugar, was so impressed that he asked me to ghost his book about his years at Tottenham. We decided to call it *Behind Closed Doors*. I also found him a publisher. Scholar, who floated Tottenham, the first club to do so, had many fascinating stories to tell and was a joy to work with. Scholar's book in turn got me a commission by Jarvis Astaire, the boxing promoter, to write his biography. Unlike Scholar, Astaire was not much fun to work with and I had to send him a legal letter to get my money.

* * *

I met my second British citizen of nowhere even more unexpectedly. One winter afternoon in 1988, sitting in front of my Amstrad, a wedding present from Tapanda and Chordi, and still pining about the novel I had never written, I got a call.

"It is Tom Rosenthal here."

I was shocked, convinced one of my friends was playing a prank. Why should Rosenthal, co-owner of André Deutsch and publisher of V.S. Naipaul, Gore Vidal, Norman Mailer and John Updike, authors I admired, be ringing me? But it was Rosenthal, and he wanted me to write *A History of Indian Cricket*, the first proper narrative history of the game in India.

I went to see Tom at his offices in Great Russell Street, not far from the TUC headquarters. A large man, he almost overflowed from his chair, sitting behind a huge desk smoking a cigar and looking like an emperor. He offered me a cigar, and I quickly discovered Rosenthal was one of the few in this country who bridged the divide between "arties" and "hearties". He didn't feel a man of literature couldn't love cricket. An MCC member, he never missed a Test at Lord's and often travelled to other grounds to see Test matches. He also sought out great cricketers and bonded with them. One of his best friends was Michael Holding, a West Indian cricketing legend and one of the greatest fast bowlers in the history of the game. Holding, along with me, was present at Rosenthal's memorial service, the only cricketer there, and I was struck by the fact that many of Rosenthal's arty friends didn't know who Holding was. That Rosenthal could have admired a cricketer like Holding was something they couldn't understand, and in her eulogy Joan Bakewell confessed she couldn't speak of Rosenthal's love of cricket.

Tom's editor provided me a template on how to write histories. John Bright-Holmes said a good history book must avoid being "one damm thing after another". Break up the narrative with pen portraits of leading figures. And start by describing a dramatic moment. My opening chapter was titled "The Day The Elephant Came to the Oval" describing that day in September 1971 when India won a Test and a series for the first time on English soil and Indian supporters paraded an elephant from Chessington Zoo

The book had been timed to appear in the summer of 1990, when the Indians were touring England. I could not have asked for better reviews. The most touching was by Alan Ross in the *Independent on Sunday*. He too was born in Kolkata and maybe this explained why he was so kind. To my great surprise the book was shortlisted for The Cricket Society Silver Jubilee Literary Award for 1990. Before the award lunch I received a letter saying I had won and would get a cheque for £500 and an inscribed parchment certificate. Derek Wyatt was also at the lunch as one of his authors was on the shortlist.

* * *

Simon Wilde, then a young reporter, had approached Derek and told him he'd discovered much new material on Ranji. He was going to India to do more research. Derek agreed to pay his travel expenses. Derek sent me Simon's draft and asked for my comments. I knew about the book as Simon had written to me asking for help addressing me as "Dear Mihir Bose". His Ranji biography, unlike many others, was not a hagiography and had fascinating new material. But the book was written in a style that didn't work. Derek agreed and asked Simon to substantially rewrite it.

A History of Indian Cricket was also responsible for me writing for the *New Yorker*, to which I had previously pitched ideas with no response.

In 1997 when the magazine devoted an issue to mark the fiftieth anniversary of Indian independence Bill Burford asked me to write an article on cricket. It seems Salman Rushdie had suggested my name. I have never met Rushdie, but I admired his *Midnight's Children*, which I had favourably reviewed. Writing for the *New Yorker* meant I was introduced to a person unknown in British journalism: the fact checker, a person who asks writers to provide verification for facts in the article. I had mentioned how the first ever Test in India was played at the Bombay Gymkhana, which then didn't allow Indian members. I had mentioned that though now it was full of Indian members, the menu still had roast beef and Yorkshire pudding. The fact checker asked me to verify this, and I rang one of my friends in Mumbai who was a member, getting him to read the menu and let me know if I was right.

But in contrast to England and America the reaction among Indians was more mixed.

* * *

Within weeks of my history being published one of India's cricketing greats reacted very angrily. That was Bishan Singh Bedi, the mercurial spinner who had enchanted me and millions of cricket fans with his magical left-arm spin bowling. He was the manager of the Indian team touring England that summer. This series was the first in England where both teams had cricket managers. The *Sunday Times* asked me to do a piece comparing Keith Fletcher, the England manager, with Bedi. During the Old Trafford Test I spent an evening with Bedi. He was outspoken. I wrote a piece contrasting Bedi with the taciturn Fletcher but did it with great affection. Bedi was incensed by the article. During the Old Trafford Test, he had come to the press box looking for me and told journalists he wanted to find "the Bengali to shove an umbrella up his arse."

I had presented the book to Bedi, inscribing on the title page "Bishan, with fond memories of his great cricketing deeds". At the Oval he came to the press box and chucked the book at me. He didn't want it. I opened it at the title page to see he had crossed out my thanks and instead scrawled this handwritten message just above my name:

> You gutter journalist, shove it up your filthy bum & enjoy being the worst historian [this was underlined] ever. "You are a cunt of the highest order"—nay, "odour"!! Try carrying this quote you swine.

However, for others it became a reference book. I was most touched when my friend Noel Rands, who played the umpire in Aamir Khan's much-heralded crossover Bollywood film *Lagaan*, which uses a cricket match to illustrate British–Indian relations during the Raj, told me the great Khan had my history in his dressing room.

* * *

I might also have written a novel for André Deutsch. In 1993 I sent Tom a synopsis called *Reuters Fart*, my ludicrous attempt to ape Salman Rushdie and Amitav Ghosh. Tom commissioned it but it never got written. It still might have had I won the *Daily Mail* novel competition where contestants had to write a chapter. A publisher had been lined up to provide a contract to the winner. John Mortimer, one of the judges, liked my chapter and complimented me on it. But Fay Weldon, another judge, felt I hadn't got the female character right. Beryl Bainbridge, the third judge, agreed with Weldon and I didn't win. I don't know whether, if there had been a majority of male judges, I would have won. More likely, the dream I had sitting in the freezing cold of my Clapham Common bedsit was never meant to come true. I have never had a novel in me.

40

TAKING ON A NATIONAL TREASURE

A few years ago, while walking along a green near my house one Saturday afternoon an elderly man in shorts approached me, and with a diffident smile said, "You don't remember me do you? I am Terry Venables". I smiled and thought how I could I forget the former England coach? For nearly two decades he had been almost a constant in my journalistic life. When I left the *Telegraph* for the BBC, the mock sports front page of the paper that I got as a leaving present showed a pensive Venables with a thought bubble reading, "That's It! I'm joining Ferguson, Allardyce and Redknapp's boycott of the BBC." Venables is the only person I have written about who sued me personally but not the paper or its editor.

Venables' death showed how much this country loved him. It came in the middle of one of the deadliest conflicts in the Middle East. Yet, while the *Times* relegated Hamas releasing a four-year old American-Israeli girl, whose parents they had murdered, to the bottom of the page, the masthead had a picture of Venables with the headline "Innovative and Brilliant." The Guardian headline was "A football romantic who made people happy." Yet, ironically, I never set out to upset Venables and my first feature on Venables was full of love. The headline "The Second Coming of Venables", summed up its gushing nature. Tottenham were playing Arsenal in the FA Cup semi-final in March 1993 and I wrote that if Tottenham beat Arsenal "then the fans at Tottenham's Paxton Road End would probably christen him the man with the magic wand." I concluded, "that whatever happens against Arsenal there is great confidence the future belongs to White Hart Lane."[1]

On the evening of 13 May, 1993, watching ITN's News At Ten at my home in Kensal Rise this world came crashing down.

I saw Peter Staunton standing outside Royal Lancaster hotel, where the football writers had gathered for their traditional eve of Cup Final dinner, buttonhole Venables as he got out of his car, asking him to confirm rumours that he would be sacked by Sugar the following day. Venables looked surprised and in a voice that was both pained and resigned, said that, yes, there was to be a Tottenham Board meeting to decide his fate. I envied Staunton his great scoop.

In fact it was a carefully staged drama orchestrated by Donna Cullen, Venables' PR. A few days earlier Cullen had gone to her meeting with Venables armed with an article I had written that month in *Director* magazine about the businessman Gulu Lalwani. Sugar had known him for twenty-five years but had fallen out with him. Culllen felt it could be used to show Sugar did not get on with people. The Staunton doorstepping had, as Cullen put it to me, "stolen Sugar's thunder."[2] But why had the Sugar-Venables take-over of Tottenham turned in two years from a dream into a nightmare? Why was Venables no longer, as the *Times* had described him, "football's renaissance man, the Leonardo da Vinci of the league"? The mystery deepened with Venables saying he did not know why he was sacked. The result was the media presented it as a capricious chairman, sacking the manager of a football club when in fact Venables was chief executive of a public company, in which he had invested nearly £3 million. The football side was actually managed by coaches.

Even Roy Hattersley was on Venables' side and, in a thinly veiled swipe at Sugar, said that football should be run by footballers rather than people who just buy their way into the club.[3]

* * *

I rang Nick Hewer and asked why had the Sugar camp kept so quiet? Nick told me Sugar could not compete with Venables on the back pages such was his bond with sports journalists. He was prepared to help me on the same basis that the FBI "deep throat" had given information to Woodward and Bernstein over Watergate.

I learnt relations between Venables and Sugar had broken down a long time ago. I also got an internal Tottenham document prepared on Eddie Ashby, Venables financial adviser. He had been a director of 43 companies, 16 of which were in receiverships, 8 in liquidation and 15 struck off. In two cases assets had been transferred prior to the appointment of a receiver. He had been declared a bankrupt on 6 June 1991, before Sugar and Venables had taken over Tottenham. Ashby was said to be actively involved in the commercial side of Tottenham's business. At one stage callers to White Hart Lane were told he was "general manager" and had a desk and secretary there.

The main article entitled 'Why Sugar tried to oust Venables' began, "Terry Venables says he does not know why he was sacked. We can tell him there were..." There was another article on the news pages headlined 'Essex Men fight for extra time at Spurs'.[4] Venables saw it as a blow below the belt. "If I could not be dammed directly, then it would be done by association."[5] The rest of the media ignored my story and continued to picture Venables as the wronged man. This narrative may have not been challenged had Venables accepted Sugar's offer to take a £3.5 million pay-off and go quietly. Venables ignored the advice of one leading football chairman to take the money. He took Sugar to court and that changed everything.

On the Sunday my story broke Sugar sitting in his dining room prepared an affidavit which narrated his version of the story. The 56-page affidavit provided Jeff Randall and me with a great scoop which made the world aware of the word "bung", until then a closely guarded football secret.

* * *

Sugar said that when in August 1992 Tottenham bought Teddy Sheringham from Nottingham Forest, Venables told him that Brian Clough, the manager, "likes a bung."[6]

Jeff and I got hold of the affidavit. The affidavit had not yet been read in court and was not privileged. We had to work hard to persuade Alistair Brett, the *Sunday Times* lawyer, to let us run the bung story. I had in the meantime been talking to the chairmen of various clubs and learnt that the Inland Revenue was investigating clubs for paying bungs. One chairman confided, there is "A lot of brown paper-bagging (making payments in cash)."

Our story, on the front page on 30 May 1993, was headlined: "Revealed: Soccer's secret world of cash backhanders" and it began: "Sensational allegations are about to plunge English soccer into crisis. They will confirm widespread rumours about a secret world of backhanders and under-the-counter cash payments including some of the biggest names in football."

Kelvin McKenzie, the *Sun* editor, who had several reporters working on the Sugar-Venables row, could not hide his annoyance that they had not got hold of the story. Jeff gave him one titbit that we had not used: that Clough liked to be paid bungs in a motorway café. This was splashed all over the *Sun* on Monday which devoted several pages to the story. Kelvin sent over a case of champagne.

Venables denied he had told Sugar any such thing.[7] Clough retorted, "A bung? Isn't that something you get from a plumber to stop up the bath."[8]

Less than two weeks after our story the Premier League set up a three-man inquiry, comprising Premier League chief executive Rick Parry, Steve Coppell, a former England player and manager and Robert Reid QC. I often spoke to Reid getting a few nuggets but it was a totally unexpected source who gave me a story which led to media speculation that I might be arrested.

* * *

I learnt that in the Sheringham transfer in addition to the invoice on which Tottenham had paid £50,000 in cash there was a second invoice from, probably, the most extraordinary company ever to invoice a football club. This company was Silver Rose International Ltd (Export), whose invoice had a long-stemmed rose imprinted on it. It was also for £50,000 and the wordings on both invoices were identical. As the football authorities did not allow the use of agents in transfers the invoice did not mention that this was payment for the transfer but "For the assistance in arranging a distribution and merchandising network" for Tottenham in America.

Silver Rose was a company in London's Finchley Road whose shop front had a sign saying "Silver Rose Undresses the World" with the lingerie displayed living up to this billing.[9]

Soon after my story appeared in my weekly Inside Sports column in the *Daily Telegraph* on Saturday 30 September 1995, Detective

Inspector Ray Needham of Chelsea CID rang David Welch saying he wanted an informal chat. He came with his assistant to the offices of the *Daily Telegraph* in Canary Wharf. He tried and failed to convince David that the Silver Rose faxes were a forgery. David gave the two officers tea and as they left he came out of his office into the sports newsroom and said, "I have just had a very strange conversation with this policeman."[10]

Needham also visited the offices of MP Kate Hoey at the House of Commons and asked Patrick Cheney, who worked for Hoey, whether Hoey had been in touch with me. Needham told Cheney that, "he had been called in to investigate the theft of documents from Venables' company Edennote. His investigation showed that, at most, there was theft of photocopying paper worth 20p." Needham explained that "this enquiry had restarted following the Silver Rose article when Venables had renewed the charge."[11]

Venables by this time had become the England football coach and a few weeks after Needham's visit, the FA announced the police were investigating a campaign to discredit Venables. Needham's visit to the *Daily Telegraph* became known and created a sensation. The *Sunday Telegraph* headline read "Venables calls in Scotland Yard" with one journalist on the paper fantasising that Needham's informal call on Welch was some sort of raid on its sister paper. Alan Hubbard in the *Observer* suggested that papers would shortly be sent to the Crown Prosecution Service and four people could be charged with conspiracy to pervert the course of justice.[12] Since Needham was investigating my Silver Rose story I wondered if I could be one of the four.

The next few days were very anxious until Peter Brandt, commander of the operational crime unit in central London, who reviewed the investigation,[13] concluded it was not a criminal matter.[14]

My Silver Rose story also saw Venables serve a "subpoena duces tecum", lawyer speak for "come to court with certain documents", on me forcing the *Daily Telegraph* to appoint Bindman & Partners to represent me. Among the documents Venables wanted was the Silver Rose invoice. Actually Venables didn't want the document, but wanted me to reveal my source. Journalists are protected from disclosing their sources by Section 10 of the Contempt of Court Act 1981. It requires something like national interest to override it. Venables' high powered QC failed to convince Recorder David Williams that I should take the witness stand and he also granted me costs.[15]

It was even more reassuring when the Premier League bung inquiry report confirmed that the Silver Rose faxes were not forgeries but "confident that the faxes were sent with a view to assisting in the making of an improper payment in relation to the Sheringham transfer."[16] The inquiry concluded that Clough had got the £50,000, but this was not unanimous as Coppell was not convinced. The FA took no action against Clough and the bungs saga did no damage to his status. I was made aware of the public mood when Clough held an open-air meeting on a Sunday evening in Derby. When I asked why he had given evidence to the Premier League inquiry the reaction of the audience made it clear this not a question that I should have troubled the great man with. The audience had come to pay homage to an English football icon not deal with his dark secrets.

While this was going on I was involved in a personal battle with Venables.

* * *

On 24 May 1996 Venables issued a writ against me.[17] It was sent to my home address claiming damages for the libel regarding an article I had written about him, on 19 September 1993, two years and eight months earlier, in the *Sunday Times*, a paper I no longer worked for. At the time the article appeared Venables had said nothing, let alone bring libel proceedings. By the time I received the writ I had forgotten I had written the article.

The most alarming thing was that neither the *Sunday Times* nor the editor was sued. Normally a person also sues the publication and its editor. The writ is normally served at the publishers' office, not at the home of the writer.

Venables was suing me to stop publication of *The False Messiah— The Life and Times of Terry Venables*. My great worry was now that I worked for *Telegraph*, would the *Sunday Times* defend me? To the great credit of the paper Alastair Brett instantly said they would. He and Jeff Randall, who had become sports editor, backed me magnificently throughout the action. To my great surprise the judge in some of the legal duels examined not just the article for libel but also the headline which, as is normal in newspapers, had been written by the *Sunday Times* subs. So, I was being held responsible for something I had not written.

By this time I had another worry.

* * *

Ashby, charged with breaking bankruptcy laws, was facing a criminal trial. My book had to come out before Euro 96 which was before the case was heard. I could face contempt of court. If found guilty I would be jailed. The only way round this was to not to use Ashby's name. I called him John Brown saying this was "the pseudonym of a business associate of Venables."

I eagerly followed the Ashby trial held at the Knightsbridge Crown Court in October 1997 but as it neared its end I was away in Toronto on work. I knew Nick Hewer was attending court and with some nervousness I rang him from Toronto to find out what had happened. He told me that the jury, after deliberating for just under five hours, had found Ashby guilty on four separate offences under the Companies Directors Disqualification Act. Judge Timothy Pontius sentenced him to four months imprisonment.

Venables had been called as a witness on behalf of Ashby but Judge Pontius said of his evidence "the jury plainly found to be at best fanciful and at worst intended by you both to deliberately and dishonestly mislead them as to the true position. I have not the slightest hesitation myself in preferring the second view."[18]

The *Evening Standard* report was headlined "Judge condemns 'dishonest' Venables"[19] and the *Times* headline was "Venables lied in court, judge said".

* * *

I had also been reporting on the DTI inquiry on Venables but every time I had a story about what the DTI had found Venables would insist the inquiry was about minor administrative errors. On 14 January 1998 the DTI produced its devastating report. Venables accepted nineteen charges of serious misconduct as a director. One of his admissions was that in order to buy Tottenham he had borrowed money against a pub called "Miners" situated in "Cleremount Road" in Cardiff. Neither the pub nor the road existed. He was fined £500,000, and given a seven-year ban as company director.[20]

Yet Venables would still not drop the libel action. It was only in April 2001, nearly eight years after my article had been published, and five years after I had been served with a writ, by which time I had divorced and moved house, that the case was over.[21]

* * *

In 1994 when Venables published his autobiography I asked Sugar to review it. By this time I had established a good relationship with him and the sports desk of the *Sunday Times* loved mocking me by shouting out, every time I got a call, "Alan Sugar on the line". Sugar wrote the review despite his lawyers advising him against it, worried it might harm the libel writ Sugar had issued against the book. Sugar was proved right for he won the libel case. The publishers paid out £100,000 to Sugar who donated it to the Great Ormond Street Hospital.[22]

Some years later I was approached by Tom Bower, who was writing *Broken Dreams*, about the dark world of the beautiful game and I was happy to provide him material on Venables and other football secrets. Tom had two chapters on Venables. He very generously told me, "You were responsible for the book. Without you the book could not have been written." This, from one of our most successful investigative writers, meant a lot to me.

* * *

By the time Bower's book was published Venables, quite unwittingly, had given me a lovely present. In December 1997 a highly placed insider at Portsmouth gave me a very confidential document about the sale in August that year of Lee Bradbury, a valuable player, to Manchester City for a reported £3m.

The document showed that one of Venables' companies had been paid a total of £352,500, described as a fee "in respect of a one-off performance bonus". This seemed extraordinary as Portsmouth were bottom of the First Division and when my story appeared on 6 December players and staff at the club had not been paid their November wages.[23]

I did not profit monetarily but the story won the *1997 Sports Story of the Year Award*.

Looking back I can see that Venables greeting me that day in west London showed how much he wanted to be loved. But while I could admire his football skills I could not ignore his business record.

41

THE MUSLIM FROM RANGOON'S LESSONS
IN RELIGIOUS TOLERANCE

When I read about the growing religious intolerance towards Muslims and other minorities in India I think of Mohammed Aly Rangoonwala.

A successful businessman in Burma, hence his name Rangoonwala, the man from Rangoon, he fled the country when it fell to Japan, walking most of the way back to India. While many Indians on the walk from Burma had suffered racial discrimination, which convinced Gandhi the British would never treat Indians as equals and give them independence, he spoke warmly of how he had been received by British officials when he got back to India. He set up business again and this initially meant hawking goods. The hard work paid off. He become one of Pakistan's leading industrialists and President of the International Chamber of Commerce.

He also played a crucial part in helping create Pakistan and was close to Mohammed Ali Jinnah, the founder of Pakistan. Yet this did not make him a bigot as I discovered when quite out of the blue Andre Deutch forwarded a letter he had sent me at their address. When we met he told me how impressed he had been by my history of the Aga Khans and felt I would be the ideal person to write the history of the Memons. He set me a simple task, "Tell us and tell others who the Memons are. We are not just a rapacious business community. Nor are we to be confused with the Mormons of America. We, our children and grandchildren need to know where their ancestors came from and what they did. We would also like to share this information and knowledge with others."

The Memons, a history of the community, was published by the Memon Foundation which Rangoonwala had set up. My only regret was he did not live to see its publication.

I felt honoured that such a distinguished and devout Muslim should ask me, a man born a Hindu, although no longer religious, to write a book about a Muslim community of the sub-continent. Rangoonwala's trust in me, and the Memons acceptance of my book as their official history, holds out hope for secularism in the sub-continent, despite the growing attacks on it.

42

HOW A MULTIRACIAL STOMACH LEADS
TO A MULTIRACIAL HEART

In 1976, as the National Front marched through the streets of this "green and pleasant land" advocating their own very particular brand of hideousness, Jill Tweedy, in her *Guardian* column, suggested that to make Britain truly multiracial, the Asians and other non-whites should learn to cook and savour Lancashire hotpot, and the indigenous whites should take to chicken vindaloo. The consequent enrichment of palates would lead to the enrichment of souls and, no doubt, in time a truly multiracial Britain would be able to appreciate the diversity of foods and culture.

I read this piece in India in my rather expensive overseas edition of the *Guardian* and in the company of a friend whose knowledge of this country was confined to the BBC World Service and the British Council. "Vindaloo?" asked my friend, enunciating the word slowly. "What is that? Is this a very new thing the English have invented?" Just to make sure, he quickly looked it up in the menu of the restaurant we were in—one of the poshest in Mumbai—and sure enough, vindaloo was nowhere to be seen. In fact, vindaloo is not an English invention but a Goan dish, and my friend did not know about it because the vastness of India means it is unknown outside that former Portuguese enclave.

Vindaloo has still not travelled much over India, but since 1976 the white British have taken to vindaloo and other Indian food to such an extent that the former Labour foreign secretary, Robin Cook, could say that chicken tikka masala becoming Britain's favourite food defined a new sense of Britishness. Certainly, in Westminster it seems there can be no political plotting without chicken tikka

269

masala and poppadoms. I could not have imagined this in 1969, when it seemed the political revolution my 1960s generation hoped for looked much more likely than this food revolution. Almost everywhere I went, I was told by the locals how much they despised Indian food, and the price of my acceptance was not to bring "my food" with me.

* * *

Seven years before Jill Tweedie's article in the *Guardian*, in the spring of 1969, the musical *Hair* opened in London's West End. The Loughborough students' union booked coaches to bring students down, and all London seemed to be taken up by this story of multiracial, multicultural love. The song "White girls love black boys and white boys love black girls" was on everyone's lips.

That night I lost my virginity to a white girl. After this rite of passage, I felt I needed a curry. I emerged into Shaftesbury Avenue and headed for an Indian restaurant, where I saw two police officers rush past me and grapple with a burly white man. The window panes of the restaurant were shattered and an Indian waiter in a bow tie held a towel to his badly cut forehead. Despite this, he could not stop the blood trickling down his white dress shirt, colouring it crimson. When I asked a passer-by, he said, "Some drunk had a fight with an Indian waiter. But then only drunks go to these curry houses. Dreadful."

I did not bother to investigate further and took refuge in Chinatown, which, by contrast, seemed a haven of calm and order. I later learnt Indian food was called "blotting paper" food, ideal for soaking up the many pints of beer a person had consumed.

In the summer at my Leicester factory, a worker warned me, "Whatever you do, don't bring your funny food here. It smells, and we cannot stand it." And a few months later, in my crummy Paddington hotel, the smile on the face of the white guest vanished as she discussed Indian food. She had just told me with a broad grin how she found the way Indians spoke English amusing because they could not pronounce *v* and made it into a *w*. But then, with a very stern face, she said, "I must tell you, we can't stand your food. It's the smell. It infects everything, and you can't get rid of it."

Forty-seven years later, in November 2016, a group of white English friends came for dinner at our home in West London. In front of them was *biryani*, *sag aloo*, mango chutney—both hot and mild—and *raita*. Pudding was *kulfi* and *gajar ka halwa*, Indian carrot cake. To complete this picture of acceptance of Indian food, it was cooked by a friend's son, also white. The guests enthused over the food, and we received letters saying how much they had enjoyed the meal.

The next day, my fitness trainer, a young man of thirty, told me how the previous night he suddenly felt the urge for curry and immediately after a training session rushed to his local Indian restaurant. When I told him there was a time when Indian food was detested in this country, he said, "I don't believe that. That must have been long before you and I were born."

* * *

When I went to my first Indian restaurants in this country, apart from the hideous décor—like a grandmother's discarded blankets—and the awful wine, Liebfraumilch and Black Nun, what struck me were the menus. They listed starters, main course, pudding. But such a three-course wonder is a western concept totally foreign to the subcontinent. In a restaurant in India the distinction made is between snacks and meals. There, every course is a distinct one and could be a main course. And during wedding feasts, or other occasions, the more courses you serve, the greater your glory. I once attended a marriage in Kolkata where a courses "race" took place between the families of the bride and the bridegroom. In Bengali weddings the bride has a reception followed by one by the bridegroom, two days later. At this wedding the bridegroom's side won as they served ninety-eight courses as opposed to the bride's eighty-six. They could not stop bragging.

Also, the western main course plus two veg is nonsensical in Indian terms. The vegetables (vegetarian meals apart), even in the most succulent of English meals, are an accompaniment only. They are meant not so much to excite the palate as to satisfy hunger, but translated into Indian terms this produces confusion. The result is you mix your *bhoona ghosh* with, say, *bhindi bhaji*, perhaps the most popular Indian vegetable in this country, and ruin the different tastes of both.

The order in Indian eating is not starter, main course, sweet, but a tandoori or tikka, which is seen as appetiser, followed by vegetables, usually eaten with some sort of Indian bread. This would be followed by fish and then meat. And if the latter has gravy, you can have rice with it. And while no western meal would serve more than one sweet dish, Indians like to serve several.

This emphasises how food plays a very different role in India compared to the west, which is particularly true in the way Indians and westerners celebrate important events. All cultures mark occasions, whether they be joyous or sad, with food and drink. A wedding could not be more different to a memorial service, but both see food and drink being served, albeit in very different styles.

But whereas in the west a joyous occasion is always marked by drink, often champagne, in India a joyous occasion is always marked by sweets. "*Mook misti koro*" "Make your mouth sweet," is a very popular Indian expression. While visitors to English homes are offered a drink, in Indian homes they are always offered a plate of sweets.

* * *

The other distinctive feature of Indian cuisine reflects the nature of migration from the subcontinent. Much of it was from what was then east Pakistan, now Bangladesh. As I have explained in earlier chapters, Bengali food is built round fish. But Bengali restaurateurs feared that, with these fishes being full of bones, the British, who use a knife and fork, as opposed to the Bengalis, who eat with their fingers, would find this impossible and be turned off Indian food. This has resulted in one of the most extraordinary features of the Bangladeshi restaurants in this country. They do not serve the food these Bangladeshis eat at home, but northern Indian cuisine, with which they were unfamiliar. But what my fellow Bengalis did do was make clever use of the Goans who had settled in this country.

During the Raj many Goans, unable to find work in Portuguese-held Goa, had been cooks on ships plying between India and the west. For them vindaloo was a staple dish. They were some of the first cooks in many of the Indian restaurants, and to cook vindaloo was natural. But whereas in Goa the vindaloo is a Goan pork dish, in Britain the enterprising Goan cooks saw no reason why it should be confined to one animal and introduced chicken and meat vindaloo. I am surprised our politicians, who never stop talking of British values, do not use the fact a regional pork dish of one country has become a national British dish where any animal meat can be used to advertise British tolerance and universality.

I must confess I have never taken to vindaloo, and in my first spell in this country struggled to find an Indian restaurant I liked. I much preferred Chinese takeaway to any Indian meal. It was only when I started working with my fellow brown articled clerks that I found a way out. They, like me, shunned Indian restaurants and searched for authentic Indian food. We found it in the most unexpected place, a restaurant run by the Indian High Commission. Not only did we enjoy the cuisine but, with almost everyone eating there being also brown, we felt we had a secret the majority of the white population was not privy to. But in 1973 two young Pakistani kids, brandishing replica guns, entered the High Commission through the restaurant and tried to hold it to ransom. They were demanding India free the 90,000 Pakistani prisoners of war they were holding following the victory over Pakistan in the 1971 war that liberated Bangladesh. The police, thinking they had real guns, shot dead the kids. The restaurant was considered a security risk and closed. We did find substitutes, but they were not quite as good. The compensation was we saved money because these restaurants took luncheon vouchers, unlike the High Commission restaurant.

* * *

All this changed in 1982 when I became the Indian food critic of *Time Out*. I had got talking *to* Jerome Burne and Don Atyeo, joint editors of *Time Out*, and when they enthused about Indian food, I told them the Indian food they ate in London was nothing like the Indian food in India. They were shocked and asked me to write an article which was titled "You can't Keep a Good Curry Down."[1] My appointment as *Time Out*'s Indian food critic followed.

For the next few years, I had wonderful Indian meals. Bangladeshi restaurant owners eager to please me would serve up food they ate at home, and nothing could be more delicious. Once when Chordi came to visit me, I took her to an Indian restaurant and told the owner I wanted authentic Bengali food. He did me proud. The meal we had was, said Chordi, the best ever Indian meal she had had. I noticed new owners emerging and the old flock-wallpaper restaurants serving Black Tower and Blue Nun, horribly sweet German wine, being replaced by the modern generation of Indian restaurants.

* * *

Even more remarkable was the growing confidence of the generation born here, who, unlike the first generation of immigrants, were willing to make television programmes that made the host community aware their society had changed—and changed for the better. In 1969 the most popular sitcom in Britain was *Curry and Chips*. Spike Milligan—who was born in India—blacked up to play an Indian waiter. His standard response to anything the customers said was "Goodness gracious me" in what Milligan thought was an Indian accent.

I first saw it in my grisly Paddington hotel. With me in the television room were a white couple who couldn't stop laughing. They turned to me and said, "Spike Milligan sounds better than the real Indians." Thirty years later, Sanjeev Bhaskar and Meera Syal would name their groundbreaking comic sitcom *Goodness Gracious Me*. One of its funniest skits was about affluent Indians in India going to an English restaurant on a Friday night. In a hilarious reversal of roles, they ask for the blandest English food on the menu while baiting the hapless English waiter. In the process, they brought out the humour that has always been part of the Indian subcontinent and showed that, like Jewish people, they were also capable of having marvellous fun at the expense of their own community.

I was made aware of the impact this had on the wider white community when the *Daily Mail* asked me to write an op-ed piece about the success of *Goodness Gracious Me*. I had written for the *Daily Mail* before, but these were generally articles discussing whether white people had been racist. My first article was about a judge who had been condemned as a racist for admonishing an immigrant from

Pakistan who, despite having lived here for decades, had not learnt to speak English. I defended the judge, saying to live in the land of Shakespeare and not speak English made no sense. But this piece on *Goodness Gracious Me* was different. It was celebrating how British society was showing its capacity to be inclusive through cuisine. And in the process had proved Nigella Lawson, the goddess of British cuisine, wrong.

In 1986, when we both worked for the *Sunday Times* and she was deputy literary editor, I had suggested an article on India. Nigella was not interested: "That's last year's fashion. This year it's Africa." The film *Out of Africa*, starring Meryl Streep, had just been released.

The hold of Indian curry on the English palate has proved to be no passing fad. It is now such an accepted part of this country that at a meeting of a board of which I'm a member the chief executive, trying to explain the strategy, made references to korma and pop-padom, as if by so whetting our appetite would make us approve the plans. Jill Tweedie would have been amazed. Indians haven't had to take to Lancashire hotpot to make vindaloo, a regional dish in India, a national dish in this country. But how much this suggests we now have a multicultural heart because we have a multicultural stomach is still open to debate.

43

THE GULF BETWEEN BLACKS AND WHITES
WHEN DEALING WITH A RACIST

In July 1995 *Wisden Cricket Monthly* had as its front cover an article by Robert Henderson entitled "Is it in the Blood?" The strapline ran "Robert Henderson examines—from a cricketing viewpoint—the sensitive matters of racism and national identity." Henderson wrote, "An Asian or a negro raised in England will, according to the liberal, feel exactly the same pride and identification with the place as a white man. The reality is somewhat different." The article concluded, "All the England players whom I would describe as foreigners may well be trying at a conscious level but is that desire to succeed instinctive, a matter of biology? There lies the heart of the matter."

Wisden Cricket Monthly was then the country's premier cricket magazine and under the same ownership as the *Wisden Cricketers Almanack*, the game's bible. The magazine's editor, David Frith, was widely regarded as a great cricket historian. The editorial board comprised, Michael Atherton, then England captain, former captain David Gower, OBE, Matthew Engel, editor of the *Wisden Almanack*; Patrick Eagar, the country's leading cricket photographer; and Frank Keating.

The article had a devastating impact on Devon Malcolm, who had grown up in Jamaica and was then England's leading fast bowler. The passage he found particularly offensive contained this line: "It is even possible that part of a coloured English-qualified player feels satisfaction (perhaps subconsciously) at seeing England humiliated because of post-imperial myths of oppression and exploitation."

In the previous summer's last Test at the Oval against South Africa Malcolm had produced one of the greatest bowling performances in the history of the game, taking 9 for 57 in 99 balls against

South Africa in the second innings, providing the platform for England to win and square the series.

Malcom persuaded his lawyer Naynesh Desai, who is of Indian heritage and knows how a person of colour can be made to feel an alien, to sue the magazine, and it settled. Desai calls it "a lucky break".

> In 1995, people didn't react to such articles as they would react now so that's why I say it was a lucky break that John Paul Getty was the owner. I got a message to say that Getty was very upset his magazine had run this sort of thing. Devon got this message as well so it must have come through the cricketing grapevine. Devon said to me "I'm being told that John Paul Getty is very embarrassed about this whole event and wants to draw a line under it." The minute the writ was issued Getty's lawyers said, "We want to settle." It went to and fro for four or five weeks and then they finally capitulated.

In the statement in Open Court the lawyer for *Wisden Cricket Magazines* agreed with Malcolm's lawyer that the "allegations were entirely untrue", "racist and highly offensive." In perhaps the most significant admission he also said, "The article was published in the belief that it was a contribution to a legitimate debate but they now accept that it ought not to have been published." Yet what is astonishing is that before this judgement, in the weeks following the publication of the article, many of the country's leading white writers and opinion-formers, despite disagreeing with Henderson, felt a debate about national identity based on what he had written was justified, even discussing whether unconscious factors affected the motivation of players.

Matthew Engel in the *Guardian* thought Henderson was talking "drivel" when he argued biology may play a part in determining whether a person wants to succeed when he is playing for England but was also complimentary about the article: "Much of it is carefully, even densely argued. He has written before on this subject and is clearly riveted, possibly obsessed by it." What he found strange was that Henderson had used "the word 'negro', which is now widely regarded as offensive outside far right-wing political circles".[1] The next day the *Guardian G2* supplement had a cover story with pictures of Chris Lewis, Phil DeFreitas and Devon Malcolm, all of them cricketers of colour, headlined "Please try harder: Race, loyalty and the big cricket test." On the inside page there was an article entitled "The man behind the row", about Henderson in which he denied his article was racist or that he was a racist.[2]

In his *Guardian* piece, John Ryle, having discussed Henderson's use of the word "negro" and what Englishness meant, made it clear:

> None of this is to suggest that Mr Henderson's article should have not been published. He is wrong for sure, about race, and the nature of dissent among non-white Britons. But he has some salient points to make about racial and cultural bias in cricketing countries other than England, which most commentators have ignored.[3]

Ian Jack, for the *Independent on Sunday*, decided to go around asking people what they felt constituted Englishness and concluded, "Nearly everybody had trouble with the idea of England." So elusive was Englishness that Jack found it almost impossible to devise a satisfactory test to prove a person was English.[4]

White reporters fanned out round the country to ask black sportsmen whether, despite their colour, they felt truly English.

Henderson's reference to the subconscious was taken up by Mike Brearley in the *Observer* on 9 July:

> I agree with [Robert] Henderson's view in his notorious article in *Wisden Cricket Monthly* that unconscious factors enter into motivation, and that a person's identifications may influence performance. No doubt his speculation about members of racially disadvantaged groups—that, even if they have been born and brought up in England, their commitment to the national side may have traces of ambivalence—could have some truth in it. However, his argument is over-speculative, partial and confused. As a result, it is also offensive.

Brearley concluded:

> Maybe DeFreitas, Malcolm and others do less well for England than they should; and maybe one cause is their lack of pride in England. But maybe not. *Maybe* [italicised in the original article]. The unconscious is a hybrid and above all elusive beast. Mr Henderson's attempt to expose it in others reveals more about his than theirs.[5]

* * *

Politicians also joined in the debate. Jeremy Corbyn wrote a letter to *Wisden Cricket Monthly* which Frith chose as the lead letter for the August issue. Corbyn agreed, "that on some levels there is a crisis in English identity as we struggle as a nation to come to terms with the legacy of colonialism and as we slowly learn that it is not OK to trash everyone because we think we are a superior race." Henderson's article, he thought, "just feeds into that 'Little Englander' mentality" and that there was "sickening racism" in the game. But his criticism of Henderson was very muted, and he was, in effect, willing to debate on race and identity with Henderson.[6] During the debate, Henderson was portrayed in the media as an unknown. He wasn't. Frith had published him before. Many of the cricket press had corresponded with him, including Engel. Nor was Henderson unknown to me.

* * *

Henderson's first letter to me had come two years before his *Wisden Cricket Monthly* piece, in August 1993, and it resulted from an article I had written on football at the beginning of the 1993–94 football season. Days before the season was due to start the Commission for Racial Equality joined the Professional Footballers Association to launch a campaign called "Let's Kick Racism Out of Football." Their aim was to put more black people in the stands— and in the boardrooms.

I wrote a think piece in the next day's *Daily Telegraph*, briefly mentioning my own problems at football grounds and highlighting that before blacks began to be targeted by football crowds, Jews had been singled out. My piece was meant to raise questions about how effective the campaign might prove given that the FA and the Premier League were convinced racism was no longer a problem in football and were very reluctant to back the campaign.

It was in response to this article that I received a thick envelope from Henderson which was more like a dissertation containing a two-page letter and three essays. The letter said nothing about racism in football. Instead Henderson accused me of totally ignoring how the English felt about racism and not understanding the resentment caused by non-white migration since the end of the

Second World War. The surprise, he argued, was the English hadn't reacted more violently. He claimed his work as an Inland Revenue investigator for several years in heavily populated immigrant areas of London had made him very aware that the attitudes of Asians towards blacks were like those of the Nazis, alleging that even educated Chinese made very derogatory references to blacks. But then he thought everyone was a racist and he admitted he was one.

The three essays very clearly set out his racist thinking. One was an eleven-page essay entitled "The Liberal Bigot", a title that summed up how Henderson loathed them. He claimed William Wilberforce was one of the early liberal bigots. Henderson defined racism as white men praising their own culture and defending their interests, something which liberal bigots saw as sacrilegious. Criticism of apartheid South Africa riled him and was for him evidence of how prejudiced liberal bigots were towards whites ruling blacks. But then liberal bigots were consumed by self-hatred. Henderson defined two kinds of liberal bigots, one with a bigger brain than the other.

There was also a seventeen-page document on "Men, Morality and International Order" in which he argued it was absurd to claim colour didn't matter. He warned that mixing either by race or culture would debase liberty and threaten the social order. He was in favour of ethnic cleansing despite all its horrors, as it would lead to peace. Nor did he join in the universal condemnation of ethnic cleansing in Bosnia by the Serbs.

The article articulated what is now called the white replacement theory: That non-whites who had higher birth rates would outnumber whites and whites would not have total control of any country in this world. Henderson's solution was mass repatriation of immigrants from Europe by paying them money to leave.

There was also a one-page note entitled "Koranic Quotations", which reproduced some of the most blood-curdling sayings from the Koran.

But all this was nothing compared to what happened when Henderson resurfaced in my life after nearly a three-year absence. Then I found myself subjected to the most disgustingly racist letters I have ever received. I felt almost irredeemably soiled and sullied by reading his correspondence. As I write this, having looked again at those letters, a chill runs through me.

* * *

Reading Henderson's article I immediately thought I had read some of this before. Going back to the essays he had send me in 1993 I was struck by how many of the themes he had articulated in them also figured in this article, albeit couched somewhat more carefully: criticism of the liberal elite for promoting multi-cultur-alism, the educationalists, politicians and the media removing any pride in being English and that "racial and cultural discrimination by coloured people has been the racism which dare not speak its name". And that apartheid South Africa could claim "good socio-logical reasons for the exclusion of non-whites, indeed perhaps better". I was astounded such an article had been published and covered the Wisden controversy at length. That winter Malcolm had what he called a "nightmare" tour of South Africa which saw him fall out with Ray Illingworth, the England manager. I reported on the ramifications of this story on 20 January 1996. Two days later came Henderson's first letter accompanied by replies he had received from various well-known individuals responding to let-ters Henderson had written to them over several years.

They included Jim Swanton, the legendary cricket correspondent of the *Daily Telegraph*, Peter Deeley his successor, Matthew Engel, Trevor Bailey and Tony Lewis. His correspondence with Tim Rice related to the Wisden article. Rice's letter called the Hit Racism for Six campaign "ridiculous".

Henderson sent me these letters because he wanted to show off that he was in touch with many well-known names. Henderson did not send me the letters he had written to these people, who were all white. But when it came to his correspondence with a black person he sent both her letter and his reply. The person was Diane Abbott, the Labour MP for Hackney North and Stoke Newington. Abbott, responding to Henderson's "Is it in the Blood?" article, had written to Henderson personally, saying the article had made her sad. She hadn't liked the words Henderson had used, which were no longer suitable when discussing race. Like a tutor dealing with a pupil who needed guidance, she urged Henderson to carry out more research, which she was sure would prove he was wrong, and she hoped her letter would make him think.

Henderson far from seeing himself as a pupil needing tutoring responded by accusing Abbott of not giving him the right of free expression. This was a favourite Henderson rant.

In a letter to me, Henderson mocked Abbott's style of writing likening it to that of a twelve year-old describing her holiday activities. He also claimed the fact Abbott got into Cambridge showed she had benefited from positive discrimination. But Abbott had got off lightly compared to what he had in store for me.

* * *

His five-page 22 January letter to me, which was copied to David Frith and Charles Moore, my editor at the *Daily Telegraph*, had a PS which described how he felt about my skin colour. In horribly graphic terms he conveyed the impression that because I was brown and my looks were unacceptable I resembled human excrement, with a smell that would be unpleasant. He thought he might be able to get Ian Hislop, editor of *Private Eye*, to include me in the "Lookalike" feature of his magazine and consoled me by saying that if I was struggling to earn a living, I could exhibit myself in a fair. Then, having converted Mihir into "Minor" and Bose into "Pose", he suggested a sign I could wear using these two names. In addition to that the sign would have a term which would identify me as human excrement.

In his letter on 11 February, again copied to Frith and Moore, he actually began the letter by addressing me using another well-known word which conveys human excrement. It went on to say I was still as fat, brown and smelling a lot more. He also said I was dishonest, a theme he elaborated in a letter he wrote the same day to Terry Venables then manager of the England football team, a copy of which he enclosed. Referring to the fact that I had written articles about Venables he set out to explain why I was deceitful. Henderson alleged that my journalistic colleagues when referring to me used a term which meant I was a turd and that was because I looked like one. This was, of course, fantasy. He also urged Venables to expose me.

On 8 March 1996 there followed the last letter I ever received from him, again copied to Frith and Moore. In this letter he again began by addressing me by a word that meant a turd. He alleged I wasn't liked by my fellow sports journalists, largely because of my personality. That I was egoistic, didn't have much brain and regarded myself highly. This letter ended with another scatological choice of words conveying my brown skin colour.

Henderson's letters to me were also threatening. In his first, 22 January letter, he said if I did not expose my white colleagues, who he alleged actually agreed with his views, he would expose me by using the ethnic press. They for this purpose, he proudly boasted, using a phrase coined by Lenin, would be his useful idiots. I wonder if the increasingly hostile and disgusting tone of his subsequent letters was due to my refusal to bow to his outrageous demands. In his letters to me Henderson gave his address and clearly felt he had no reason to hide his views from a man like me.

I had never received such letters in all my years of journalism and reading them made me feel how could a human being ever have such thoughts about another human? I felt very strongly I must respond to Henderson. Keith Perry was also outraged, feeling what Henderson had said was disgusting. But Arthur Wynn-Davies, the *Telegraph* lawyer, told both of us we shouldn't react. Keith was approached by Andrew Hutchinson, then assistant editor, and told not to do anything about the letters. Keith recalls, "I got the impression that they were wary of him." Neither Keith nor I were given any explanation why we should stay silent.

I have never believed the argument often trotted out—in my experience nearly always by white people—that racists are fools and idiots. Some may be, but many aren't. What was surprising is that very knowledgeable men, who aren't remotely racist, weren't alerted to the perils posed by Henderson when they saw the reference to biology in his article. Instead, many of them focussed on the language he used, in particular the word "negro" and did not try and examine where this so-called human being was really coming from.

I utterly reject Henderson's arguments that whites are secret racists which they hide when talking to non-whites. But what the Henderson saga showed is that there is a great contrast between how a black person and a white person, even if both of them are anti-racists, can see the issue of race.

In the *Observer*, Victor Ubogu, the Nigerian-born Bath and England prop who had come to England at the age of three, had said:

> There is no point in the magazine saying the article is part of a legitimate and interesting debate. It is crap, pure and simple ... It's almost not worth replying to this guy, for to do so lends a substance and status to his remarks they don't merit...Far better to ignore the bloke and let actions speak for themselves.[7]

But this was not how Donald Trelford, former editor of the *Observer*, who, like me, was a columnist in the *Daily Telegraph*, saw it. Henderson had tried to interest him on the theme of his Wisden Cricket Monthly piece, but Trelford wasn't tempted. The reason Trelford gave was very revealing: "But it wasn't the intolerance that stayed my pen but the fact that his arguments did not add up."[8] Trelford felt what Henderson "yearns to recover is a gritty Englishness", that he was "hopelessly out of touch with modern British society". Trelford, revealingly said, that this did not sound "so much like racism in the sense of colour prejudice" but admitted that his "coloured friends" disagreed with him. I knew and liked Trelford but on this issue I was with his "coloured friends".

Much is made of Voltaire's saying, "I detest what you write, but I would give my life to make it possible for you to continue to write." I cannot give my life to defend Henderson's right to write what he did about me. Sometimes the line must be drawn. On race the agenda cannot be set by a person like Henderson. I would like to think we have moved on from 1995.

44

SPEAKERS AND THE BBC

In a sense, working for the BBC was my Olympic dividend. Some-time after London won the Games, I had a chat with Roger Mosey, then head of BBC Sports, discussing why the BBC didn't have a sports editor. The BBC covered events on the field of play brilliantly, but what about the commercial world of sports? Roger agreed that with the Olympics coming to London they needed to appoint a sports editor. By then the coverage of sports news, business and politics had moved on dramatically since I had started the "Inside Sports" column in the *Daily Telegraph* in 1995. Five years later, Simon Stone was appointed the Press Association's first sports news correspondent; his bosses told him, "Do what Mihir Bose does." While this was flattering, it was also a challenge. Simon's brief showed that while I had for some years had the field virtually all to myself, all the other sports editors now felt the need to have a dedicated sports news correspondent. By the time London won the bid in 2005, they were snapping at my heels.

My appointment as the BBC's first sports editor didn't meet with universal approval. On social media there were comments that this was political correctness. I would like to think my permanent skin tan wasn't the reason. Charlie Sale in the *Daily Mail* wondered how the BBC could appoint a 60 year old. The BBC journalists union voiced their objection that an external candidate had been selected when there had been two internal ones. Whatever the reasons one thing is certain: unlike the official of All India Radio, Fran Unsworth, who was on the BBC board that choose me, didn't ask me for perfumes from Harrods. Such a thought wouldn't have occurred to her.

I had a producer Jon Buckley, a devoted Liverpool supporter, who had worked for Channel 4 with several distinguished correspondents. Like everyone at the BBC, he had a nickname, "Buckers". He quickly gave me a nickname, "Speakers", after the Bose music system speakers. The problem was getting on the air.

* * *

Although I had started in journalism as a broadcaster, worked for the BBC and presented programmes for different television stations, the BBC felt I needed to be tutored before I could be allowed into people's living rooms.

I had tutoring sessions with Julian Worricker, a broadcaster. Not long before I joined Julian had also tutored Robert Peston, who a year earlier had succeeded Jeff Randal as business editor. Julian would later tell me, "When I was told I was going to do a little bit of work with you I remember thinking to myself Mihir knows what he is doing in front of a microphone." Julian had often interviewed me on his shows and our sessions were like being back on one of his programs.

I also had sessions with a pronunciation coach, Elsbeth Morrison, and spent some time making sure I pronounced the name of Roman Abramovich, the then Chelsea owner, properly.

What was new was learning how to do the piece to camera. While it looked spontaneous, in reality it was written out and memorised, and then, after various takes, a final version was recorded for the package which was broadcast. For the first few weeks Buckers would take me up to the terrace of Television Centre and I would practise doing a piece to camera. This meant practising the walk, what I should do with my hands, and what I should look at as I spoke. Andrew Marr was believed to have set the standards for the most imaginative use of the hands during a piece to camera. I was advised to copy it. As for the walk, Buckers would often come up with some very imaginative ones and once, when I was broad-casting from Beijing in the lead-up to the 2008 Beijing Olympics, he got me to emerge from behind a group of people, recreating, as Caroline said, a scene from the children's book *Where's Wally?* Although I liked to think I avoided looking like a wally.

I did get the knack of it and Buckers and other producers kindly called me "one take Speakers" which was very flattering.

Then there was the "two-way", where the presenter asked questions I had to answer. An old BBC hand told me that many journalists recorded their answer on a tape machine and had the machine in their pocket and played it as they talked to the presenter. But I preferred to ad-lib, confident I could give a reasonable answer to the question.

However, despite my training going well there was the feeling that for my debut on the Ten O'Clock News I should have an exclusive. I finally made it thanks to Tessa Jowell, who, after I had taken her for lunch to the Reform Club, revealed to me the true and quite staggering cost of London 2012. It was considerably higher than what we had been told it would be when the bid was won. What's more, she said, the Treasury and Gordon Brown, who had reluctantly backed the bid, were proving really difficult and refusing to approve the budget. It was on deep background: I could use the information but, of course, not name her as the source.

But before I could go on air I had to get Peter Horrocks, then head of BBC News, to approve. Everybody at the BBC feared his intellect. I didn't find it difficult to convince Peter. The only problem surfaced as our meeting was coming to an end, when he said I should ring the press office of the Department for Culture, Media and Sport and ask them for their reaction. This surprised me and indicated a huge difference between the BBC and the written media. If this had been the *Daily Telegraph* or the *Sunday Times*, the editor would have instantly said "Go ahead." I told Peter ringing the press department would serve little purpose. First, they wouldn't know, and second, they would check with the minister and her officials, who would deny it. This is exactly what happened. The press office also started putting it around that the story wasn't true. But I knew it was and insisted we run it.

The advice I was given before I went on the set of the Ten O'Clock news was "Mihir, when you get on the air, make sure your tie is right. If not, viewers will wonder about your tie and by the time they start paying attention to what you are saying, you will have finished speaking."

My story was well received except by Neale Coleman, one of Ken Livingstone's closest advisers who I had got to know well. He sent me a message saying I was no better than a tabloid journalist who always got stories wrong. A few days later, Jowell confirmed in Parliament the figure I had given. Coleman apologised but suggested I must have got the story from a Treasury source who intended to make trouble. I couldn't let on who my source was.

My years in the written media had made very aware that competition within media organisations was always more intense than that between rival publications. At the *Sunday Times* we thought we were far superior to the *Times*—we also made a lot more money and at the *Daily Telegraph* the *Sunday Telegraph* wasn't highly regarded. Yet the rivalry between the *Ten O'Clock News* and the *Today* programme was on an entirely different level.

This became very evident to me when I was tipped off that George N. Gillett Jr, an American businessman, was about to complete his deal to buy Liverpool. My source said I could reveal that the deal was done before it was even announced on the Stock Exchange. I promised to do that on the Today programme. The various BBC outlets list the items that will be on the programme and as soon as it was circulated, Craig Oliver, then editor of the Ten O'Clock News, rang me to ask that I break the story on his programme the night before rather than on Today. I had to tell Craig I couldn't agree to his request.

Oliver had a reputation for not liking sport. What he didn't like were stories about what happened on the field of play. If there were stories that resonated beyond the field of play, he was always interested. Craig took some persuading about stories, but he agreed to two of mine which had nothing to do with sport.

In 2007 he agreed for me to go to India to do a piece on the sixtieth anniversary of India's independence. What convinced him was when I said I was a "Midnight's Child" as well. In 2008, when I told him this marked forty years since Enoch Powell's "Rivers of Blood" speech and I had arrived in this country a few months later, he again agreed to a piece on that subject.

Jeff had told me how the BBC had its own caste system. The Ten O'Clock News was the high-caste Brahmin of the news order and editors preferred to appear there, shunning the Six O'Clock News, which was considered of lower caste.

Buckers would often tell the producer of a programme we had a story only to be met with "It is not on the wires." This would prompt Buckers to say, "Yes, because Mihir has got a scoop." Even then it would take some work for the producer to be convinced.

One story I had no problem getting on the air was the Premier League's plan for a 39th game to be played abroad. I was intrigued when it was announced that there was to be a meeting of the clubs followed by a televised press conference. This suggested that something very significant was going to be decided. As the meeting was going on I rang Peter Kenyon. He whispered to me on his mobile phone details of the 39th game. I revealed the story much before the press conference which ignited a protest from fans even as the Premier League was holding its press conference. It gave the fans' campaign a momentum helping scupper it. This so angered the Premier League that for years they refused to give me interviews.

However, I could not get on air the story that Bob Woolmer, coach of the Pakistan cricket team, had not been murdered by illegal bookmakers. His death in a Kingston hotel after Pakistan had unexpectedly lost a World Cup match to Ireland had led the Jamaican police to announce that he had been strangled. The media speculated this was the work of illegal bookmakers who had lost out.

But after months of ridiculous theories as to how Woolmer was murdered a very well placed source told me that the Home Office pathologist Dr Nat Carey had concluded Woolmer was not strangled. But the BBC wanted someone to come on the record, which was impossible. The Woolmer saga also showed how some Commonwealth countries still relied on the mother country. The investigations started with a former Scotland Yard man, Mark Shields, then the Deputy Commissioner of Police in Jamaica, and ended at the Home Office.

There was one story I got on the air which I did not expect to and involved the use of Punjabi words which the Australians considered racist. An Australian cricketer, Andrew Symonds, who was of mixed race, accused an Indian player, Harbhajan Singh, of calling him "a monkey". Harbhajan claimed he had said in Punjabi "teri maa ki", which means mother fucker. Symonds, not knowing Punjabi, had interpreted "maa ki" as monkey. All this had been complicated by Indian prudery. At the initial hearing into this incident Harbhajan had not admitted to using these words. While Indians use a lot of swear words they are never used in formal company and never in front of respected elders. That hearing had taken place in the presence of Sachin Tendulkar and Harbhajan could not admit to having used such words in the presence of the great god of Indian cricket.

When I told my BBC bosses the story it took them some time at their morning news conference to understand the real meaning of "teri maa ki". When they did they allowed me to break the story.

Being on air did mean I was coming into people's living room and I suddenly found people stopping me in the street and treating me as if we knew each other. However, because the public fund the BBC some feel they own BBC staff. Once, when I was having a haircut at my local barber's, a customer who had just had his hair cut said, "Remember, we are paying for that haircut."

Despite all this, the BBC remains one of our great institutions, a testimony to the capacity of Britain to create organisations people the world over respect and admire. For me the BBC will always be summed up by Rajiv Gandhi only believing his mother, Indira, had been assassinated, when told it had been broadcast on the BBC by Sir Mark Tully. There is no other broadcast organisation in the world which generates such trust. It would be a pity if this unique British institution, the like of which doesn't exist anywhere else in our world, is damaged. It would be another example of the British not being able to appreciate their wonderful creative genius.

45

TEA WITH CHERIE BLAIR AND LONDON 2012

On the first floor of the Reform Club, sandwiched between the Smoking Room and the bridge room, is a room which is very special for me and my wife Caroline. This is where the general committee of the club meet and where I had wooed her, when we were both members of the general committee, making history by becoming the only Reform committee members ever to get married. This is where, a year after our marriage, in summer 2003 I had tea with Cherie Blair. It was not love but sports politics that was on the agenda. I was there to explain to the Prime Minister's wife what would be involved should she become leader of London's bid for the 2012 Olympics.

It had come about because David Welch asked me to spearhead a *Telegraph* campaign for London to bid for the 2012 Olympics. David, unlike other sports editors, did not care much for football; his passion was racing. A British bid seemed a hopeless cause. Birmingham, once and Manchester, twice, had failed miserably, convincing the British that the French-dominance of the IOC meant a British bid was always doomed, a sentiment Tony Blair shared.

Worse, as I was reporting every day, Britain seemed incapable of staging major world sporting events. The British had given back the 2005 World Athletics Championships because the Blair government could not afford to build the required facilities at Picketts Lock. Rebuilding Wembley Stadium had developed into a not very funny soap opera. The Millennium Dome was another drain on resources. The government had had to bail out the Manchester 2002 Commonwealth Games. Both on Wembley and Manchester 2002 I had built up excellent contacts. These provided me with quite a few scoops, though my revelations of the funding problems of Manchester had so upset Howard Bernstein, the chief executive of the Games, that he slammed down the phone on me.[1] Years later I would be told by one adviser to Tessa Jowell, the Secretary of State for Culture, Media and Sport that they dreaded my calls on Wembley and Manchester.

However, my calls must also have impressed Jowell who would often ask me whether I felt it was worthwhile Britain bidding for the Olympics. I told her that the Birmingham and Manchester bids had been viewed by the IOC as the British not being really serious about the Olympics. London would be different. Also, as one IOC member had put it to me, "The British government needs to show they want the Games." The IOC, I told Tessa, behaved as if it was a sporting nation state and to succeed the British would have to come to terms with that.

The problem was a sceptical Treasury. The Chancellor Gordon Brown, who both knew and loved football, had set his heart on getting the World Cup back to this country. He had no interest in the Olympics and made it clear he would not give any money for an Olympic bid. It was when I told David Welch this that he decided that one way to push the government would be to start a campaign for a London bid.

It was launched in October 2002. Normally such campaigns get a reaction from the rest of the media. This time the only reaction was from the *Daily Mirror* which opposed it. Privately many of the journalists dismissed it as another illustration of a bizarre Welch obsession with the Olympics. This was after all the editor who not only sent a large team to the 2000 Sydney Olympics but based himself in Sydney during the Games.

A few weeks later I was in Mexico City for an IOC meeting and decided to poll members on whether London should bid. My poll found that they all supported the idea. The session also showed that the British Olympic Association (BOA) was willing to use their best weapon, their chairman the Princess Royal, to nudge the government.

She had been an IOC member for sixteen years but while she dutifully attended every session, she said little or nothing, did not sit on the various IOC commissions and, unlike other European royals, shied away from making any comments at IOC meetings, remaining silent even during the corruption crisis. I had noticed that when IOC members broke for lunch she did not mingle with her fellow members but ate on her own with her security team. One IOC member had told me with real sorrow in his voice, "Your Princess never talks to her fellow members. Perhaps she does not feel we are good enough to have a conversation with". Another prominent IOC member had told me, "If she did not turn up we would not miss her."

But now she publicly backed London bidding and agreed that London was the only British city that would find favour with her fellow IOC members. She did though sharply dismiss any idea that Prince William could lead the bid team. "Has somebody suggested that? I would suggest he did not bother." However, when I asked her whether she would be happy lobbying her fellow members she looked hard at me and said, "Lobbying is not a word that suits me somehow. But talking is easily done. My role will be to keep up with what is going on and stay close to developments."

However, despite this unprecedented Royal approval, and an opinion poll showing that 75 per cent were in favour of a bid, there was much scepticism among MPs. Over the next few months, I wrote a series of articles on how the government, by refusing to come to a decision, was giving a head start to Paris, New York and other cities which had had already entered the 2012 race. I was told of Cabinet meetings where Jowell would make a presentation but there would be no decision. To be fair Blair had other things on his mind having decided in March 2003 to join America's invasion of Iraq.

Then quite suddenly it all came together in the Downing Street garden. Blair would later tell me he told Jowell:

> What happens if we lose, we're going to get slaughtered. I don't want to be humiliated by the French. She said—and she knew exactly how to put this to me, "You know this is not the Tony Blair I know, cautious and timid." So, I said, "Oh all right, let's give it a go then."[2]

I soon learnt that Jowell's good friend, Cherie Blair, who had encouraged her husband to back the bid, wanted to head the London bid. When I told David this he decided that the ideal combination would be a joint leadership team of Seb Coe and Cherie Blair. Coe was a columnist for the *Daily Telegraph*, so all that remained was to get Cherie on board.

* * *

I approached Michael Beloff, the QC who shared Cherie Blair's barristers' chambers and was a fellow member of the Reform. He agreed to arrange a meeting with Cherie which is how Cherie, David, Beloff and I were in my favourite committee room that summer afternoon.

I explained to Cherie that bidding meant hanging around the hotel lobbies of the world cosying up to fairly old, invariably male, members of the International Olympic Committee. That for all the grandiose talk of Olympic members that hosting the Games went far beyond sport and would change the country, the decision to choose the city was more like an election of the committee members of a local golf club. And like the members of a golf club the members of the IOC, ranging from royalty to associates of former dictators, saw the Games as their personal property of which they were fiercely protective. They regarded bid leaders much like medieval kings did emissaries of foreign countries, except these sporting monarchs would not be satisfied with mere trinkets.

None of this daunted Cherie Blair and it soon became clear that she was keen to lead the bid. Our meeting ended with her saying, "Of course he will have to be consulted." She did not have to specify who he was. The meeting was deep background which meant I could write about her interest in the bid without giving any details as to how I knew about it. This was followed by other exclusives about how the British Olympic Association welcomed her interest in the bid and that she was being interviewed by headhunters Saxon Bamoflyde.

David was delighted and so eager for Cherie Blair to head the bid that sometimes I got the impression he had fallen for her. So, when the head-hunters decided that she did not "have all the skills required to be considered as a bid leader" David could not hide his disappointment. I would later hear that her skills were not the only factor. The security services were worried about ensuring the safety of the Prime Minister's wife as she went round hotel lobbies canvassing IOC members.

To make matters worse for David, Seb Coe was also rejected. He did not stand a chance. I had reported on 9 May 2003 that the Cabinet sub-committee Misc 12 was now chaired by John Prescott, who had taken over from Jack Straw. While Straw might have accepted Coe, for Prescott Coe was ruled out having been a former Conservative MP. I had also reported that the head-hunters were looking at various other candidates who, much to my surprise, included Barbara Cassani, the American businesswoman who had masterminded Go, British Airways' low-cost airline. Ken Livingstone, the London Mayor, despite his reputation as the symbol of the hard left, was impressed with her business skills and she got the job. David did get part of his dream team, although he had to wait a year when, after London had come a poor third to Paris and Madrid in the IOC's evaluation of the cities, Cassani resigned. Coe was now the inevitable choice to take over.

That Coe, with his great Olympic record, would strike an instant rapport with IOC members was not a surprise. What surprised me was that on becoming leader Coe began to play the multi-racial card. He told me how his mother had an Indian background. Once, while other bid members looked under pressure, he calmy sipping jasmine tea told me, "I am coping with the pressure. Maybe it is my Indian heritage". This was a reference to his mother who had recently died. He also went to Delhi and spoke at the Asian Olympic Council emphasising his Asian links. It was clear that the traditional British bidding style of cosying up only to white Australians, Canadians and New Zealanders had been ditched. I was to see the results of this a year later when, in July 2005, the IOC met in Singapore to decide who would stage the 2012 Olympics.

* * *

The year since Coe took over had not been all plain sailing for London 2012 with the Royals in particular not providing the support for the bid that was considered crucial. On 14 January 2005 I wrote a piece in the *Telegraph* saying that Princess Anne was not doing anything to lobby her fellow IOC members. One of them told me, "You know how the Princess Royal could help this bid? All she had to say to some of the IOC members, my mother has a house in central London, why don't you come and have tea there". But no such invitation to her mother's home came. At this stage the Royals were not doing well. Prince Harry had sported a Swastika. Worse still, the Queen was reported to have said that Paris would win the race to stage the 2012 Olympics. A Palace spokesman had tried to distance the Queen from the bid saying, "We cannot say specifically that the Queen supports the bid because there is a political element to it". I pointed out that as constitutional monarch the Queen had to be careful. The Spanish King had actively campaigned for Madrid. His Greek-born wife Sophie had spent much of the 2004 Athens Olympics virtually camped in the Hilton, the IOC's hotel, ceaselessly buttonholing IOC members. The British royal family could not be expected to do that. However, unlike the Manchester and Birmingham bids no other Commonwealth cities were in the race. "Then", I wrote, "it would not have been right for the Queen to go out to bat for a British city. But now there is nothing to stop her— or her daughter—from doing so."

Not only did the Palace ignore my advice but in the months that followed the London bid organisers also made mistakes and when I interviewed Juan Antonio Samaranch, despite the fact that his favourite son Coe led the London bid, he told me Paris would prevail.

But then London played its Tony Blair card, and the tide began to turn. A few weeks before the vote I broke the story that both Tony and Cherie Blair had written to IOC members asking to meet them when they were in Singapore. It seemed that the husband-and-wife team had divided up IOC members between them. Tony Blair was making IOC members feel they were just as important as the world leaders he always met. The effect was dramatic.

I realised this when a senior European member of the IOC, who was widely respected and well connected told me, "I was surprised to receive this letter and it shows how much the British Prime Minister and his wife care about the bid". I had marked him down as voting for Paris but he now felt that not only was the race too close to call, but that London could prevail.

The vote in Singapore was on the eve of the G8 summit in Gleneagles which Blair, as host, had to preside over. He and his advisers decided on a clever wheeze: go to Singapore for a few days before the vote, meet IOC members individually and then leave just before the vote pleading high matters of state.

* * *

Talking to IOC members it was clear to me that New York and Moscow did not stand a chance. They were waging a private battle to make sure they were not the first city to be eliminated. The key city was Madrid. Madrid was being heavily promoted by Samaranch and, while he was no longer President, most of those who would vote had become members while he was President and revered him. At one session I had heard one IOC member describe him as a father. Should it be a fight between Madrid and London Samaranch could take Madrid over the line. To win, London had to avoid Madrid in the final.

A few days after I broke the Blair letter story Jowell asked what I thought would happen. I told her that Madrid was back in the race and could not be ruled out. She told me that until about a month ago the London bid team had thought apart from Paris, New York might threaten London's chances. Now they thought Madrid would pose a real challenge. If London got in the final with Paris than the race would be decided on how the Madrid votes were divided between the two. If the split worked in London's favour, London could win.

I rang Graham Sharp of William Hill and put £100 on London at 7–2. I was confident this would not be a losing bet. However, a few days later I was consumed by the fear that I might not live to see another day, let alone make money from William Hill.

* * *

I could not have felt more secure on that glorious sunny afternoon that June as I emerged from my home in West London to drive to Harrow to pick up my daughter. As I approached my car parked just round the corner from my house I noticed a young, well built, quite handsome black man standing on the other side of the road. I paid no attention having other things on my mind. I was debating which route to take. But my greatest fear was that Caroline would discover I'd picked up a piece of rye bread as I left the house. She has always warned me about snacking and as we both work from home I was worried she might see me from her office window.

I got into the car but could not drive away immediately. I had parked the car under a tree, the windscreen was filthy, and I switched on the windscreen washers to give it a clean. As I did so, I noticed the man walk past me on the passenger side. I had a feeling that all was not well, so I quickly started the car. Suddenly, he was standing by the driver's door, opening it and shouting: "Get out." As I pulled at the door he gripped my arm and shouted. "Do you want to die?". He repeated the words again, motioning with his other hand as if he was carrying a gun or a knife.

Since my silent answer to his question was no, I did not want to die, and certainly not at that moment in a suburban side street, I stopped resisting and was pulled out of my car.

My first dread, as the man climbed into the driver's seat, was that he would try to run me over. I hurried to the pavement and watched as he tried to reverse the car. Then after a few jerks and a crashing of gears, he drove off. It felt rather strange, being left in the quiet little street still bathed in wonderful sunshine.

I ran—half stumbled—home but once I had closed the front door I felt very calm. I walked up to my wife's office saying, "You won't believe what happened".

The next few minutes passed in a daze. My wife sat me down, dialled 999 and helped me find my car registration number. The police swiftly circulated a description and soon we were told there had been several sightings. By this time two plain-clothes police-men had arrived. But even as I told my victim's story I felt a sense of shame that I had not fought my attacker, the same feelings I had experienced all those years ago when Chelsea fans had set upon me. The police reassured me I was not a coward but had done the right thing.

As they drove us to the station to take my statement, one of them heard on his walkie-talkie that my car had been found. It was a write-off. The robber had cuts and bruises and was on his way to hospital where he was kept under arrest. Sarah Sands, editor of the *Sunday Telegraph*, showing characteristic sympathy, asked me to write a piece about my experience. Ma would say when a major calamity had been averted, "*Farah par howcha*". What she meant was a minor mishap had prevented a much greater tragedy. I had lost the car but saved myself from being killed or badly hurt. I felt comforted by that thought as I flew to Singapore.

* * *

In Singapore I had barely entered the foyer of the IOC hotel when I realised how different this Coe-led London Olympic bid was to the Tony Banks World Cup one. Austin Sealey, the IOC member for Barbados, looked at me and said with a laugh, "What you guys doing? You are going to win". Sealey was a great Anglophile, but this was no joke. As he told me of how London had campaigned I began to think that this time William Hill would send me a cheque.

London was certainly doing things differently. At the Raffles City Convention Centre, a glitzier version of Brent Cross and the first shopping centre to host a session of the IOC—two huge hotel towers that made the place look like a multi-layered doughnut—there was no sign of London. They were secreted away at a holiday resort, planning what Seb Coe had called "the narrative of the bid". For the other bid cities camping out in the foyer of the convention centre, London's absence provoked mirth and one French source asked me sarcastically, "So have you been to your English hideout? Are they going to storm out of it and ambush us French?" Even when the London bid team, led by Coe and, soon after, Tony Blair arrived at the Raffles Convention Centre the French seemed to think it was all a bit of a media blitz.

Blair had arrived in Singapore with his reputation in Britain at a historic low because of the Iraq war. But not for the first time it turned out a leader shunned at home glows with magic when abroad. A security cordon had been thrown round the shopping centre's lifts as word spread of his arrival. I had come to the foyer to buy a coffee but where the coffee stall normally stood there were now men in suits with bulging pockets. A crowd, many of them clutching shopping bags, quickly gathered. While Livingstone, in blue shorts and clutching a shopping bag as if he was heading for the beach did not attract any attention, Blair brought shoppers and shopkeepers to a standstill. I found myself behind Claire and Vivian, two Qantas air hostesses, Jenny from Idaho and an elderly Chinese woman.

As we waited for Blair, Claire got her camera ready, while Jenny kept saying, "Do you know Idaho, that is where potatoes come from". The Chinese woman clutched an autograph book and put her fingers to her lips every time I asked her whether she admired Blair as if this were a state secret.

As the security team talked on their mobiles Blair emerged from the lift to come within touching distance of Claire and Jenny offering the smile that had once so dazzled the British public. The effect was immediate. The shoppers burst into applause and the Chinese woman was so overawed that she dropped her autograph book. Claire, however, kept her nerve and managed to get a picture "I don't fancy him", she insisted, "You would have to be desperate to fancy a politician, but he is the British Prime Minister, and I got a great picture" she added skipping away to resume her shopping. Watching Blair at work a French source had told me, "I didn't think he was running for office in Singapore". The tone was mocking but Blair was soon at work undermining the French.

* * *

This he did by meeting around sixty of the IOC members in his hotel room. The French complained how Blair talking to these IOC members in his hotel suite was blocking up elevators in the hotel. But when I met some of them, they were in raptures: "Your British Prime Minister knew my name", laying great emphasis on British. Blair was well briefed on their record in the Olympic sport they had excelled in and used this to flatter them. I was struck by the fact that he did not ask any of them to vote for London instead told them of London's legacy plans and underlined the government's commitment to the bid. One IOC member I spoke to immediately after his meeting with Blair told me, "I will not tell you whether I shall vote for London or not. But let me tell you that your Prime Minister is very impressive."

Such was the Blair effect that an IOC member who had returned from a meeting with him told me, "London will win by three votes.

I have never seen anything like this by the English". He was also impressed that the Princess Royal was at last acknowledging the existence of her fellow IOC members. "Even Her Royal Highness is campaigning and talking to IOC members."

On the day of the vote, I wrote in the *Daily Telegraph* that Madrid held the key to London glory. The French had behaved like a football team 1–0 ahead with ten minutes to play. London had come to Singapore as underdogs but:

> If London can get a good majority of Madrid votes it will squeeze past Paris. The theory has been that London cannot do that because Madrid's mainly Latin and South American voters are more likely to feel at home with Paris. However, judging by the mood in the Madrid camp there's a real anger with what is considered a French bias in the IOC, particularly in the way the evaluation report was glowing about Paris but nit picking about Madrid. This may induce some of the Madrid voters to swing to London. That should be enough to give London a small winning margin. However, if they stick to their natural inclination and go for Paris then the French capital could win.

My feeling that London could win was bolstered when I spoke to an IOC member from the Indian sub-continent. He pulled me to one side and said in a conspiratorial tone, "The game is on. London could win." Talking to IOC members and drawing up a list of how they might vote I worked out London could win by three votes.

The presentation by the cities showed how adaptable the English could be. The French had glamour with Catherine Deneuve featured. London had decided they would not try and have Helen Mirren to match her but Coe speaking of how choosing London would send a clear message to the young of the world of what sport can do. Blair was on video talking in French. Kai Holm, the member from Denmark could not hide his surprise as he told me, "Today the French behaved like the English and were all buttoned up, the English showed their passion and won".

After the presentations the IOC members had a break before they voted. I was waiting outside and I saw one member I knew walking to the lavatory. I joined him and as we stood at the urinals he told me, "The French are so arrogant. It will be a London-

Madrid final." Then I met the IOC member who had been so impressed with the Blair letter and when I pressed him on the vote he said, "London could win".

I immediately rang William Hill and put another £250 on London, hoping Madrid would not reach the final round of voting. My concern was that if it did the Spanish capital would beat London and this was also the fear of Simon Clegg, the chief executive of the British Olympics Association. The first two cities to fall were no surprise, Moscow then New York. The crucial round was the third. Would Madrid eliminate Paris? It was close, one IOC member failed to vote, and we had the final I and the London team wanted: a straight fight with Paris.

We had to wait for an hour after the vote to find out how it had gone to fit in with television presentations organised for the results announcement. During this wait several members of the London team went through a rollercoaster of emotions. No one more so than David Beckham. As he walked into the Raffles Ballroom for the announcement he saw that the Paris team was arranged to the right of IOC President Jacques Rogge. They were all linked together in the way football teams are before a penalty shootout. All the photographers were on their side as if they expected Rogge to open the envelope and say, "The host city for 2012 is Paris".

There was only one photographer on the side of the London team. Beckham turned to Clegg and asked, "Is this normal?" and Clegg, who until then was sure London had won, began to feel that perhaps London had lost.

I was on a gantry outside the Ballroom broadcasting to Sky when Rogge, who had told me how he loved cricket, "fascinating game, what statistics", opened the envelope and said, "The host city for 2012 is London."

After the vote, while much was made of Beckham's presence, I was sure it was Blair who had turned the tide. He had timed his visit to Singapore just right. Jacques Chirac, the French President, had come too late and met no one, to the annoyance of many IOC members. Hilary Clinton had looked very wooden and had kept the press waiting for an hour before emerging from her aircraft. While the Americans had Muhammad Ali, he no longer had the aura of being the greatest. The Blair effect was very clear. Sir Steve Redgrave, chairman of the IOC Athletes' Commission said, "The one single factor was the Prime Minister being here." Dick Pound, the IOC member from Canada, and chairman of the World Anti-Doping agency, was certain, "I think he made the difference." Irish IOC member Patrick Hickey was even more precise. "This is down to Tony Blair. If he hadn't come here I'd say six to eight votes would have been lost. The four votes that were in the final round were definitely down to him."

The *Daily Telegraph* headlined my piece, "Blair the key to how London won Olympic race."[3] Cherie may not have led the bid but her husband had shown how British soft power can be used, something post-imperial Britain does not always appreciate.

I returned home to find a cheque from William Hill waiting for me but I had got one thing wrong. London had not won by three votes but by four.

46

NELSON MANDELA DEFINES WHAT
FREEDOM MEANS

My meeting with Nelson Mandela came about because of four very different men, two British and two South Africans, and occurred as a result of an event that I loathed.

For me the struggle against apartheid had always been one of the great moral issues of our times. I could not understand how sports fans, while proclaiming they were anti-racist, could not see that the world could not play sport with the apartheid regime. I was often the main speaker opposing motions at cricket societies, debates calling for the boycott to be lifted. During such debates those in favour of lifting the boycott would recycle the lies of the white regime that changes would come faster if there was no boycott.

In the summer of 1989, Ali Bacher, the captain of the last white cricket team to play international cricket, and running the white cricket body, announced that sixteen English cricketers would play in a rebel tour in his country. I rang Dominic Lawson, deputy editor of the *Spectator*, suggesting an article. In my piece I made it clear that I saw Bacher's rebel tour as a threat to organised sport. Despite the tone of the article being against the line of the paper, Dominic ran the piece exactly as I had written it but suggested that in future when writing against the grain of the paper I should not take such a tough line. What I could not have anticipated was the unexpected fallout from its publication.

Nick Gordon, then editor of You, the *Mail on Sunday* magazine, was so impressed he suggested I fly out to South Africa to interview Bacher. Bacher was due in London and we met for lunch at a hotel in Surrey. He thought Gordon was editor of the *Spectator* and was very chuffed such a prestigious magazine wanted to interview him.

Bacher would reveal years later that money for these rebel tours came from South African taxpayers. It was to make the world believe that apartheid South Africa was a perfectly normal place. Bacher encouraged me to visit South Africa, promising free access.

* * *

Mandela was still in Robben Island and most white South Africans did not even know what he looked like. No photograph of him had been permitted in the South African media since he was imprisoned in 1963. Even Bacher's wife Shira had never seen a picture of Mandela. But then the white world knew nothing about the non-white world as I discovered on my first Saturday night in Johannesburg.

I had returned to my hotel clutching the early edition of the *Sunday Times* of South Africa. A young black boy was sitting on the pavement just outside the entrance selling papers. As he saw me he said, "Indian" and thrust a copy of the *Sunday Times* at me. I was about to say I had a copy when I saw a front page that looked very different and I though this might be a later edition. When I compared the two edtions I discovered that the first copy of the *Sunday Times* which I had picked up in the white area of Johannesburg was for white people. The copy the black boy had given me was an Indian edition where the white edition was wrapped round a supplement containing a whole sheaf of news about Indians. It was only distributed in the Indian areas. The Indians read what the whites did but the whites were spared any Indian news.

A couple of years later this was to result in one of the most bizarre incidents I have ever seen in a press box. The Indian cricket team was making its first ever tour of South Africa, sixty years after India had made its Test debut. On the Sunday of the first Test in Durban the *Sunday Times* ran a feature on the Indian bowler Manoj Prabhakar having become a sex symbol in South Africa. The Indian journalists were much amused by the article. The *Daily Mail* reporter was eager to read it. But he could not find it in his edition and was puzzled. I explained to him that the Prabhakar story was only in the Indian edition since it was only Indians who found him sexy, there was no way the whites could. The white edition that the

Mail man had did not have the article. I went up to him, "You are missing out because you are white. Here, have my Indian edition."

* * *

Since that first to South Africa I had got to know and like Ali Bacher. In 1991, following Mandela's release, South Africa finally had its first truly non-racial cricket body and Bacher decided to have a celebratory dinner. He wanted the great and good of world cricket to be there, but he knew nobody from India and turned to me for help, asking for the names of Indians to invite to the black-tie event in Sandton, the exclusive white suburb in Johannesburg.

I immediately suggested Sunil Gavaskar. I also gave Bacher names of some prominent Indian cricket journalists. It was Gavaskar's presence that led to the Mandela visit.

Bacher had also invited Sir Gary Sobers. Bacher took both Sobers and Gavaskar to the township and, at my suggestion, got Gary to bowl to Sunil. The picture made the headlines in the South African media the next day. Sobers also met Mandela. This made Imtiaz Patel, a South African proud of his Indian origins who worked for Bacher, determined that Mandela should also receive a great Indian cricketer. The result was that I, on the Sunday morning following the dinner, tagged along with Gavaskar to Mandela's home. It was a few months since his release and he still lived in Soweto in, the palatial home that Winnie Mandela had built while Mandela was in prison. Hidden behind high walls it looked like a house from the white suburbs of Johannesburg transplanted to the township.

We were led up a small flight of stairs to a room dominated by a huge oil painting of Robert Mugabe on one wall. In the middle was a long V shaped table filled with the presents and gifts Mandela had acquired from his various foreign travels since his release. But what looked like the office of a company chief executive, turned into a throne room when Mandela arrived, dressed in a tie and a jumper. His associates, who had been milling round in the room, withdrew to a distance whispering softly, "Madiba", father, the term invariably used to refer to him. As he began talking it became obvious that he quite liked using the royal we, reflecting his own royal roots.

Mandela was very aware of how sport could be used to usher in the rainbow nation telling us, "De Klerk [President of white South

Africa] has made it clear in our conversations 'Look if you would make it possible for All-Blacks to come here, then we can smash the system.'"

Since his release he had travelled the world and wherever he went cricket came up. Bob Hawke, the Australian Premier, had mentioned it, and when he stopped over in London to meet John Major, one of the first issues the British Prime Minister raised was whether Mandela would allow the South Africans back into cricket. "You know," said Mandela, "Mr Major seemed more interested in cricket than the issues." As he recounted the story he was overcome with laughter.

Mandela had never played cricket but he told us about watching the Australians playing a Test match in Durban in January 1950. Like all black spectators he had to watch behind cages which kept them separate from the whites. Mandela and his fellow black South Africans wanted Australia to win and were overjoyed that a wonderful innings by Neil Harvey led the visitors to victory. When I asked him whether he congratulated Harvey, perhaps asked for his autograph, Mandela tensed up and said, "No, no we could not do that. We could not approach him. Had we tried, we would have been thrown out."

Six years later, the Australians had toured India. At Mumbai's Brabourne Stadium Harvey put to the sword the bowling of my boyhood hero, Subash Gupte, one of the finest leg spinners in the history of cricket. But, while he broke my heart—no young boy likes to see his hero humiliated—I could not help but admire Harvey's batting. Where my experience differed from that of Mandela was nobody told me where to sit and I would have had no problems approaching Harvey for his autograph.

I was born free, thanks to the previous generations of Indians who had sacrificed so much to win our freedom. I, a nine-year old boy, could show my feelings when a man who was thirty years old could not. Mandela and his fellow non-whites had to wait another thirty-eight years before they were at liberty to do what comes naturally to all sporting fans. While, in the wider scheme of things, these are simple sporting emotions they sum up what freedom meant; that morning in Soweto Mandela brought that home to me.

47

UPSETTING THE CHURCHILL LOBBY

In the autumn of 2016, over lunch with Paul Lay, then editor of *History Today* I mentioned how, contrary to popular misconception, the British Raj didn't hate the Muslims but the Hindus, and that Churchill had wanted to destroy them. I had written for Lay often and had got on well with him. I had been a guest of his at the Savile, his London club; he had lunched with me at the Reform, and he commissioned me to write a piece.

My article began by quoting from the diaries of Churchill's Downing Street secretary John Colville about what Churchill had said in February 1945, on his return from Yalta, over dinner with Colville and Air Chief Marshall Sir Arthur Harris. "The PM said the Hindus were a foul race 'protected by their mere pullulation from the doom that is their due' and he wished Bert Harris could send some of his surplus bombers to destroy them."[1]

I went on to point out this wasn't an isolated anti-Hindu view. Three years earlier Churchill had told Ivan Mikhailovich Maisky, the Soviet ambassador in London, that, should the British be forced to leave India:

Eventually, the Moslems will become master, because they are warriors, while the Hindus are windbags. Yes, windbags! Oh, of course, when it comes to fine speeches, skilfully balanced resolutions and legalistic castles in the air, the Hindus are real experts! They're in their element! When it comes to business, when something must be decided on quickly, implemented, executed—here the Hindus say "pass". Here they immediately reveal their internal flabbiness.[2]

Churchill wasn't the only one I quoted. The article also gave examples of British historians and writers expressing their hatred for the

Hindus and admiration of the Muslims going back to the early years of the nineteenth century.

Soon after the article was published in the December 2016 issue of *History Today*, Paul Lay rang me to say he had received an email from the historian Andrew Roberts which contained a letter about my article signed by Roberts and eleven others, including well-known historians and members of the Churchill family. Roberts, in his email to Lay, bragged he had organised the letter in an hour and hoped Lay would be impressed. The twelve could have been fourteen. Roberts had also tried to contact Edwina Sandys and Professor Warren Kimball, but as they were in the States, he hadn't heard from them.

The letter lodged a "protest" about my statement that Churchill wanted to destroy Hinduism. Its signatories brushed aside Churchill's remark to Colville and Harris as "one admittedly intemperate remark reportedly made by Churchill" which couldn't be the basis of what they described as "a completely unrecognizable theory that he wanted to 'destroy' a religion followed by hundreds of millions of people, several million of whom were serving as volunteers in the armed forces of the Crown at the time." The letter concluded by wondering how "as respected a journal as *History Today* should stoop to claiming that Churchill ever wanted to 'destroy' the majority population of a country that was the jewel in the crown of an Empire to which he was so dedicated."

However, this was no drunken remark. The evening in question takes up two pages not only Colville's diaries but also of Martin Gilbert's official biography of Churchill, and, Hindus apart, Churchill was very perceptive about Britain's position in the post-war world: "We would be weak, we should have no money and no strength and we should lie between the two great powers of the USA and the USSR."

What made the letter all the more curious was how Roberts and his group dealt with Beverley Nichols, author of *Verdict on India*, a book which had much impressed Churchill for its portrayal of Hindus. Colville had given Churchill the book before his trip to Yalta. Churchill read it while aboard *HMS Orion*. On his return from Yalta, when Colville asked him about the Nichols book, Churchill said he had read the book "with great interest" and this had led to his remarks of Hindus being a foul race.

Given Churchill's praise for Nichols' portrayal of Hindus, I had quoted a couple of passages from the book to illustrate how Nichols saw the Hindus. Hindu art, Hindu music, he wrote, was "to most Europeans ... not only quite incomprehensible but actively repulsive".[3] Gandhi, then in a British jail, was featured in a chapter entitled "Heil Hindu" and portrayed as a fascist, and Hindus were described as worse than the Nazis:

> Congress is the only 100 per cent, full blooded, uncompromising example of undiluted Fascism in the modern world ... Just as every Nazi is a superman, so every Brahmin is "Bhudeva", which means "God on earth". And Congress is, of course, a predominantly Brahmin organisation. Secondly it is Fascist in practice. It is a Gandhi dictatorship ... The German "Heil Hitler" has a striking equivalent in the Indian Gandhiji ... The resemblances between Gandhi and Hitler are, of course, legion.[4]

Nichols also drew a damning contrast between the two great symbols of Christianity and Hinduism:

> The symbol of Christianity is the figure of our Lord on the cross— the figure of the perfect Man, who, even if we deny him divinity, has given the world its most beautiful legend and its most exalted code of conduct. The symbol of Hinduism—or rather one of the most widely revered of its many symbols—is the figure of Ganesh, half man and half elephant.

Then, describing his visit to a Ganesh temple, he wrote:

> The sun shone on a tiny building of crumbling brick, and inside this building the monster squatted, awaiting us. It is carved from a single hulk of black, shining stone, and his trunk and his misshapen limbs contorted like angry serpents. The forgotten sculptor who had evoked this creature from the rock, so many centuries ago, was a genius but he was—I felt—an evil genius, a man possessed. For this Ganesh was imbued with a malevolent life; in the fading light his limbs seem to twitch, as though impelled by ancient lusts. He could escape if he wanted; a flick of that sinuous trunk, a gesture of those twisted arms, and the walls would crumble, and he would walk abroad in the darkness. Christ and His cross, giving to the world a last, shining phrase—"Forgive them for they know not what they

do"—Ganesh in his cave, twisting his trunk, riding in a chariot driven by a mouse. Can any but a fanatic seriously contend that these two symbols are worthy of equal honour in the Hall of Universal Religion?[5]

Any Hindu reading such an account of Ganesh, one of the most beloved of Hindu gods, would feel the writer was echoing how Nazis had portrayed Jews. Yet it was about this book that Churchill wrote to his wife, "I think you would do well to read it. It is written with some distinction and a great deal of thought. It certainly shows the Hindu in his true character."

Nichols had gone to India on a trip which, according to his biographer, because of wartime restrictions had to be approved by Churchill's government. His journey had taken place when a famine was raging in Bengal which killed 3.5 million Bengalis. While Churchill resisted diverting shipping to feed Bengal, he was keen to get food to Greece, where a famine caused by the Nazi occupation killed an estimated 300,000, and at the Cabinet meeting of 24 September 1943 Churchill made it clear that, "the starvation of the anyhow underfed Bengalis is less serious than sturdy Greeks." The official status of Nichols can be judged from the fact he had claimed to be a journalist but stayed as a guest of the viceroy.

Churchill's endorsement of Nichols was all the stranger because Nichols couldn't have been more opposed to Churchill on how to tackle Hitler. Before the war, Nichols had made speeches for the Hitler Youth and entertained Joachim von Ribbentrop for lunch at the Carlton Hotel so the German could spell out Nazi policies on Germany's ex-colonies. He had also seen Oswald Mosley, the leader of the British Union of Fascists, as the man to unite the country and prevent war. Even after Dunkirk, impressed by Hitler's "appeal to reason" speech, Nichols felt a peace deal could be done. All this had made me describe him as a man with strong Nazi sympathies.

But Roberts and his friends took umbrage, calling this "incorrect" and claiming Nichols was "a strong peace activist." They didn't seem to see the contradiction that Churchill should have admired a book by a man who wanted peace after Dunkirk. This is when Churchill had made his great speech about fighting on beaches, which has always been seen as the clarion call in the war to fight Hitler.

The fact is Nichols had written about India because, as his biographer put it, "He saw it as a means of proving his patriotism." The book served as a very useful propaganda tool used by the Churchill government to discredit the Congress, particularly in America, where there were demands for Britain to give India independence, something that worried Churchill.

It also didn't go down well with Roberts and his friends that I'd mentioned how during the war Churchill had even lied to President Roosevelt, claiming the majority of Indian solders fighting for the Allies were Muslims, when they were Hindus. He had also stated the Gurkhas, who are Hindus, had a "somewhat childish mentality". They chided me for not naming sources. But the house style in *History Today* doesn't allow footnotes giving sources. Had I been asked to give sources, I could have supplied several.

Churchill had never concealed his hatred for Hindus. In a speech on 12 December 1930 he had warned that one consequence of the British withdrawing or giving up control could be "a Hindu despotism supported by an army of European mercenaries".[6] A few months later, in a speech in the Albert Hall on 18 March 1931, he had predicted, "There can be no doubt ... that the departure of the British from India ... would be followed ... by a reconquest ... of the Hindus by the Muslims". In the speech comparing the Muslims with the Hindus he had said that they were "a race of far greater physical vigour and fierceness, armed with a religion which lends itself only too readily to war and conquest. While the Hindu elaborates his argument, the Moslem sharpens his sword."[7]

The speeches were published in 1931 in a book titled *India*. It ended with promotional material on The Indian Empire Society whose council had thirteen members, eleven whites and two Muslims. No Hindus.

Paul Lay's initial reaction to the letter from Roberts and Co was that it was no bad thing to upset the Churchill lobby, and his email to me enclosing the letter said he thought I might enjoy it. I didn't enjoy the final paragraph, which compared me to David Irving as a revisionist historian, a comparison I felt was a libel. Roberts admitted to Paul it was a mistake, and it was removed. Paul agreed I would get a chance to write a rebuttal to the letter, and I duly sent a detailed one. However, it was never published; Paul explained the publisher felt it would serve no purpose but merely lead to a game of claim and counterclaim. Paul also told me how he'd been invited to have dinner with Roberts. I am sure he had an excellent dinner. However, Paul and I have never enjoyed another lunch together. Geoffrey Wheatcroft says in his brilliant book *Churchill's Shadow* that there is now a Churchill cult in this country. Just as there is of Gandhi in India. How very ironical.

48

BRITISH MORAL CAKEISM

Some years ago, when the Indian President made a state visit to this country, the first such visit in nineteen years and only the third ever, I was invited to Buckingham Palace along with some 300 other Indians living in this country. This was showcasing the success of British Indians: rich businessmen, members of the House of Lords and well-known entertainers, all sipping champagne and eating tikka masala. British businessmen were also dotted around, hoping to tap into the growing Indian market. In the palace ballroom, the Queen and Prince Philip watched a Bollywood dance performance, the first time such a spectacle had been seen there.

The evening featured an exhibition in the Picture Gallery of the *Padshahnama*, the illustrations commissioned by the seventeenth-century Mughal emperor Shah Jahan, the man who built the Taj Mahal. A leaflet explained that 200 years or so later, as the British conquered India, these were presented to George III. They are now one of the greatest treasures in the Royal Collection. The exhibition was no doubt intended to make the Indians feel at home, but one Indian turned to me and asked: "Presented? Surely it should say stolen?" A look at his face told me he wasn't joking.

Many Indians also believe the British stole the Koh-i-Noor diamond, taking it after defeating the Sikhs. Lord Dalhousie, the man who conquered the Sikhs, made no secret of how he had acquired it, dismissing "old women" in London for criticising his rapacity:

Whatever my affectionate friends in London-hall may think...[I] regarded the Koh-i-Noor as something by itself, and with my having caused the Maharaj of Lahore, in token of submission, to surrender to the Queen of England. The Koh-i-Noor has become in the lapse of ages a sort of historical emblem of conquest in India. It has now found its proper resting place.[1]

This was "confiscation" of enemy property which was justified not least because it would help pay for the war. It was something all conquerors in history have done and on that basis the British are perfectly entitled to retain it.

The problem is the British pretend it was a gift willingly given by Duleep, the boy king who submitted to Dalhousie, to Victoria. This is a classic illustration of the British desire to occupy the moral high ground. The British as conquerors weren't the first or even the most rapacious looters. All empires have been based on loot and Indian history is full of such looters, many much worse than the British. Nadir Shah carried away the Peacock Throne of Shah Jahan, the man who built the Taj Mahal, to Persia and so much wealth that the Persians got a three-year tax holiday. Nobody in India has ever asked Iran to return it because Nadir Shah never claimed it was a gift.

Conquerors are also ruthless, and some British historians themselves have compared the behaviour of their countrymen in India to the Nazis. After crushing the Revolt of 1857 and retaking Delhi, Captain William Hodson stripped naked the three Mughal princes who had commanded the uprising in Delhi and shot them out of hand. He then stripped the corpses of their signet rings and armlets and pocketed them, helping himself also to their bejewelled swords. Michael Edwardes, in his *Red Year*, writes, "The signal vengeance was by no means over, nor was there any cessation in the amount of innocent blood ruthlessly shed, for the city of Delhi was put to the sword, looted and sacked with the ferocity of a Nazi extermination squad in occupied Poland."[2]

Niall Ferguson in *Empire* describes how, just after the British had lifted the siege of Lucknow, a young boy supporting a tottering old man approached the city. A British officer, convinced all Indians whatever their age must be rebels, brushed aside his plea for mercy and shot the boy. Three times his revolver jammed, the fourth time he succeeded, and then the boy fell. Ferguson writes, "To read this story is to be reminded of the way SS officers behaved towards Jews during the Second World War."

However, for Ferguson there is a but:

The British soldiers who witnessed this murder loudly condemned the officer's actions, at first crying "shame" and giving vent to "indignation and outcries" when the gun went off. It was seldom, if ever, that German soldiers in a similar situation openly criticised a superior.

And with Ferguson's "but" we come across a central plank of the British Empire. The annual report the Secretary of State for India presented to Parliament was titled *Moral and Material Progress in India*. The British were claiming not only that they were improving the economic condition of the Indians—which they didn't succeed in doing—but that they were also improving their morals. India's many other conquerors didn't feel the need to morally justify their conquest. This is what sets the British apart and it is by their own moral standards they must be judged.

* * *

As far as India was concerned, this British desire to feel good started when Parliament held an inquiry in 1773 as to whether Clive had behaved dishonourably in the way he had won the battle of Plassey in 1757 which launched the empire in India. Colonel Burgoyne, proposing the motion, described Clive's actions as crimes that would have shocked human nature even to conceive. Clive took the high moral ground, saying "Am I not rather deserving of praise for the moderation which marked my proceedings? ... I stand astonished at my own moderation!" Parliament rebuked Clive for making money but also said he "did, at the same time render great and meritorious services to this country".

Macaulay applauded the decision describing it as "discriminating justice" and contrasting it with the cruel treatment of Louis XV's government of their countrymen who like Clive had furthered their country's interest in Asia. As Nirad Chaudhuri, a biographer of Clive, put it, by those same moral standards, if applied to Clive, "the very establishment of British power in India ... was naked aggression and usurpation, if not robbery. England could not retain the stolen goods if they called Clive a thief."[3]

And the British claim that Clive had to wage war against Siraj to avenge the Black Hole atrocity, an event much disputed by historians, as Chaudhuri notes, "Retrospectively ... served to throw a moral halo over the British conquest of India, as if it was God's punishment for iniquity."

This moral desire to justify conquest went hand in hand with painting a picture of the suffering endured by the British conquerors. Winston Churchill, in his November 1929 article in the *Daily Mail*, wrote about "the willing sacrifices of the best of our races" for "the rescue of India from the ages of barbarism". Churchill was echoing Rudyard Kipling, who, in his 1917 *Barrack-Room Ballads and Other Verses*, wrote of how the Indian Civil Service:

> die, or kill themselves by overwork, or are worried to death or broken in health and hope in order that the land may be protected from death and sickness and famine and war, and may eventually become capable of standing alone. It will never stand alone, but the idea is a pretty one and men are willing to die for it, and yearly the work of pushing and coaxing and scolding and petting the country into good living goes forward.

Reading this one might come away with the idea the empire was a Victorian NGO and the British had gone there because Indians begged them to. The true story is that in February 1583 Elizabeth I, a beleaguered queen threatened by Europe's then most powerful kingdom, Spain, wrote a begging letter to Akbar, the Mughal emperor, describing him as "the most invincible and most mighty Prince ... Invincible Emperor" to allow her subjects to trade with India. The letter went on to speak of the Indian Emperor's "humanity", how the English Queen would be "greatly beholden" if he would treat her subjects "honestly" and grant them "such privileges as to you shall seem good".

India then was the second most powerful economic country in the world, after China. In 1700 the tax revenues of Aurangzeb, Akbar's great-grandson were £100 million, and Aurangzeb's annual income was said to be $450 million, more than ten times that of his contemporary, Louis XIV.[4] Even in 1750, two centuries after John Newby arrived with Elizabeth I's letter, India's share of world manufacturing output was 24.5 per cent, while Britain's was 1.9, China being the leader at 32.8 per cent. In 1880 India was bottom with 2.8, Britain top, with 22.9. In effect, Britain deindustrialised India in the process of becoming the world's greatest industrial power.[5] Between 1757 and 1947 the British per capita income in real terms grew by 347 per cent, that of India 14 per cent. Britain's former colony America could protect its industries behind a high tariff wall, India could not and in 1896 only 8 per cent of the cloth Indians consumed was made in India.

But many in Britain don't know these facts, as I discovered, much to my surprise, when speaking to Stephen Fay, my old *Sunday Times* colleague, who often commissioned me to write for him and valued my Indian contacts. When he asked Chris Blackhurst to write an article on *hawala*, the ancient Indian banking system, he asked me to provide Chris with contacts in Mumbai, which Chris found very useful. Stephen dismissed the idea that before the British arrived India had had a thriving manufacturing industry, albeit pre-machine age, but some years later he came up to me and sheepishly admitted he had been wrong.

* * *

The real charge against the British is not that they looted India but that they committed the greatest infanticide in intellectual history, disowning their own Indian intellectual progeny. Nirad Chaudhuri called this "The Great British Betrayal". Arthur Koestler in *The Lotus and the Robot* wrote, "European rule in Asian countries was based on force ... We ruled by rape, but influenced by seduction."[6] The problem was the British were horrified to find Indians had been seduced by their culture. Macaulay won the argument to have Indians educated in English, saying, "all the historical information which has been collected from all the books written in the Sanskrit language is less valuable than what may be found in the most paltry abridgements used at preparatory schools in England." In contrast English "stands pre-eminent even among the languages of the West ... Whoever knows that language has ready access to all the vast intellectual wealth which all the wisest nations of the earth have created and hoarded in the course of ninety generations."[7]

Yet nearly a century later, the reason the British Cabinet in its crucial meeting in 1917 gave for not giving India self-government was it "would simply mean setting up a narrow oligarchy of clever lawyers."[8] In other words, disowning the very class of Indians Macaulay had said would be "Indian in colour and blood, but English in taste, in opinions, in morals and in intellect".

My Bengali ancestors were keen on acquiring Britain's intellectual wealth, but Kipling branded them "babus" and ridiculed their claim to be acquainted with Shakespeare. In 1913, when Rabindranath Tagore, much influenced by British education, became the first non-white to win the Nobel Prize for literature, Kipling wrote to his friend Rider Haggard: "Well, whose fault is it that the Babu is what he is? We did it. We began in Macaulay's time. We have worked without intermission to make this Caliban."[9]

This desire to shun Indians eager for British education and culture ran deep. Beatrice Webb and her husband, Sidney Webb, who visited Peshawar in 1912, were "amused" that the British considered "the wild Pathans (Afridis and Afghans) ... far superior to the Hindoos!", despite the fact that "they are cruel and treacherous, shockingly addicted to unnatural vice and habitually given to stealing each other's wives; that murder and robbery are so common as not to be deemed crimes" and that the British didn't think "that even in a couple of centuries, the Pathan may develop into anything like a civilized people." Twenty years later, the British plotted against the chief minister of a North-West Frontier Province who was a Muslim doctor, Khan Sahib, educated in India and at St. Thomas' Hospital in London whose wife was the daughter of an English farmer. Gerald Curtis, the British Deputy Commissioner of Hazara district, was deeply unhappy Khan Sahib "was bent on promoting a more egalitarian society." The British were delighted when he lost power, the province never took to the secular ideas Khan Sahib was preaching, and today it is the land of the Taliban. What would the west not give for another Khan Sahib?

Not that such rejection dimmed Indians' love for the icons of British culture, an adoration which was dramatically emphasised in 1964 by the Bengal government's response to the four hundredth anniversary of Shakespeare's birth. The British in India had never honoured their greatest playwright, preferring to call one of the main streets of Kolkata "Theatre Road". Now the Bengal government renamed it "Shakespeare Sarani", Shakespeare Road. This was done when many of the British road names were being changed into

Indian ones. For my fellow Bengalis there was no contradiction. The names they were changing were those of their former imperial masters. Shakespeare was universal and he belonged not just to Britain but to the world.

One of the saddest legacies of British rule is that they left behind no cultural imprint of the kind the Hindu–Muslim interaction produced. Indian classical music is a blend of Hindu and Muslim music and represents one of the greatest examples of the fusion of two very different religious and cultural traditions. This remarkable coming together produced some of the greatest classical musicians of India helped by the patronage of the Muslim courts. Nothing like that happened under British rule with the British doing nothing to introduce western classical music into India. The result was India got its first and only professional symphony orchestra in 2006, 59 years after the British had departed. In contrast China, despite never being a British colony, has 70 orchestras. The Indian orchestra made its first tour of Britain only in 2019 and British reviewers thought it had a long way to go.

The linguistic synthesis of Hindus and Muslims also produced a language, Urdu, a blend of the Persian and Sanskrit. Although I don't know Urdu, my knowledge of Hindi, derived from Sanskrit, means I can converse with Urdu speakers. It enriches my meeting with Pakistanis, whose national language is Urdu.

In contrast, in 1942 George Orwell saw no future for English in India, thinking it might "survive as a pidgin English useful for business and technical purposes." Orwell didn't think his novelist Indian friends, like Mulk Raj Anand and Ahmed Ali, were "likely to have many [Indian] successors". Orwell was proved wrong, but that came through the work of the first generation of free Indians, led by the trailblazing success of Salman Rushdie's *Midnight's Children* in 1981.

The British could claim this cultural self-loathing served them well. Charles de Gaulle acknowledged:

We pretended to turn negroes into good Frenchmen. We had them recite, "The Gauls were our ancestors" … [That] was not very bright. That is why our decolonization is so much more difficult than that of the English. They always admitted that there were differences between races and cultures.

However, this English admission has left a legacy which is now proving a burden.

All this was compounded by the British, unlike like the Romans or the Mughals, not seeking matrimonial alliances with the rulers they had conquered. The Mughals saw marriage to Rajput princess as cementing alliances. Both Akbar's son Jahangir, and Jahangir's son Shah Jahan, had Hindu mothers. No member of the British aristocracy, let alone the royals, married into families of Indian rulers. British monarchs had no problems seeking marriage alliances with European royalty even those they had fought but similar matrimonial ties with Indian royalty were anathema. In 1926 when retainers of the Nizam of Hyderabad, Britain's greatest princely ally in India, went to a London show where there were scantily dressed white women Lord Birkenhead, Secretary of State for India, immediately wrote to the Viceroy. "Few things are more damaging to our prestige as a people than the exposure of the bodies of white women before Indians". In the closing years of the Raj Leo Amery, Churchill's Secretary of State for India, regretted that the British had not allowed Indian princes to marry British women. But even here there was a racial element. He felt such marriages would have produced a stronger breed of Indian males.

* * *

One problem in claiming this moral high ground is that the British, confronted by examples of cruel and violent behaviour during imperial rule, refuse to believe it. I was made aware of this during the discussions that followed the first night of my play *The Black Man's Burden*. One member of the audience argued the Amritsar massacre was the fault of India because the British had been affected by the conditions in India—the heat, the dust, the squalor—which led to the loss of their high moral values. That evening I could hardly believe what I was hearing. Now I realise that member of the audience only knew one face of Britain, the one described by Orwell:

> The gentleness of the English civilisation is perhaps its most marked characteristic. You notice it the instant you set foot on English soil. It is a land where the bus conductors are good-tempered, and the

policemen carry no revolvers. In no country inhabited by white men is it easier to shove people off the pavement.[10]

But there was another face, which the non-white colonies saw, a duality well summed up by Pietro Quaroni, Italy's ambassador to Afghanistan, after a visit to India in 1938. There was, he said, the metropolitan face of Magna Carta, Habeas Corpus, the Mother of Parliaments, which only Westerners saw. But there was also the imperial face presented in the British colonies, "of how to rule and how to ensure obedience. With this second England, it is unwise to take liberties."

However, this imperial face didn't stop the British taking the moral high ground when judging other countries' misdeeds. The nineteenth century, in particular Victorian Britain, had been a great century of western moralistic intervention in many parts of the world, what today we call human rights issues: the anti-slavery campaign, the outcry against Belgium's dreadful colonial rule in the Congo, and agitation against the Ottoman Empire's treatment of its subject races. Byron led the Greek fight for freedom; Gladstone, aroused by Turkish atrocities against the Bulgarians, wrote his famous pamphlet *Bulgarian Horrors and the Question of the East*. The great irony here, as the American historian Gary Bass points out in *Freedom's Battle*, is "at the height of British public rage over the Bulgarian horrors, an epic drought took the lives of untold millions of Indians."

* * *

One man who knew these two faces well was the man considered the greatest Briton, Winston Churchill. In September 1897, the 23-year-old Churchill, then a soldier with the British Army in India, took part in a punitive raid to put down rebellious tribes in the Mamund Valley of India's North-West Fronter Province. In *My Early Life* he wrote:

We proceeded systematically, village by village, and we destroyed the houses, filled up the wells, blew down the towers, cut down the great shady trees, burned the crops and broke the reservoirs in punitive devastation.... Whether it was worth it, I cannot tell. At any rate, at the end of a fortnight, the valley was a desert, and honour was satisfied.[11]

Churchill had no problem justifying what he called "the questions which village-burning raises", writing in *The Story of the Malakand Field Force* (1898):

> Their villages are made hostages for their good behaviour … Of course, it is cruel and barbarous, as is much else in war, but it is only an unphilosophic mind that will hold it legitimate, to take a man's life and illegitimate to destroy his property.[12]

Churchill was well aware of the metropolitan face. "In official parlance the burning of villages is described euphemistically":

> One member of the House of Commons asked the Secretary of State whether, in the punishment of villages, care was taken that only the houses of the guilty parties should be destroyed. He was gravely told that great care was taken. The spectacle of troops, who have perhaps carried a village with the bayonet and are holding it against a vigorous counterattack, when every moment means loss of life and increase of danger, going round and carefully discriminating which houses are occupied by "guilty parties", and which by unoffending people, is ridiculous. Another member asked, "Whether the villages were destroyed or only the fortifications." "Only the fortifications," replied the minister guilelessly. What is the actual fact? All along the Afghan border every man's house is his castle. The villages are the fortifications, the fortifications are the villages. Every house is loopholed, and whether it has a tower or not depends on its owner's wealth. A third legislator, in the columns of his amusingly weekly journal, discussed the question at some length, and commented on the barbarity of such tactics. They were not only barbarous, he affirmed, but senseless. Where did the inhabitants of the village go? To the enemy of course! This reveals, perhaps, the most remarkable misconception of the actual facts. The writer seemed to imagine that the tribesmen consisted of a regular army, who fought, and a peaceful, law-abiding population, who remained at their business, and perhaps protested against the excessive military expenditure from time to time. Whereas in reality, throughout these regions, every inhabitant is a soldier from the

first day he's old enough to hurl a stone, till the last day he had the strength to pull a trigger. After which he is probably murdered as an encumbrance to the community.[13]

Churchill's response was very frank: "I do not believe in all this circumlocution."[14] Modern British politicians are unable to justify the cruelty of imperial rule. When, in 2009, the true story finally emerged of the barbarity by which between 1952 and 1960 the Mau-Mau rebellion in Kenya had been crushed, the government settled with the claimants and there was an apology by William Hague, the Foreign Secretary, in the House of Commons.

* * *

But should the British or anybody else apologise for past wrongs? This raises the question of Apology and Acknowledgement with a capital *A* and Gratitude and Guilt with a capital *G*. I cannot understand why describing some awful act by the British during the empire means the descendants of those who committed the act should apologise. They need to acknowledge what happened, not offer excuses for it.

Similarly, I don't see why the descendants of the conquerors should feel guilty about what their ancestors did. If they feel guilty, should I be grateful my ancestors were conquered by the British?

That the conquered should feel gratitude was a view often expressed by the British during the empire. It wasn't uncommon for the British to say the Indians needed to be civilised. Winston Churchill put it very bluntly in a speech at the Trade Hall in Manchester on 30 January 1931, when he said the vast majority of Indians "are primitive people." And in the *Daily Mail* article I've already briefly quoted from, he defined the British mission as ensuring India "its ceaseless forward march to civilisation".

But, while I don't accept my ancestors needed to be civilised by the British, I'm aware they had many faults and, as rich landlords in East Bengal, dreadfully oppressed poor Muslims.

Some years ago, I visited Ramchandrapur, my ancestral village in the Barisal district of Bangladesh. The day we visited B.M. College in Barisal, where Baba had studied, an article in one of the country's most prominent English dailies had taken my ancestors to task.

"Hindus treated the poor and uneducated Muslims as outcasts and not worthy of any big consideration in social and political matters."

That morning my wife and I were sitting in the principal's office at B.M. College, with plates of delicious Bengali sweets and tea in front of us, and it was clear this past still rankled. This is even though the Muslims in Ramchandrapur have done well. There is only one Hindu family there, who are very poor and have memories of awful treatment at the hands of the Muslims, including their women being raped. The village has a resplendent mosque, while what the locals call a Hindu temple is an idol in an open ground looking like it has been discarded. Nevertheless, I must acknowledge my ancestors behaved dreadfully. I don't see why I should apologise.

This acknowledgement is necessary because we need to understand the past. I accept the past is nuanced. Nothing exemplifies this better than the debate about slavery. While its evils cannot be wished away, the idea descendants of slaves, centuries later, should get reparations is absurd. Nor do I have any problem with the British claiming the moral high ground in saying the Royal Navy did much to eradicate slavery. For me the problem is, what we are presented with is severely edited, which leads to distortion. The Europeans were not unique in having slaves, nor even the first. But in other societies slaves could not only be free but became kings. India has what historians call the Slave Dynasty, representing ex-slaves who became kings. And one of these kings, Shams ud-Din Iltutmish, who had been sold as a slave when a boy, became the first Muslim sovereign to rule from Delhi and is considered the effective founder of the Delhi Sultanate and one of the best mediaeval Indian rulers. There is no such example of a former European slave taking the throne.

William Wilberforce led the campaign to abolish slavery and also wanted to get rid of Hinduism, stating in the House of Commons that missionary access to India was "the greatest of all causes, for I really place it before the Abolition [of the Slave Trade]." Comparing Christianity with Hinduism, he told the House of Commons in 1813, "our religion is sublime, pure and beneficent [while] theirs is mean, licentious and cruel," sentiments not dissimilar to those Churchill expressed a century and half later. Wilberforce described

Hindu deities as "absolute monsters of lust, injustice, wickedness and cruelty". So, if when talking of Wilberforce I were to raise his views about Hinduism, would this make me a "woke warrior"? Surely it would simply mean I was presenting Wilberforce in the round as he truly was.

It is the European failure to do so and persist in presenting the European version of history as the universal history that is a major problem. The Machiavelli–Chanakya problem.

49

DID MACHIAVELLI PLAGIARISE CHANAKYA?

Machiavelli needs no introduction. Yet nearly 2,000 years before Machiavelli wrote his book on statecraft, *The Prince*, an Indian called Chanakya wrote a book on the same subject called *Arthashastra*. Even in that age before social media, ideas along with goods did travel between continents, and it is not inconceivable that *Arthashastra* reached Florence. Machiavelli may or may not have known about this book, although reading the two books you may get the impression Machiavelli plagiarised Chanakya. Machiavelli was a failed theoretician, Chanakya helped build one of India's greatest empires, the Mauryan dynasty. He was the adviser to Chandragupta, who inflicted a crushing defeat on Seleucus Nicator, one of the generals Alexander had left behind when he withdrew from the Punjab, a victory which Indira Gandhi referred to when India defeated Pakistan in 1971 and liberated Bangladesh.

Some of the advice Chanakya gave Chandragupta was striking. On corruption he said, "Just as it is impossible to know when fish, moving in water, are drinking water so it is impossible to know when officers appointed to carry on tasks are embezzling money." As for what a king should do, he said, "A ruler should win over his people by seduction: a king should know how to perform magic tricks to give him an aura of miraculous powers and should make liberal use of manipulation."

Indian schoolboys know of both Machiavelli and Chanakya, and when India became independent it named the diplomatic enclave in New Delhi "Chanakyapuri" (the city of Chanakya). Yet few in the west know of Chanakya, and even scholars of erudite books on Machiavelli don't mention him. On the rare occasions European historians refer to Chanakya, they call him "the Machiavelli of India" when in reality Machiavelli should be called "the Chanakya of Italy". Max Weber, the German sociologist, got it right when he commented that *Arthasastra* made *The Prince* look "harmless". These aren't the only illustrations of an edited history presented in the west.

Perhaps the best example is the name of "Everest" given by the British to the highest mountain in the world. Not that it was a nameless mountain. Straddling two countries, it had several Nepalese names and a Tibetan one, *Chomolungma*, "Mother Goddess of the World", which was published in 1733 on a map in Paris. What the British did was estimate its height for the first time. That was the work of the Geological Survey of India of which George Everest was the head. However, the man who actually estimated the height wasn't Everest, who had retired by then, nor any of his fellow Brits. It was an Indian, Radhanath Sikdar, a Bengali mathematician and surveyor, who worked for the Geological Survey. However, Everest's successor decided Peak XV, as they called it, should be called "Everest" because, he said, that was a name the whole world knew. Observe the contrast between British schoolchildren and their Indian counterparts. The British know the name of Everest. The Indians know who both Everest and Sikdar are. But by not learning about Sikdar, the modern British miss out on the achievements of their ancestors. It was the British who had set up the Geological Survey of India, an institution which hadn't existed before in India, and also started the process of mapping India, something Indians had never before done. Sikdar was also the product of the education system Macaulay had introduced. By not acknowledging him, the British once again show their sad inability to acknowledge their own intellectual progeny.

The counting system we have is, probably, the most glaring example of how what we call "world history" is really Europeans looking at the world, with the rest of the world having a walk-on part. While the Greeks developed the counting system the whole world uses, they could do so because of the work of an Indian mathematician who, unlike the Greeks, understood the vital significance of the number zero. Zero is central to the numbering system because it is what's called a "spacing number". As Simon Singh explains in *Fermat's Last Theorem*, it helps us distinguish between 52 and 502, 52 being ten times 5 plus 2, 502 being a hundred times 5 plus 2. The Greeks, having got the number from Babylonians, hated zero, and Aristotle wanted it abolished as a disruptive number, because dividing a number by zero produced a meaningless answer. But Indian mathematicians rejected this view and, as Singh, explains:

> The seventh century scholar Brahmagupta was sophisticated enough to use division by zero as a definition for infinity ... As well as adding zero to the mathematical vocabulary, they replaced the primitive Greek system with the counting system which has been universally adopted. Once again, this might seem like an absurdly humble step but try multiplying CLV by DCI and you will appreciate the significance of the breakthrough. The equivalent task of multiplying 155 by 601 is a good deal simpler.

So, if we are to have a true world history, shouldn't we be saying the Greeks marketed the counting system but this wouldn't have been possible without the contribution of the Indians. Otherwise, we are presenting what is indeed a hugely distorted picture. The confusion this can cause is enormous. When I mentioned this at one dinner party, my host, unable to accept what I was saying, turned to Alexa. But Alexa was unable to help, probably because it had not heard of Brahmagupta. It's interesting that the name Baba gave me was derived from Varahamihira, a sixth-century Indian astrologist and astronomer whose main work was a treatise on astronomical mathematics. He was called "Varaha" or "Mihira" and Baba took the Mihir from there.

To make history truly universal British schoolchildren, like Indian schoolchildren, should learn about both Sikdar and Brahmagupta. But this would be condemned as a supreme example of wokery. The result of this imbalance is that we, the descendants of the conquered, always carry two bags, one containing the conqueror's history, the other, that of the conquered. Descendants of the conquerors, like my wife, only have to worry about the conqueror's bag. What we are witnessing now is an effort by the descendants of the conquered to equalise these historical weights and move towards a truly universal history.

This isn't always easy, and sometimes I avoid doing it even when I'm aware it needs to be done. On 16 August 2018 Aretha Franklin, the American singer, songwriter and pianist died. That night I was doing the "Paper Review" on the BBC News Channel with Baroness Ros Altmann. I feel very close to Ros, not only because we are both passionate Tottenham supporters, but because the night she'd made her debut I'd reassured her she'd be fine, as indeed she was. Since then, we'd often done the papers together. Aretha Franklin's death was an obvious story. The next day's papers described her as the "queen of soul". I had no problem with that. But "greatest singer"? What about Lata Mangeshkar, the "nightingale of India", whose songs captivated many more millions, not just in India but the Middle East, Africa and even Eastern Europe. But that night, discussing the papers I didn't mention Lata because I knew I'd have to explain who she was and the whole question of playback singing in Bollywood movies. I went along with the papers' accolades for Aretha Franklin.

As it happened, when Lata died four years later, ITV decided her death should be recorded and interviewed me. I was surprised because the British media had taken little interest in her before that. But the reporter had read my history of Bollywood, which has a chapter on Lata. He didn't need playback singing to be explained to him. He was also a person of colour, and I wondered if that connection had prompted this desire to make sure ITV recorded her death.

The remarkable European domination of the world for four centuries has meant the way the Europeans look at the world is taken as the standard, universal view. There is, of course, nothing wrong in Europeans presenting their version of history. What I would like to see is Europeans accept that's what they're doing. Their failure to accept means that I, like other non-Europeans, feel we are the great "other" who must always remain outside this wonderfully constructed European tent. I can't mention Lata when discussing Aretha Franklin because few in Britain outside the Asian and African diaspora would know who she is.

No subject cries out more for a truly global perspective than the histories of the two world wars.

50

ORWELL'S "NOT COUNTING NIGGERS"
IS STILL RELEVANT

In August 2020, as Britain celebrated the seventy-fifth anniversary of the victory over Japan in the Second World War, the *Times* printed a letter of mine:

> Today's celebration to mark the victory over Japan also sees Indians celebrate 73 years of independence, India having won its freedom from British rule exactly two years after Japan's defeat. This was not a coincidence. Despite being beaten, Japan's war in Asia destroyed the mystique of white supremacy and made European rule in Asia impossible. All the European powers had gone into war determined to hold on to their colonies. After the war the British were the first to realise this was impossible. The French and Dutch did not and fought to retain their empires before admitting defeat. That Japan seeking its own empire driven by a belief in Japanese racial superiority had, quite unwittingly, become the liberator of Asia was, perhaps, the most unexpected consequence of the Second World War.

The letter didn't go down well with the *Times* readers. One of them was so offended by my reference to "white mystique" that he asked "Why are you living here under white mystique, why don't you go home?" It showed how many are still in denial about the Second World War. One man who wouldn't have been shocked is George Orwell.

In the *Adelphi* magazine in July 1939, he wrote an article on the subject which is still relevant more than eighty years later. It was entitled "Not Counting Niggers".

An American writer Clarence K. Streit, had argued that if the world's democracies formed a united states of democratic countries

335

with a common government, common money and completely free internal trade, the dictators would crumble before a shot was fired. Streit's fifteen democracies which included the USA, France, Britain, were all white countries, many of them containing dependencies full of colonial peoples, including the US, which then ruled the Philippines. Streit didn't believe non-whites could ever rule themselves and that Indians should be treated "much the same as we treat politically our own immature sons and daughters".

Orwell wrote:

> ... Mr Streit has coolly lumped the huge British and French empires—in essence nothing but mechanisms for exploiting cheap coloured labour—under the heading of democracies! ...The unspoken clause is always "not counting niggers." For how can we make a "firm stand" against Hitler if we are simultaneously weakening ourselves at home?... What we always forget is the overwhelming bulk of the British proletariat does not live in Britain, but in Asia and Africa. It is not in Hitler's power, for instance, to make a penny an hour a normal industrial wage; it is perfectly normal in India, and we are at great pains to keep it so. One gets some idea of the real relationship of England and India when one reflects that the *per capita* income in England is something over £80 and in India about £7. It is quite common for an Indian coolie's legs to be thinner than the average Englishman's arms. And there is nothing racial in this, for well-fed members of the same race are of normal physique; it is due to simple starvation.[1]

European democracies did go to war "not counting niggers", making it clear that the much-advertised fight for freedom from Nazi tyranny did not extend to their colonies. Churchill, having signed with Roosevelt the Atlantic Charter, which promised freedom to conquered peoples, returned to tell the House of Commons its provisions didn't apply to India or Britain's other brown and black colonies. Australia said the White Australia policy was sacrosanct, and De Gaulle, leading the free French, summed up the view of many in France that the end of the war would see France resume, indeed strengthen, its pre-war colonial rule. In Tehran in 1943 when Roosevelt proposed to Stalin that the way to get the British out of India was "reform from the bottom, somewhat on the Soviet lines",

Stalin rebuked him, saying, on the contrary, the British Empire should be enlarged not reduced, with the British given bases and strongpoints throughout the world on the basis of trusteeships.

I was reminded of Orwell's "not counting niggers" phrase in April 2021.

* * *

An investigation by a special committee of the Commonwealth War Graves Commission found that at least 116,000 predominantly African and Middle Eastern First World War casualties "were not commemorated by name or possibly not commemorated at all." That figure could be as high as 350,000. Most of the men were commemorated by memorials that didn't carry their names. The investigation also estimated that between 45,000 and 54,000 Asian and African casualties were "commemorated unequally".

In a letter to the *Times* I mentioned that "Then the British did not allow Indians to be officers." My letter provoked outrage from some British officers of the armed forces. A colonel wrote to me that "throughout the Indian Army at the time there were Viceroy Commissioned Indian and Nepalese officers."

Yes, they were called officers, but they ranked below the white British officers, who were known as the "King's Commissioned Officers" and who could command both British and Indian troops. The "Viceroy Commissioned Officers" could only command Indian troops, were paid much less and had vastly inferior accommodation and hospital facilities compared to the white officers. In my reply to the colonel, I quoted from George Morton-Jack's excellent book *The Indian Empire at War* that the Indian army was based on:

> denying Indian recruits equality of command with their white officers.... All the positions of high command were reserved exclusively for British officers, of both the Indian and British armies.... To be a serving Indian soldier, therefore, was to join a regiment, never to leave it, and never to be treated as the equal of a white man.[2]

Morton's subtitle *The Untold Story of the Indian Army in the First World War* makes clear this is not known. The response to my *Times* letter showed people don't want to know.

I cannot blame them as the history of the Second World War is an exercise in cherry picking. Yes, more than two million Indians volunteered to fight with the British. But what happened in India after Gandhi launched his Quit India campaign in 1942? Such was the scale of the revolt that General Rob Lockhart, Military Secretary in the India Office wrote, "India must be considered as an occupied and hostile country". To hold India Britain used fifty-seven and a half infantry battalions and 35,000 men, re-introduced the Whipping Act, in 538 instances troops opened fire and on six occasions rebel territories were bombed from the air. And there was collective punishment with an entire village or community fined if any of their members were involved in the uprising. But true to the principles of divide and rule Muslims were exempt from collective fines. And taking the moral high ground Leo Amery told the Commons whipping was being "administered by a light rattan cane and not by the 'cat'". Until this becomes part of the war story we will remain in the world Orwell so brilliantly described.

51

HOW THE BRITISH RAJ PIONEERED
IDENTITY CULTURE

Whenever the argument is raised that modern woke warriors are playing identity politics, I think of the gymkhanas along Kennedy Sea-Face in Mumbai. There they are in bricks and mortar a lasting legacy of the Raj, advertising distinct religious identities. There is a Parsee Gymkhana, a Hindu Gymkhana and a Muslim Gymkhana. The Raj had provided the land for them to build their own gymkhanas, each fronted by a lovely cricket square. As I was growing up, Shankar would often drive me there so I could watch the cricket being played. The setting could not have been more beautiful. Across the road was the Arabian Sea, and to enjoy cricket against that setting with a lovely sea breeze blowing was idyllic.

During the Raj, these gymkhanas formed the cornerstone of the most extraordinary cricket tournament in the history of sport. The Parsee, Hindu and Muslim teams advertised the British view that India was made of many religious communities with the colonial power ensuring harmony and fair play. However, there was no Christian team. To field one would involve including Indian Christians, and the British would then have played alongside brown cricketers. The British team only had people of pure European blood.

Organising sporting teams based on colour wasn't remarkable. In America until 1947 Major League Baseball didn't allow black people, which led to the creation of the Negro League. Until the 1990s, South Africa had all-white sporting teams. But never in the history of sport had there been a tournament where there were three teams based on religion playing against one based on race. It was a unique British sporting creation.

It was only in 1937, nearly half a century after such matches had first begun, that a "Rest" team, composed of Indian Christians, Anglo-Indians, and other minorities, like Jews, joined the tournament. A star of this assorted team was India's leading Christian cricketer, Vijay Samuel Hazare, who in 1952 led India to her first ever Test victory, as it happened, against England. In his memoir, *A Long Innings*, Hazare writes:

> My side, the Rest, clashed against the Europeans. As if to punish them for keeping us out of the tournament so long, we thrashed them, totalling over 400. I scored my first century in the carnival when I made 182 against them, and but for dropped catches we could have won by an innings.

The British can certainly claim that, unlike white South Africans or Americans, they played cricket with the Indians and that Indian cricket derived dividends from this remarkable identity-based cricket tournament. There was excellent cricket, and it provided a platform for cricketers who dominated the first wave of the sport in India until well into the 1950s. When in the 1980s I wrote my history of Indian cricket, I met some of the men who had watched it, and they all expressed their deep affection for this tournament. And despite the religious strife that swept the country, leading to the mayhem of partition, no violence marred these matches.

Identity cricket was the icing on the identity cake, which included having separate electorates for elections to provincial assemblies. In the elections in Bengal, for instance, only 48 of the 250 seats could be elected by the general franchise. For the rest, there were twelve very distinct electorates, with seats reserved for people based on their identity. Seats were reserved for Hindus, who were further subdivided, with reserved seats for the Hindu scheduled castes, for Muslims, Europeans, Anglo-Indians, Indian Christians, representatives of commerce and industry, and the universities. There were also reserved seats for women, who were further divided into three categories: women in general, Muslim women, and Anglo-Indian women. Full universal suffrage without any reserved seats, the type we in this country recognise as democracy, was the work of Indian politicians after independence.

The British, worried by the growth of the Congress Party, also actively promoted Muslim identity. When in October 1906 the

Muslim elite of India presented to Lord Minto, the Viceroy, a petition pleading that the Muslim community should be given special privileges, the *Times* described the petition as "the only piece of original political thought which has emanated from modern times".

The way the British used tremendous skill, ruthlessness and great cunning to fashion identity into a mighty weapon with which to run their great empire has to be admired. What has changed is that in our day, the blacks, the LGBTQs and many other minorities are copying what the Parsees, Hindus and Muslims did on the cricket field more than a century and a half ago. Our problem in this very different world is to find a way to make identity politics irrelevant, but a start would be to acknowledge it has always existed.

52

MY COLLABORATING FAMILY

I'm having dinner in a London club. Portraits of the greats of British military history, generals, admirals, hang on the wall. We've reached the port, at which point the subject turns to the empire, and I say the British could never have ruled India without the help of millions of Indian collaborators.

So far, the conversation has been very amicable. But now, as a I use the word *collaborator*, my companion, who is white British, freezes, and after a long pause says, "Not collaborators, but assisters." This is not the first time I had met a Brit who just wouldn't accept Indians had collaborated with the British.

At the height of the Raj there were only 150,000 Englishmen in India. Hitler was so impressed by this that when he ordered Operation Barbarossa, his attempt to conquer the Soviet Union, he told his troops they should emulate the British Empire in India, that a small force of Germans will rule a vast land. Stalin, too, was astonished by how few British ruled India, as he told Churchill at one of their wartime meetings. In February 2015, at the launch of the Channel 4 series *Indian Summers*, the fact there were so few British colonisers in India was prominently displayed. At the after launch party I said to one young white Englishwoman it would be interesting to see how the series would deal with Indians who collaborated with the British. The moment I uttered the word, she exclaimed, as if I had uttered an obscenity: "That is not a word you can use!"

I am always surprised by such an attitude, for the British could never have conquered or ruled India without the help of a large army of Indian collaborators. At the Battle of Plassey Clive had almost three times as many Indians as British and lost four Europeans but fourteen sepoys, Indian soldiers. Nearly a century later, thousands of local troops helped the British to defeat their fellow Indians and quash the revolt of 1857, an achievement in which the Sikhs took great pride. Without these Indian collaborators, the British would have been turfed out of India a century before they left.

Even the Amritsar Massacre, the worst atrocity of British imperial rule, where the British commander General Reginald Dyer ordered his soldiers to open fire at a peaceful crowd of 25,000 people gathered in a park, the actual shooting was done by Indian soldiers from the 54th Sikhs, 59th Scinde Rifles (Frontier Force), and 1st/9th Gurkhas. The soldiers were from various communities—Hindus, Muslims, Baluchi, Gurkha and Pakhtun. One Gurkha would later tell a British officer, "Sahib, while it lasted it was splendid, we fired every round we had."

In Michael Ondaatje's novel *The English Patient*, a character says of the Indian soldier Kip, "What's he doing fighting English wars?" What Kip was doing was extending British dominions and preserving their rule. In all except the Boer War, in which, as a war between white tribes, it was considered inadvisable to have brown soldiers, real-life Kips fought for the British. In India, I can find evidence of it in the most unexpected places. I am on the top of a fort in a former princely state, and I find Chinese guns. They turn out to be those brought back by Indian soldiers who helped the British crush the Boxer Rebellion. During the half-century before 1914, Indian troops served in more than a dozen imperial campaigns, from China to Uganda. So great was this reliance that in 1878 the Liberal politician W.E. Ford complained the government was relying "not upon the patriotism and spirit of our own people but on getting Sikhs, Gurkhas and the Mussalman to fight for us".

A popular music hall jingle of the time went:

We don't want to fight.
But by Jove if we do
We won't go to the front ourselves,
We'll send the mild Hindoo.

The Indian Army even at peace time was twice the size of the home army and Lord Salisbury described India "an English barrack in the Oriental Seas from which we may draw any number of troops without paying for them." While my ancestors weren't soldiers, they were also collaborators and greatly benefited from "assisting" the British.

* * *

My ancestors were *zamindars*, landlords, *zamin* being the word for "land". But they didn't own their land. Before the British arrived, land was owned by the ruler and *zamindars* acted as agents of the state, collecting from the cultivators who tilled the land and passing it on to the ruler.

This system was changed by Lord Cornwallis, who made no secret of his belief in the racial superiority of the European: "Every native of Hindustan I verily believe is corrupt." Indians were barred from serving in the British administration. However, Cornwallis knew the British needed Indian collaborators, and this is where my family profited.

What Cornwallis did was make my ancestors absolute owners of the land. Cornwallis also fixed the revenue my *zamindari* ancestors had to collect. For the British this was a win-win situation. The work of revenue collection, a tedious process, was being done by the Indians so the Europeans could concentrate on the more lucrative businesses which made much more money. The *zamindars* had an incentive to collect as much as they could because every rupee more than what they had to pay the British was pure profit. It also made India more like the society the British understood, one with a landed aristocracy; the British had found it its absence from India puzzling. It meant my Hindu ancestors, who lived in what is now Bangladesh and were a minority, ruled over their Muslim subjects. If the price was that they had to bow to the foreign conquerors of their land, they were happy to do so.

Cornwallis' reform also helped produce what is known in Bengal as *bhadralok*, literally "well-behaved people", who in Britain would be classified as upper-middle class. For all the British distaste for the caste system, they had in effect created a new one. This was definitely a case of Indians of a certain class benefiting from a British racist.

Not that collaborating with the British meant they got to know them; the British were not interested in being anywhere near the Indians. My family come from Barisal but, as Jon Wilson puts it in

India Conquered, "the Collector decided to move his office to a different town to get away from the influence of local pawnbrokers twenty miles away."

However, this didn't make my family any less keen to serve their new British masters. A perfect illustration of this was provided by *Dadu* who, as I've explained, I called "grandfather" even though he was Baba's (my father's) uncle. As a Bengali he couldn't join the army as a solider because, according to the British martial race theory, Bengalis were considered racially incapable of fighting. So he qualified as a doctor, came to Britain, became a fellow of the Royal College of Surgeons and joined the Army Medical Corps. He served in the British army until they left India, and I remember him in retirement in Pune, living in a wonderful house, not far from where the British had built their cantonment (army garrison) after they conquered that part of India. He was very proud of his garden, tended by a *mali*, a gardener, who made sure Dadu always won the prize for the best garden in Pune. In the evening, as Dadu sat in his garden on wicker chairs, with the bearer serving whisky, he would be visited by serving Indian officers. We felt very proud of the way they paid their respects to him.

It was Baba who was the great rebel in our family. His father, my real Dadu, who died before I was born, had brought him up to continue our family's historic role as collaborators. After getting his degree under the educational system set up by the British, Baba, through my Dadu's influence, had secured a government job. This was considered priceless because it meant job security for life and on retirement, money from his provident fund, the Indian pension. There seemed no reason to believe the British would ever leave India. But Baba wanted India to be free.

On 6 April 1930, as Gandhi took a lump of mud and salt from a beach in Dandi on the west coast of India, breaking British laws and launching the second and the most successful of his civil disobedience campaigns, a thousand miles away and sitting in his government office in Barisal, Baba decided he could no longer collaborate with a foreign government. He resigned his job and made a dramatic exit from his ancestral home. Travelling by boat from Barisal, he went to Kolkata, from where he took the train to Allahabad in northern India, which acted as the headquarters of the Congress party, to join the Freedom Movement. But this didn't work out. He never told me why. He couldn't return home and decided to travel to Mumbai. There, unable to find work, he sat on a low wooden stool on the pavement opposite Victoria Terminus, the grandiose railway station built by the British, and wrote letters for illiterate Indians. Then, quite by chance he met another Bose, who was not related. He had set up Bengal Waterproof, the first company in India to manufacture raincoats and other rainwear products, which promoted its goods under the catchy name of "Duckback". He wanted Baba to take charge of Duckback's operation in the city, which Baba did. Baba eventually died in Mumbai. He never returned to Barisal.

Baba accepted eighteenth-century India was bound to fall to a foreign power and the British were the best of the foreign bunch. Baba hoped India would be free, but the British withdrawal in 1947 came as a surprise. That summer, looking forward to the cold-weather season, Baba had gone to his tailor and ordered several double-breasted suits. But then in August, much to his surprise, the British suddenly upped and left. Baba never wore the suits; he felt wearing such suits, which had been modelled on those then popular in Britain, after the British left might suggest he still hankered for the Raj. They hung in the tall teak wardrobe in his bedroom. Growing up, I would often use its full-length mirror to practise my cricket strokes, and every now and again open it to look at the suits. They still looked new and evoked an image of the post-war England of the 1940s, the suits I saw people wearing in *Brief Encounter*. The fact these suits never left Baba's wardrobe has always made me reflect that historians often miss out the things that can really affect our daily lives. So, for all the copious writing about the effect of the British withdrawal from India, I haven't read anything about how the British leaving India meant Indian men like my father had suddenly to change their wardrobes.

On Indian Independence Day Baba always hoisted the Indian tricolour—until demonstrators demanding the Portuguese leave Goa stole the flag. It astonished Baba that any Indian could do such a thing.

* * *

Looking back, I can see now that during my childhood my parents also struggled with the contradictions of collaboration, though they never discussed it. So Dadu would tell us stories of how he was part of the first British contingent to arrive in Singapore after Japan's surrender in 1945. Yet Singapore was the base of Subhas Chandra Bose, who had raised an army to fight the British from Indian POWs held by the Japanese. Dadu would just have missed Bose, who had fled the city just days before the British arrived. Bose never returned to India; his plane crashed in Taipei a few days after Japan's surrender.

There was much talk of how wonderful India would have been if Bose had returned. Dadu never discussed Subhas Bose. We never asked him. It is as if they were two separate worlds. Dadu would have been told by the British that Subhas Bose was a traitor, but I was brought up to revere him as an Indian hero who had given his life to free India. I loved Dadu and would never have thought of him as a collaborator.

For the British, Dadu was a "loyalist", the word the British used to describe Indian collaborators. The implication was that India was a country which the British had created and only by serving the British could an Indian prove he was a loyal citizen. As H.R. James, Principal of Calcutta's Presidency College, told his students, "One thing that patriotism in Bengal should not do is to direct the national spirit into an attitude of hostility to British rule. There would be something I should call patricidal in such an attitude."

It's taken me a long time to accept this historical truth of my family's collaboration with the British. My friend Quaiser happily jokes about the fact he comes from a family of real traitors who betrayed India to the British. This is a reference to his being a descendant of Mir Jaffar, general of Nawab Siraj-ud-Daulah's army, who sold himself to Clive. The British can never forget, let alone forgive, the treachery of Philby, Burgess and Maclean, but for many Indians Mir Jaffar stands on a different plane because his treachery meant a foreign power conquered India.

* * *

I first began to appreciate the relationship between the British and Indian collaborators when I read Lord Lytton's *Pundits and Elephants*.

It is 1923. Gandhi's first campaign of non-cooperation had made it difficult for Lord Lytton, governor of Bengal, to find collaborators. He sends for Mullick and asks him if he would take up the post but warns it would be a sacrifice not a promotion:

"Are you prepared to exchange a bed of roses for a crown of thorns?" I asked.

He asked for 24 hours to think the matter over. When he returned, he told me he had consulted Sir Campbell Rhodes, the chairman of the British Chamber of Commerce, with whom he had often sparred across the floor of the Legislative Council, and asked him, "The Governor has asked me to become a minister. Shall I accept?" Rhodes had replied, "Well, Mullick, if you are thinking of yourself, don't. If you are thinking of your country, do."

"That was enough for me," said Mullick, "and I have come to accept your offer."

Observe the wonderfully skilful way Lytton and Rhodes have spun the story of collaboration, something no other conqueror in history has matched. Indians imprisoned and even killed by the British fighting for their freedom are supposedly having such a good life that they are lying on a bed of roses. In contrast, the Indian collaborator, who as minister would enjoy a very privileged life, is portrayed as the nationalist wearing "a crown of thorns". Rhodes even pictures those seeking to free India as selfish, while serving the British is patriotic.

Yet Lytton was no despot. Son of a Viceroy, he briefly served as Viceroy himself. Educated at Eton and Cambridge, Lytton was well ahead of his times and an advocate of female suffrage. His sister, an active campaigner for women's rights, suffered greatly when she was imprisoned.

Lytton's book was published in 1942, in the middle of the epic fight to defeat the Nazis and their superior white-race theory and when paper was in short supply. Yet it was not considered at all contradictory that, when it came to India, Lytton was also advancing a race theory. But while Nazis didn't believe the non-Aryans, Jews and Roma people could ever prove themselves the equal of the Nazis, and they had to be destroyed, as millions were, Lytton held out hope that if Indians sat at the feet of the British long enough, they would eventually be able to match the British, the representatives in India of the superior European race, be"as good as any European in public life." This difference is crucial and shouldn't be ignored, but nor should my family be called "assisters" when they were collaborators.

53

WHO ARE YOU?

English football fans have a song which goes "Who the f*** are you?" It's directed at the supporters of the rival team and isn't meant as an inquiry. They know very well which team they're playing. Their song expresses their great joy that their team is winning and mocks the supporters of the defeated opponents.

It resonates with me because it raises the profoundly serious question of my own identity. It's one I've wrestled with all my life. And in the half century I have lived in Britain, my answer has changed. From a very early age I was made aware this was a very loaded question. Unlike the British, who can broadcast their regional identity secure in the knowledge they aren't putting the existence of their nation at risk, when we were growing up, we couldn't. India was struggling to prove Churchill wrong when he said "India is a geographical term. It is no more a united nation than the Equator." We had to demonstrate that India wasn't a country which had been held together only because of the British "nanny". India had been a country long before the British arrived.

Those who chose not to assert their Indianness were pilloried, which led to a rift between Satyajit Ray and Raj Kapoor, the two titans of Indian cinema, that was never healed. When Ray accepted an international honour, he said, "I am a Bengali filmmaker," but Kapoor angrily asked him "Why can't you say you are an Indian filmmaker? For God's sake!"

The two men represented very different cinematic traditions and also had very different ideas of what it meant to be Indian. Ray was the last great product of the Bengali renaissance that had sought to revitalise a dying Indian culture in the nineteenth century, assimilating the best of British influences. Raj Kapoor wanted to broadcast his Indianness. His most famous song showed him playing a rustic, carrying his clothes wrapped round a stick on his shoulder, ambling along a dusty Indian road singing that, while his shoes were Japanese, his trousers English and his hat Russian, his heart was Indian. Despite my Bengali background it was Kapoor with whom I sympathised.

The only thing worse than not saying you were an Indian was to talk about your religion. A person who did so was called a "communalist", which meant they were a religious bigot. So keen were Indians not to mention the word *religion* that newspapers reporting religious riots would describe them as "communal riots", well aware people would know what this meant: Hindus and Muslims were killing each other. Not till years later, when I went to the European continent and saw the word *communal* used in its true sense, did I feel comfortable using it.

And it is only now, after almost fifty years of living in this country, that I have no hesitation in saying I'm of Bengali origin and a Hindu. Britain has helped me to discover my ancestral roots. But while I feel liberated, I'm aware many of my fellow white British citizens are going through a crisis as they try to come to terms with the new multiracial world that has emerged. The result has been that, like the word *communal* in India, in Britain the question "Where are you really from?" has become loaded. There is a wide gulf between whites and non-whites as to what it really means.

It's a question nearly all non-whites are asked. I have been asked it many times. Initially I used to bristle, but now I say, "You mean what is my race, my ethnicity?" The moment I say that, the person will back away, much as Indians do when the word *communal* is used. I then say "No problem, I'm of Indian origin." While the white person is in effect saying I'm different, even implying I'm an outsider, I don't see it as racist. It would only be racist if the fact that I'm of a different race was used to discriminate against me. I have always thought we should be careful to use the R-word—racism can be weaponised. At social gatherings remarks meant innocently can provoke intense suspicion.

I was made aware of this at the Buckingham Palace reception, which I have referred to previously, in the lead-up to the Indian president's visit. A man in front of me in the queue to be presented to the royals, a Mr Patel, was told by the Duke of Edinburgh "There are a lot of your relations here tonight." I'm sure the Duke meant well, but it so puzzled Mr Patel that he kept asking me: "Did he mean there are a lot of Patels here, or," and he dropped his voice at this point, "did he mean there are a lot of wogs here?"

The word *racist* shouldn't be scattered round like confetti. I know because I have been showered with the racist confetti and even called a racist by a fellow Indian.

It came at an election forum in 2015, where the panel comprised Michael Gove for the Conservatives, Ivan Lewis for Labour and Baroness Kramer for the Lib Dems. I had asked why people from seventy-two countries who weren't citizens of this country were allowed to vote in British elections. I was struck by how the politicians shied away from the question.

Lewis disapproved of my even raising the issue. Baroness Kramer, who didn't seem to know non-citizens could vote, justified it on the grounds that this was a wonderful example of British eccentricity, when it is actually one of clinging to an empire relic, as is the non-domicile tax privilege. Gove said he didn't want to see any change in the franchise. But it was the reaction of a businesswoman from India that was extraordinary. She said she worked and lived here, paid her taxes, so why shouldn't she vote? This led her to calling me racist. She was, of course, being ridiculous. Had she been a British citizen living in India, even if she had lived there for years and paid all her taxes, she would never be allowed to vote. This is true of nearly every country, including the US. Rishi Sunak may have had a US green card, but as a British citizen he could not have voted in US elections.

* * *

Despite the many books written about non-whites having always been part of this country, until the post-war migration of West Indians and people from the subcontinent, Britain was a white country, and that is how its greatest writers saw it.

In his 1942 book *The Lion and the Unicorn*, George Orwell wrote that while

> a Scotsman ... does not thank you if you call him an Englishman ... somehow these differences fade away the moment that any two Britons are confronted by a European. It is rare to meet a foreigner, other than an American, who can distinguish between English and Scots or even English and Irish.

Orwell did have Indian friends, but there were so few people of colour in Britain then that it wasn't surprising he saw Britain as a white society. Almost two decades later, Arthur Koestler could take pride in being a European and not seeing Europe as multiracial. In 1960 in *The Lotus and the Robot*, after returning from India and Japan, he wrote, "I started my journey in sackcloth and ashes and came back rather proud of being a European."[1] What made him proud was that in Europe "common denominators weave their fabric across territorial and racial boundaries … Europe is the only continent among the ancient geographical divisions of the world where the ethnic mosaic forms a recognizable cultural pattern."[2]

By "racial boundaries" Koestler didn't mean non-white people: then the fact that Europe was white was taken as read. Sixty years later, people talking of Europe's racial boundaries must take into account the presence of non-whites in Europe. This problem is complicated by the struggle Europeans have to describe them.

Back in 1969 all non-whites were called "coloured", a word not remotely considered a slur, whereas the word *black* was.

Now, after trying many other words, non-whites are referred to as "people of colour". What does that make my dear wife and her family, who are white? Are they colourless? What it means is white is the default colour. If you are white, your colour doesn't have to be mentioned. It is taken for granted. Colour is only relevant for those who aren't white.

* * *

The reason for this confusion is that whites don't seem to understand that the modern world we live in was created by their ancestors. They may or may not glory in it, but that is an historical fact non-whites cannot dispute. Yes, I do have my Indian culture, but the world culture is European. And also, historically Europe has been an exporter of people, creating many "Europes" round the world.

I'm always struck by the resonances of such migration. American presidents talk proudly of their European heritage, and Joe Biden regularly emphasises his Irish roots. Argentina won the 2022 football World Cup with a team wholly of European ancestry. Some years ago, when Mauricio Pochettino, then manager of Tottenham Hotspur, took the team to Italy for a European match, he spoke of his links with that country because his ancestors had migrated from Italy to Argentina. I have no such link with any country in Europe apart from the fact that, in the hoary past, my Aryan Hindu ancestors were said to have migrated to India from Europe, something now disputed by Hindu fundamentalists.

Against this, the only significant import of people into Europe over that period were the gypsies who migrated from India. But, despite living for centuries in Europe, they remain the great outsiders whom the Nazis considered "inferior" and killed an estimated half a million of.

The British can understand the migration of white people from Australia, New Zealand, Canada and South Africa. They are members of the wider British family scattered round the world. For example, Ben Stokes, who was born in New Zealand, captains the England cricket team. But Moeen Ali, whose parents were born in Birmingham but are of Pakistani origin, had to fight very hard to convince his teammates he has an English grandmother called Betty Cox. Indeed, the then England captain Andrew Strauss, born in Johannesburg to English parents, found it impossible to understand.

Back in 1942 Lord Linlithgow, Viceroy of India, wrote to Churchill's war cabinet:

> Cabinet will agree with me that India and Burma have no natural association with the empire, from which they are alien by race, history and religion, and for which as such, neither of them have any natural affection, and both are in the empire because they are conquered countries which have been brought there by force, kept there by our controls, and which hitherto, it has suited to remain under our protection.

We have moved a long way and I have no doubts about the societal changes since I arrived in 1969 and whose significance should not be underestimated.

My wife's family illustrates how dramatic the changes have been. My marriage to Caroline would have pleased Half Pant. While she isn't the titled lady he advised Indians to marry, nor did she trap me by jumping out of the closet in my bedsit, Caroline is a Cecil whose ancestor William Cecil was chief adviser to Elizabeth I. Her great-great-grandfather, the Marquis of Salisbury, was three times prime minister of this country and was succeeded by his nephew Arthur

Balfour. Salisbury was also Secretary of State for India. Caroline and I have a historical connection in the sense that I lived in the road named after Dadabhai Naoroji, the first Indian to be elected to the House of Commons. Before he won his seat, Salisbury said the British wouldn't vote for a black man.

In the late 1960s, Caroline's sister Jenny went out with a Pakistani called Sadat. Caroline remembers going for a meal in London with Jenny and Sadat and being made to wait to be served so long that they left the restaurant. Now all this seems prehistory. When I first went to meet Caroline's family in the house she grew up in, my brother-in-law David opened the front door with a bottle of champagne in his hand. I enjoy joking that when he doesn't greet me with champagne, will it mean I'm no longer welcome? In fact, I couldn't have been more warmly welcomed, and Caroline's nephew is married to a woman of Chinese origin. Jenny's son, George, hearing of the ceremony of *onnaprashan*, where the mother's brother feeds the child their first morsel of cooked food, had similar ceremonies for his two sons Edwin and Hamish, sitting on the laps of their uncle.

The story of Peter and Ann and the role they played in my life and marriage also puts the whole question of race on a very different level.

Back in 1986 I did something I hadn't expected and behaved like the stereotypical immigrant from the subcontinent. As Ma kept reminding me, I was thirty-nine years old and hadn't settled down. It was getting late if I wanted to have children. But despite having a number of girlfriends in this country, I never seemed to meet the right one. Eventually I gave in to Ma's persistence and agreed to have an arranged marriage. Ma organised it all in the classic fashion. She placed an ad in a Bengali paper in Kolkata. A broker was hired. I met a number of young ladies, and I was immediately taken by the beauty of Kalpana.

Kalpana came to England to visit her sister and brother-in-law and we married in London. Since the wedding wasn't in Kolkata, I organised it.

We had a registry-office marriage followed by a Hindu ceremony in my flat. A fire was lit in my drawing room and Kalpana and I walked round the fire seven times while a Hindu priest intoned verses in Sanskrit. This recreation of the classic ancient Aryan marriage ceremony—fire validating the marriage—in North London that July afternoon fascinated my English friends, who had never seen anything like it. One of them did say that Ma blowing on the Hindu instrument called the *saka* sounded like someone farting.

I hired a limousine to take Kalpana and me to the Savoy for the night and then we went on honeymoon to Oban in Scotland.

Our marriage lasted twelve years and we had a lovely daughter. Peter and Ann became a big part of our lives. If fictionalised, the bonds they formed with us—and particularly with my daughter— would have been dismissed as unbelievable.

I'd met them the year before I married. It had been a wet summer and I was glad to be going on holiday. As I waited at Gatwick for the delayed British Caledonian flight to depart for Crete, I got talking to Peter and Ann. They were both retired. Peter had been a policeman, Ann had worked in the health service. On the first night at our hotel, I saw Ann reading *The Aga Khans*. She initially refused to believe I was the Mihir Bose who had written the book. Peter couldn't believe I was unable to swim and made it his mission to teach me. He said I needed to practise at his local pool. Holiday friendships don't often last. Peter's determination to teach me swimming made ours a life-long one. We developed a wonderful Sunday ritual. Each week, I drove to their home in Whitton, near the Rugby Football Union headquarters at Twickenham. Peter and I went to the local pool, and he stood on the edge of the pool shouting "Keep going, keep going!" It wasn't easy, but slowly I learnt to swim. After the lesson, we returned to his house, where Ann had a wonderful breakfast of toast, butter, marmalade and tea waiting for us.

Such a friendship might have dissolved after my marriage to Kalpana. But it prospered. Peter took on the task of teaching Kalpana to swim. Kalpana cooked wonderful Indian meals which Peter and Ann loved. It was the birth of our daughter that made this English couple truly part of the family. It came three years after our marriage. One November morning, as I waited in the anteroom of Hammersmith Hospital, a nurse came and told me I had a daughter, whom we named Indira. We also gave her a middle name, Ellora, after the great caves in Maharashtra. I felt it would come in useful should people find Indira difficult. That would turn out to be the case when she went to work in Rome.

Ann couldn't have children and Peter would often joke about how a West Indian woman had told him she would get him a woman with wide hips who would bear his children. While Ma came to stay with us quite often, she didn't want to live in England, and Peter and Ann almost seamlessly came to act as Indira's grandparents. Peter called her "Indie", and Indira became the grandchild they could never have. Indira saw more of Ann than most children see of their grandparents because Ann spent two nights a week with us when Peter went to look after his ailing brother. Peter and Ann joined us on our holidays, and to watch Ann and Peter with Indira was to witness the remarkable bonds of love and affection that can develop between people despite the very evident racial differences.

* * *

I'm aware that to some of my fellow non-whites I'm a "coconut", a derogatory epithet meant to describe people who are brown outside but really white inside, always trying to replicate white behaviour and curry favour with the whites. Much as I love coconuts, I have never wanted to be one. I also realise that, because I wasn't born in this country, my views on race are likely to be different from those who were. This was very evident some years ago when I chaired a session at the Chiswick Book Festival discussing *The Life and Times of a Very British Man*, the autobiography of Kamal Ahmed, who was then at the BBC. Kamal was born in this country to a Sudanese father and an English mother. When I spoke of how things had changed for the better, Kamal pointed out that, unlike me, people who are born here expect to be treated as equals. It is their entitlement, not a privilege extended to them.

My daughter looks at the world very differently from me. Unlike me, she didn't choose to live in this country. This was the land where she was born and she is entitled to everything it has to offer. She should be treated as much part of this country as any white person.

Unlike France where the Algerian War of Independence saw the collapse of the Fourth Republic, the return of Charles De Gaulle and a Presidential system of government, in Britain the fall of its non-white empire had no impact on its domestic politics. This is despite the fact that it fought vicious wars but they are so little known that historians Christopher Bayly and Tim Harper called their book about the ones in Asia *The Forgotten Wars*. The balm for the loss of the empire is provided by the Commonwealth as was vividly demonstrated when Charles was crowned King with the impression created Charles was head of state of all the Commonwealth countries when he is head of state of fourteen Commonwealth realms. King Charles has no authority over India which has half the population of the Commonwealth and whose Prime Minister did not even attend the coronation.

The British don't mind even trenchant criticism about their imperial past provided there is praise for their culture, something Nirad Chaudhuri exploited to the full. He dedicated *The Autobiography of An Unknown Indian* to the memory of the British Empire: "All that was good and living within us was made, shaped, and quickened by … British rule". Published just four years after India had won freedom, it provoked a storm. Chaudhuri was denounced as the "poodle" of the English, he lost his job with All India Radio, which left him so poor that to write his next book he had to borrow a typewriter from the writer Khushwant Singh. He moved to Oxford, where he continued to criticise India, even provoking newspaper headlines like, "Mahatma Gandhi worse dictator than Hitler". He loved flaunting his knowledge of western literature, history, music and wine to British visitors: "I am what I am on account of British rule in India … Doesn't that show the nobility of the project?"

Yet in *Thy Hand, Great Anarch!*, the second volume of his autobiography, he referred to the British in India as the Nazis of their age, describing the behaviour of the entire British community with "all classes of Indians" as "arrogant to the point of being indecent" and remarking that the women "showed themselves collectively to be vixens."[3] He was just as scathing in *The Continent of Circe*:

> After the Japanese attack on Malaya, the British in Calcutta squealed as we never thought such fire-breathing heroes could … They wanted fighter squadrons to be sent out even from Britain, because they thought there was nothing more urgent than the protection of their skins, the skins of men who had done everything in their power to ruin and destroy the British Empire in India by their lack of intelligence, arrogance and intransigence.[4]

Yet the book won the Duff Cooper Prize in Britain—established in honour of the man who had said freedom would bring no benefit to

India—because Chaudhuri said Indians were really Europeans and could only redeem themselves by returning to the superior European culture. He also wrote a biography of Robert Clive which was so full of praise that his publisher, Ursula Owen, couldn't get over the fact any Indian could be adulatory of the man who looted and conquered his country.

The present generation cannot accept the nuanced view that British culture is wonderful but badly served by the actions of individual Britons.

* * *

I have often wondered what would have happened had I gone to America to study in 1968, as so many of my schoolmates and college mates had done. How different the story of subcontinental migration to America has been compared with this country. Unlike the migration from the West Indies to the United Kingdom, Asian migration cannot be symbolised by the arrival of one ship, the *HMT Empire Windrush*.

There were two distinct migration streams from the subcontinent. The first, known in the community as "the direct flight" migrants, arrived soon after the end of the British Raj and were mainly migrants from rural Punjab and Gujarat and a large number of Muslims from Mirpur in Pakistan-Kashmir and Sylhet in what is now Bangladesh. Most of them did not speak English and had not even lived under the Raj. The second wave was of the Indians who, in the days of the empire, had been encouraged by the British to migrate to East Africa and act as middlemen between them and the Africans. But when the African countries became independent from Britain in the 1960s, most of the Indians came here.

In contrast, America had racist policies that kept Asians out until the mid-1960s. When America removed these barriers and for the first time lived up to its oft-repeated claim to be the land of immigrants, the migrants from the subcontinent weren't the rural poor as they had been in this country, but the educated middle class like my schoolmates and college mates. This group has done very well. I would have been part of it had I secured the foreign exchange required. One schoolmate went on to work for the *New York Times*.

But he did so after getting a journalism degree at an American university. I bluffed my way into journalism, and I'm not sure I could have done that in America.

I was lucky that I arrived in this country when there were many in the higher reaches of journalism with a romantic view of India and memories of the Raj. There might have been a touch of paternalism, from which I clearly benefited. Even Michael Wharton, who wrote the Peter Simple columns in the *Daily Telegraph and* whose view of the empire could not be more removed from mine, was kind to me.

As I have grown older and felt less of a marginal person in this country, I have become more comfortable with my Indian roots. At a party to celebrate my seventieth birthday, I joked about how Hindus divide life up into twenty-five-year spans. For the first twenty-five years a person is looked after by his parents. Between twenty-five and fifty it is his responsibility to look after his parents. Then between fifty and seventy-five his children look after him. On reaching seventy-five he takes his *lota*, or pot, and his *kambal*, or blanket, and heads for the forest to meditate and prepare for the afterlife. I brought the house down by suggesting that if, on reaching seventy-five, I should try going to Epping Forest with my *lota* and *kambal*, I wouldn't be made very welcome. I would not have dared make that joke when I first arrived in this country.

I can also talk about how I see Yudhishthira from the *Mahabharata* as the perfect human being.

Yudhishthira, the eldest of the Pandavas, always spoke the truth. The exception was to help win the epic battle against his Kaurava cousins, who were considered unbeatable because they had the greatest warrior in their army. The Pandavas' plan was to convince the Kauravas' warrior his son was dead and to so dishearten him that he couldn't fight. Yudhishthira was the only person he would believe. The warrior's son had the same name as an elephant, so Yudhishthira uttered the son's name saying he was killed, adding "the elephant" in an inaudible whisper. The warrior was so devastated that he was slain, and the Pandavas won.

I know the *Mahabharata* means nothing to most people in this country and, until more recently, I would not have told the story because I would have felt it emphasised my alienness. Now the fact that I'm different isn't something I feel I have to hide. Unlike the novelist Jhumpa Lahiri, who feels she is "a writer without a definitive language, without origin, and without definition," I feel I have a language and Britain is my home.

My country of origin still raises hackles. When I was interviewed for Christopher Hitchens' brilliant documentary on Mother Teresa, the much honoured saint of the city of my birth, I endorsed Hitchens' view that she presented herself as serving the poor but having a very political agenda in regarding abortion as murder and courting the corrupt rich, like Robert Maxwell, and accepting honours from despots, going so far as to lay a wreath at the tomb of Enver Hoxha, Albania's Stalinist murderer. As I said in the programme, the worship of this Albanian woman showed India was still unable to shake off its Western moho, love, and the West using the supposed sacrifice of a Westerner to behave in the old colonial mould of feeling better helping the poor third world.

I cannot, of course, hide my colour. The question of colour divides white and non-whites. At a seminar on sport some years ago, I narrated stories of the racism I had suffered when covering football. A middle-aged white man said he had been abused for being a Luton supporter. He couldn't understand that, while he could conceal his Luton allegiance, I couldn't hide my brown skin.

David Baddiel in *Jews Don't Count* has argued that in all the discussion about racism the discrimination suffered by Jews has been ignored. There can be no denying the dreadful suffering of the Jewish community through the centuries, much of it at the hands of white Europeans. As a boy in Mumbai, long before I was aware my colour made a difference, I discussed antisemitism and the Holocaust with Shirley, Didi's Jewish friend. However, Jews aren't so obviously visible as "people of colour". For years, I didn't know David Pleat, the football manager, was Jewish. Even players of Pleat's very fine Luton side didn't know. Pleat is the Anglicised version of Plotz, the family surname of Pleat's Lithuanian ancestors. In Anthony Clavane's *Does Your Rabbi Know You're Here?*, the classic study of Jews in English football, the chapter on Pleat is called "The Invisible Jew".

When Jim Pegg rang to tell me David Robson had become sports editor of the *Sunday Times*, he mentioned David was a Leeds supporter. (Leeds was then seen as a "dirty" side, whose players won through foul play.) He didn't mention he was Jewish, something I learnt only years later, and that Robson was an anglicisation of his name.

Both Irving Scholar and Jarvis Astaire weren't keen to talk about their Jewishness. Scholar told me a story of Luton fans singing "The Jews are on their way to Auschwitz" when Spurs were playing there, but he wouldn't let me mention it in the book. Astaire wouldn't allow me even to mention that he was Jewish.

Despite all the pogroms and the Holocaust, Christians cannot deny their Jewish heritage. The King James Bible talking of Jesus mentions "Born is the King of the Jews". This is also a carol I sing during Janet's Christmas Eve party. There is no Hindu god who could be described as King of the Jews. I come from a very different religion and a very different world.

The question that remains is how such differences can be seen not as barriers, but as spurs to bring people together.

That would require this country's chequered history to be reconciled. Britain has attempted such a reconciliation in a very British way. If you walk from Embankment to Parliament Square, you first see the statue of Queen Boadicea, who fought the Romans. Should the Romans return, they would see it as rank political correctness. She was a savage queen; the Romans were the civilisers. But the British rightly celebrate the fact that she fought and died to keep her people free. Margaret Thatcher was honoured to be compared to Boadicea.

Then, as you walk up to the Houses of Parliament, there within the Palace of Westminster is the statue of Oliver Cromwell. Here is the man who beheaded a king in a manner never done before or since. After the monarchy was restored, Cromwell's body was dug up from his tomb at Westminster Abbey. His head was stuck on the top of Westminster Hall and his corpse, after being put on public display at Marble Arch, was dumped in a pit somewhere underneath what is now the Marble Arch-Hyde Park Corner interchange. His bones lie under the road there to this day.

The monarch passes by Cromwell's statue every time he or she addresses Parliament. Every year the Cromwell Society gathers at his statue on his birthday. Some years ago, I witnessed the event. What took place was a very British game. A group of Irish protestors stood outside Parliament with placards reminding everyone about Cromwell's cruelties in Ireland. They told me how proud they were to have forced the Society to celebrate inside the Palace of Westminster rather than at the foot of the statue. They sounded as though they had finally scored a great victory over the enemy they can neither forgive nor forget. Yet the Irish are family, with the Irish rugby team representing the entire island including Northern Ireland and Tony Blair's children having Irish passports.

The four statues facing Cromwell in Parliament Square are also trying to reconcile the imperial past. Immediately behind Churchill's statue is Gandhi, as if the "half-naked fakir" is guarding his back. To one side of the square is Jan Smuts, who led the Afrikaners in the Boer war against the British and was then reconciled to their rule, became a great friend of Churchill and part of his War Cabinet. He had negotiated with Gandhi but never shed his belief in white supremacy. Now, almost opposite him is Nelson Mandela, whose rainbow nation would have horrified Smuts.

Yet this imperial reconciliation is very different from erecting the Cromwell statue. That was hugely controversial yet it did not signal the British wanted a return to republican government. As the homage to Queen Elizabeth II made clear, the monarchy has never been more popular. In contrast, the empire, unlike the monarchy, cannot be restored. Also, Gandhi's imperial backstory is little known. I realised this when I went to see the play at the National Theatre about Gandhi and his assassin, Nathuram Godse. Gandhi's role in India's fight for freedom came as such a surprise to an elderly white woman sitting next to me that she said, "I didn't know he was so anti-British." Given such ignorance, a proper reconciliation will not come easily.

Growing up, I was very aware that India, with its complicated history and many conquerors, would struggle to reconcile its past. Reading Indian history and tales of lost battles made me cry. I debated the great "What if" of Indian history, the Maratha defeat in the second battle of Panipat, in 1761 to the Afghan invader Ahmad Shah. A victory then would have made the Marathas the supreme power, and it is unlikely the British would have been able to conquer India. Then I didn't think the British had any problem reconciling their history, particularly given they have repelled all conquerors for a thousand years. Now it is evident the country's reconciliation with its imperial past is fraught. But, judging by the changes I have seen since 1969, I have more confidence in this country doing so than India or America, with its legacy of slavery.

NOTES

4. MUMBAI'S VERY OWN DOWNTON ABBEY

1. Arthur Koestler, *The Lotus and the Robot*, Hutchinson,1960 p. 15–16.
2. Ibid. p. 161.

11. WHY THE WEST GETS CASTE WRONG

1. Abraham Early, *Gem In the Lotus*, Phoenix 2004 p. 96.

18. TOILETS, WATER AND BENGALIS

1. Jeremy Seabrook City Close-Up, Penguin 1971, p. 44–45.

36. HOW MY OUTSIDER STATUS HELPED ME EXPLORE THE SECRET WORLD OF SPORTS

1. *The Glory and the Grief*, George Graham, Andre Deutsch, 1995, pp. 3–15.
2. *Guardian*, 22 February 1995.
3. *The Glory and the Grief*, op. cit., p. 196.
4. *Daily Telegraph*, 18 March 1995.
5. *Daily Telegraph*, 6 March 1999, 12 March 1999 and 18 February 2000.
6. *Daily Telegraph*, 20 March 1999.
7. *Daily Telegraph*, 18 February 2000.

37. I WON'T TALK IN FRONT OF THAT LITTLE SHIT

1. *Daily Telegraph*, 12 June 1999.
2. *Daily Telegraph*, 19 March 2000.
3. *Daily Telegraph*, 1 July 2000.
4. *Daily Telegraph*, 3 July 2000.

38. THE A, B, C, D ROADS CRICKET MURDER

1. *Daily Telegraph*, 20 December 2001.

40. TAKING ON A NATIONAL TREASURE

1. *Sunday Times*, 4 April 1993.
2. Mihir Bose, *The False Messiah*, Andre Deutsch, 1996, pp. 250–253.
3. Ibid., p. 268.
4. *Sunday Times*, 16 May 1993.
5. *Venables, The Autobiography*, Penguin, 1995, p. 372.
6. Sugar affidavit, 21 May 1993 quoted in *The False Messiah*, p. 191.
7. Venables affidavit, 21 June 1993, ibid., p. 192.
8. Ibid., p. 192.
9. *Daily Telegraph*, 30 September 1995.
10. *False Messiah*, pp. 383–384.
11. Ibid., pp. 387–388.
12. Ibid., p. 392.
13. *Daily Telegraph*, 18 November 1995.
14. *The False Messiah* pp. 393–394.
15. Ibid., pp. 397–398.
16. FA Premier League Inquiry Section G, p. 100, also p. 144.
17. In the High Court of Justice, Queen's Bench Division 1996-V-No. 304.
18. *Times*, 25 October 1997.
19. *Evening Standard*, October 24, 1997.
20. Statement of Facts Not in Dispute in the High Court Chancery Division Companies Court No 007550 of 1995 pp. 21–22.
21. Letter dated 5 April 2001.
22. Alan Sugar, *What You See Is What You Get*, Macmillan, 2010 p. 386.
23. *Daily Telegraph*, 6 December 1997.

42. HOW A MULTIRACIAL STOMACH LEADS TO A MULTIRACIAL HEART

1. *Time Out*, 23–28 April 1982.

43. THE GULF BETWEEN BLACKS AND WHITES WHEN DEALING WITH A RACIST

1. *The Guardian*, 3 July 1995.
2. Ibid., 4 July 1995.
3. Ibid., 7 July 1995.
4. *Independent on Sunday*, 9 July 1995.
5. *Observer*, 9 July 1995.
6. *Wisden Cricket Monthly*, August 1995.
7. *Observer*, 9 July 1995.
8. *Daily Telegraph*, 6 July 1995.

45. TEA WITH CHERIE BLAIR AND LONDON 2012

1. *Daily Telegraph*, June 22, 2001.
2. *London Evening Standard*, July 24, 2011.
3. *Daily Telegraph* July 7, 2005.

47. UPSETTING THE CHURCHILL LOBBY

1. John Colville, *The Fringes of Power*, Weidenfeld & Nicolson, 2004, p. 534.
2. Gabriel Gorodetsky (ed.), *The Maisky Diaries*, Yale University Press, 2015, p. 421.
3. Beverley Nichols, *Verdict on India*, Jonathan Cape, p. 122.
4. Ibid., p. 122.
5. Ibid., p. 161.
6. Winston Churchill, *India*, Thornton Butterworth, 1931, p. 40.
7. Ibid., pp. 126–128.

48. BRITISH MORAL CAKEISM

1. The Duleep Singh Correspondence cited in Christy Campbell, *The Maharaja's Box*, Harper Collins, p. 41.
2. Michael Edwards, *Red Year*, Hamish Hamilton, p. 59.
3. Nirad C. Chaudhuri, *Clive of India*, Jaico, pp. 465–469.
4. Angus Maddison, *The World Economy*, and John Kautsky, *The Politics of Aristocratic Empires*, cited in Shashi Tharoor, *Inglorious Empire: What the British Did to India*, Hurst, pp. 2, 219.
5. Paul Kennedy, *The Rise and Fall of the Great Powers*, Unwin Hyman, p. 149.
6. Arthur Koestler, *The Lotus and the Robot*, Hutchinson, p. 278.
7. Minute on Indian Education, 2 February 1835.
8. Minutes of 214 meeting of War Cabinet, 14 August 1917.
9. Nirad Chaudhuri, *Thy Hand Great Anarch*, Chatto & Windus, p. 672.
10. George Orwell, *Collected Essays Vol II: The Lion and the Unicorn*, Penguin, 1971, p. 79.
11. Winston Churchill, *My Early Life*, Reprint Society, p. 158.
12. Winston Churchill, *Frontiers and War*, Penguin, pp. 118–119.
13. Ibid., pp. 117–118.
14. Ibid., p. 119.

50. ORWELL'S "NOT COUNTING NIGGERS" IS STILL RELEVANT

1. *The Collected Essays, Journalism and Letters of George Orwell Vol 1*, Penguin, pp. 436–437.
2. George Morton-Jack, *The Indian Empire at War*, Little Brown, pp. 53–55.

53. WHO ARE YOU?

1. Arthur Koestler, *The Lotus and Robot*, p. 285.
2. Ibid., p. 283.
3. Nirad Chaudhuri, *Thy Hand, Great Anarch*, Chatto & Windus, p. 61.
4. Nirad Chaudhuri, *The Continent of Circe*, Jaico, pp. 143–144.

GLOSSARY

anjali	the offer of prayers to a Hindu deity
Annaprashan	a child having its first morsel of solid food
ayah	maid
baba	father in Bengali. In Hindi it means child
babu	clerk
Baniyas	merchants
Baperbari	father's house
bhadralok	gentle folk standing for upper classes
Bhai	the name I called my maternal grandmother
bhakti	devotion
bibi	wife
Bilayat Ferot	England returned
Bilayater Moho	An infatuation for England
bindi	spot applied by women to the centre of the forehead
boroghor	big house
boromashi	big maternal aunt, eldest sister of mother
burra sahib	top boss
bustee	slum dwelling
chana	chickpeas
chappals	sandals
chokra	servant boy
choona	limestone paste
Chordi	The name I call my second sister
crore	100 lakhs = 10,000,000 (10 million)
crorepati	Indian equivalent of a millionaire
daddyji, mummyji	"ji" added to name to denote respect
danadar	low priced sweets
Desh	Native land
desi	homegrown

dhoti	garment loosely draped by males around the lower half of the body
Didi	The name I call my eldest sister
didima	maternal grandmother
diksha	blessing
gadi gora	carriages
gamcha	small towel
ghati	workers from the ghats near Mumbai
ghulam	slave
goo	shit
gotra	the Indian equivalent of clans where the people are followers of a particular sage
hagga	to have a shit
hartal	strike
hathacora roti	handmade flat bread
jati	hereditary castes
jeelapies	fried leaf-shaped sweets
jhata	father's older brother
jhatema	paternal grandmother
juldi	hurry
kabaddi	Indian sport
kakima	paternal aunt, wife of father's brother
kaku	paternal uncle, father's younger brother
kulo koli	embrace
kurta	garment worn by males on the top part of the body
lakh	100,000
Ma	mother in Bengali
macher jhol	fish curry
maha	great
maidan	an open space
Maiji	mother in Marathi
majarjhar	Middle room
mama	mother's brother
mamima	wife of Mama
mandir	temple
mashi	mother's sister
memsahib	white woman

misti dahi	sweet yogurt
mouj	fun
muni	sage
mutu	piss
pan	betelnut leaf
panda	a Brahmin who performs religious ceremonies
pandal	marquee
panch	five
payesh	Bengali rice pudding
peons	servants who work in offices
pind-daan	offering tributes to one's ancestors
pishi	father's sister
pranam koro	touch the feet
prasad	food blessed by the gods
puja	worship of Hindu deities
rosogoolas	syrupy Bengali sweets
sadhu	religious man
sahib	white man
sandesh	dry Bengali sweet made from cheese
Seth	boss
shamiana	marquee
Sharab is haram	drinking is evil
sonar Bangal	golden Bengal
Sradda	ceremony after a Hindu funeral equivalent to a wake
suttee	widows killing themselves after husband's death
Swadeshi	self-rule
tamasha	fun and frolics
thakur	a Brahmin cook
Tik hai	alright
tika	holy mark
unki	his
varna	skin colour
yaar	pal or mate
zamindar	landlord

ALSO BY MIHIR BOSE

HISTORY AND BIOGRAPHY

Silver: The Spy Who Fooled the Nazis

From Midnight to Glorious Morning? India Since Independence

The Lost Hero: A Biography of Subhas Bose

Bollywood: A History

Lion and Lamb: A Portrait of British Moral Duality

False Messiah: The Life and Times of Terry Venables

Michael Grade: Screening the Image

The Aga Khans

The Memons

Narendra Modi—The Yogi of Populism

BUSINESS

The Crash: the 1987–88 World Market Slump

Fraud: The Growth Industry of the 1980s (co-author)

How to Invest For a Bear Market

Crash! A New Money Crisis: A Children's Guide to Money

Insurance: Are You Covered?

William Hill: The Man and The Business (co-author)

CRICKET

A History of Indian Cricket (Winner of the 1990 Cricket Society Literary Award)

ACKNOWLEDGMENTS

This book has been a wonderful lockdown present. I have been wanting to write it for a long time—both a memoir and a look at how Britain has changed since I arrived here in 1969. I had often discussed it with Michael Dwyer, then suddenly in the middle of lockdown Michael rang suggesting I write it and offering me a contract. Many years ago, I had tapped into Rachel Dwyer's (Michael's wife) unrivalled knowledge of Bollywood when writing my history of Bollywood. So, this continues my Dwyer link. There is a wonderful Indian saying called maska lagoa, which means buttering up. I am not maska lagoaing when I say cannot think him enough and also for the wonderful way he and his staff have handled the book.

I have debts to many people for their help and encouragement over many years some of whom are acknowledged in this book. But there are many others. I would like to thank Barbara Schwepcke and Harry Hall of Haus for providing me the scope to air some of the themes which have always been of interest to me in the books I have written for them. Over the years many others have provided me various media platforms to look at subjects that fascinate me and articulate my views. They include David Robson, David Davidar, Martin Liu, Leo Hollis, Jeremy Robson, Sarah Sands, Peter Burns, Nick Gordon, Kathy Rooney, Bill Campbell, Neville Moir, Susan Grice, Colin Chapman, Jane Camillin, Alan Sutton, Peter Furtado, Aienla Ozukum, Max Hastings, Charles Moore, Veronica Wadley, George Bickerstaff, Stuart Rock, Graeme Wright, Mathew Engel, Steve Cording, Tim Nichols, Doug Wills and Martin Doyle. My journalism and books would have been much more difficult but for the help of people who have so willingly shared their knowledge and expertise. They include Shyam Benegal, Phillip Knightley, Roy Hodgson, Ron Noades, Sunil Gavaskar, Subhas Gupte, B.S. Chandrasekhar, Budhi Kunderan,

ACKNOWLEDGMENTS

Ravi Shastri, Stella Thomas, Andre Odendaal, Peter Hain, Tim Bell, Ken Trood, Carmen Callil, Brian Wenham, Paul Fox, Hunter Davies, Mark Lawson, Julian Amery, David Astor, Lord Boothby, Sir Hugh Greene, Martin Gilbert, Margaret, the Duchess of Argyle, Arianna Stassinopoulos, Philp Ziegler, Lord Derby, M.R.D. Foot, Rupert Hart-Davis, Ian Stephens, Sir Robin Mackworth-Young, Donna Cullen, Sharad Kotnis, Gillian Greenwood, Kishore Bhimani, Raj Singh, Swapan Dasgupta, Papu Sanjgiri, Ayaz Memon, Hubert Nazareth, Chris Haynes, Patrick Cheney, Kate Hoey, Brian Cooper, David Dein, Daljit Sehbai, Dr Sayed Wiqar Ali Shah, Anita Bose, Tapan Raychaudhuri, Rajneesh Gupta, Veena Baswani, Paul Myners, Bipin Patel, Edward Griffiths, Andrew Cecil, Majid Ishaq, Robert Bourne, Malcolm Roberts, Colin Gibson, Brian Oliver, Noel Rands, Igal Yawetz and Nick Hewer.

Jeremy Butterfield and Rose Chisholm have been very helpful. I am as ever indebted to Naynesh Desai. My daughter Indira has provided me an insight into how her generation sees issues.

Above all I must thank my wife Caroline, my rock, for her unfailing support and wonderful encouragement helping make this book possible.

Mihir Bose
London
January 2024